NORMA

★★★★★★★★★★★★★★★★★★★★★★★★★★

THE STORY OF
NORMA SHEARER

Books by Lawrence J. Quirk

The Films of Joan Crawford
Robert Francis Kennedy
The Films of Ingrid Bergman
The Films of Paul Newman
The Films of Fredric March
Foreword, Photoplay Magazine Anthology
The Films of William Holden
The Great Romantic Films
The Films of Robert Taylor
Some Lovely Image (a novel)
The Films of Ronald Colman
The Films of Warren Beatty
The Films of Myrna Loy
The Films of Gloria Swanson
Claudette Colbert: An Illustrated Biography
Bette Davis: Her Films and Career
(Update from 1965)
Lauren Bacall: Her Films and Career
Jane Wyman: The Actress and the Woman
The Complete Films of William Powell
Margaret Sullavan: Child of Fate
Norma: The Story of Norma Shearer

NORMA

★★★★★★★★★★★★★★★★★★★★★★★★★★

THE STORY OF NORMA SHEARER

Lawrence J. Quirk

ST. MARTIN'S PRESS • NEW YORK

Library of Congress Cataloging-in-Publication Data

Quirk, Lawrence J.
  Norma : the story of Norma Shearer / by Lawrence J. Quirk.
    p. cm.
  ISBN 0-312-01798-7
  1. Shearer, Norma. 1900–   . 2. Motion picture actors and
actresses—United States—Biography. I. Title.
PN2287.S37Q57 1988
791.43'028'0924—dc19
[B]   87-36696
                                                       CIP

First Edition
10 9 8 7 6 5 4 3 2 1

FOR ALBERT B. MANSKI

A loyal and dedicated Shearer admirer

Contents

Acknowledgments

Of all the film personalities I interviewed, knew, admired, and sometimes loved, in over forty-two years in journalism, Norma Shearer was the closest to my heart and lingers most fondly in memory. She was high on the list of those favorites of mine about whom I collected reminiscences and other material over those four decades, with a view to one day writing her biography.

I wish to tender my sincere thanks to
my editor, Toni Lopopolo.

I also wish to acknowledge the kindness and cooperation of those living and dead, those named throughout this book and those who requested not to be named, all of whom shared their memories of Norma Shearer with me.

Also my gratitude to Douglas Whitney, who lent me many fascinating pictures of Norma for the illustrations, and to writer-film historian Albert B. Manski of Boston, to whom this book is dedicated, who lent me photographs, letters, clippings, and other memorabilia. And a special note of thanks to Leatrice Gilbert Fountain, who provided me with valuable material on her father John Gilbert's relationship with Norma, and to Doug McClelland, Anthony Slide, Barry Paris, John Gallagher, DeWitt Bodeen, and James Robert Parish.

Also my appreciation to Ernest D. Burns of Cinemabilia, New York; Mark Ricci and The Memory Shop, New York; Dorothy Swerdlove, Dr. Rod Bladel, and their associates at the Billy Rose Theater and Film Collection, New York Public Library at Lincoln Center; The James R. Quirk Memorial Film Symposium and Research Center, New York; Mary Corliss of the Museum of Modern Art Department of Film's Photo Archives; Jerry Ohlinger's Movie Material Store, New York; the staff of the Margaret Herrick Library of the Academy of Motion Picture Arts and Sciences, Hollywood; Terry Geesken of the Museum of Modern Art Film Library; and Phototeque. And to the British Film Institute, London; Manuel Cordova; Ben Carbonetto; Eduardo Moreno; Lou Valentino; John W. M. Phillips of London; Jack Caravela; Robin Kessler; John Cocchi; Jack Jacobs; Myron Braum; and the company that now controls the old MGM.

Also thanks to James E. Runyan, William Schoell, Michael Ritzer, Arthur Tower, John A. Guzman, Don Koll, Mike Snell, and Jim McGowan.

Introduction

Norma Shearer was always someone special to me. My mother, Margaret Connery Quirk, herself a budding actress at the time, had known Norma in New York early in her career, and used to tell me much about her. My uncle, James R. Quirk, editor and publisher of *Photoplay Magazine* in its great era, 1914 to 1932, had once been in love with her. I, too, had fallen in love with Norma, in 1932 at the age of nine, when I saw her in *Smilin' Through*. Now Norma and I have come full circle, fifty-six years and a lifetime later, with the writing of this biography. Meeting and coming to know Norma rank high among my memories of Hollywood, which, during my career as a writer, editor, and author, I visited frequently.

There simply are no stars like Norma Shearer today. She had glamour, intrinsic class, a distinctive style, and an authoritatively compelling aura about her that make most of the pretenders to today's stellar thrones shrink by comparison. She had an individual stamp, a shimmering radiance, and a poised self-containment that far transcend the conveyor-belt mystiques of most of her singularly faceless counterparts of the late 1980s.

The absence from the contemporary scene of authoritative screen personalities such as Norma Shearer is symptomatic of all that is wrong with today's Hollywood. Shearer, along with Garbo, Swanson, Crawford, Davis, Stanwyck, Garson, Loy, and Dietrich, was an original. You would never lose *her* in a crowd, as you can (quite easily) many of today's female "stars." Shearer's day—1920 to 1942—was the era of the lionesses, and along with such magnificent colleagues as Garbo and Crawford—for years they were the great threesome of Metro-Goldwyn-Mayer—she made the MGM trademark lion roar as it has never roared since.

Indeed, Norma Shearer truly became the lion's consort, not only as the wife of MGM's creatively gifted production boss, Irving Thalberg, but by virtue of her hard-won position during the 1930s as the First Lady of the Screen. She collected six Academy Award nominations and won once, for *The Divorcee,* in 1930.

No divorcée was she in private life. She remained Thalberg's wife until his death in 1936, and when she finally remarried in 1942, she remained married to Martin Arrouge until her death forty years later. Her friendships and associations along the way were to prove, for the most part, equally constant.

Norma Shearer was, however, human, and she possessed in common with others a full share of foibles, vanities, and unpredictabilities of character and mood. She had a strong will and a fierce need for power, plus a determination to set her stamp upon the cinema scene of her time. She could be ruthless when put upon, responding with a force, and even a vindictiveness, that often surprised her colleagues, who mistook her ladylike poise, controlled affability, and tact for vacillation or gracious compliance, and who failed to grasp that her highly romantic nature and outlook on life pointed not toward sentimentality but toward idealized self-projection.

Norma could be exasperatingly—some thought monstrously—vain about matters in which she had trained herself to be an expert: camera angles, correct lighting effects, the most flattering costuming, the proper mounting and showcasing of her vehicles. In her unremitting, highly ambitious struggle through those years from put-upon bit player to all-powerful superstar, she exhibited jealousy, resentment, assorted one-upmanships, titanic rages, and a contemptuous unwillingness to suffer fools gladly, all of which won her a full quota of enemies. On the other side of the coin, her proven and often-implemented capacities for friendship and loyalty won her an equal number of devoted friends and admirers.

Norma once said, "It is impossible to get anything major accomplished without stepping on some toes; enemies are inevitable when one is a *doer*." She also made no bones about subscribing to the sixteenth-century Italian philosopher Machiavelli's famed apothegm: "It is a mistake to be *too* good when surrounded by others who are *not* good." Such tough movie moguls as studio head Louis B. Mayer and Loew's president Nicholas Schenck were to find that this ostensibly patrician lady carried a clenched iron fist beneath her velvet, Adrian-designed glove when she felt the stakes high enough to use it.

Both as artist and woman, Norma Shearer was the essence of passionate sensibility combined with a highly sexed nature, both on-screen and off. Yet despite her obsessive pursuit of love's ultimate fulfillments, she was not to know them totally until the age of forty-two. Passionately interested in the male sex from childhood, she palled around with boys, often besting them in sport as early as age ten. Straight through her childhood and later into adolescence, she formed intense emotional attachments to boys whose handsomeness and/or charm particularly moved her. One of them she was to lose to an early death, a grief she was to recall into old age.

Oversupervised and hampered by a mother who had her full share of neurotic sexual repressions and who attempted to fill her daughter with paranoid fears of the all-men-are-beasts-and-after-just-one-thing stripe, Norma tried to govern her persistent emotional and physical needs during her early Hollywood years, although she consistently fell in love with men who were wrong for her, and who often were married. Some of these were father figures who represented a compensation for a father whose character weaknesses she felt had caused him to fail her. She ran afoul, emotionally, of supervirile ladies' man Victor Fleming when he directed her in an early picture; she developed destructive "supercrushes" on such handsome coactors as John Boles and Malcolm McGregor, both of whom failed to reciprocate her feelings. Meanwhile she enjoyed consoling herself by fending off, with an artful flirtatiousness born of a steadily growing disillusion, the markedly unsubtle advances of such Hollywood wolves as her costar Lew Cody, while playing with the affections of other actors: sensitively lovelorn Ralph Forbes, innocently boyish Johnny Mack Brown, and that tormentedly compulsive womanizer Jack Pickford, the ill-starred younger brother of the famed Mary.

After a few other involvements, including one with the talented director Harry d'Abbadie D'Arrast, and editor Jimmy Quirk of *Photoplay,* she settled on producer Irving Thalberg, who by 1927 had already done much for her career at MGM and who, she knew, would do even more for her were she Mrs. Thalberg. But Irving also brought out in her a compassion and concern and a maternal, nurturing streak, as he was frail in health and dogged by a heart condition that was to cause his early death. Unfortunately, all her loving concern did not translate, after marriage, into the ultimate sexual and romantic fulfillment that she craved. Irving invested what energies he could summon into his high-powered producing career, and does not seem to have had much left over for the pleasures of the bed. During the Thalberg marriage (1927 to 1936) there were many rumors that Norma, profoundly frustrated sexually, resorted to discreet affairs with available young men.

According to director George Cukor, in this period Shearer even had an affair with an actor considered exclusively gay, William Haines, who told Cukor, "She was one woman who really got a *rise* out of me, and for *me,* that's saying a *mouthful!*" There were also rumors, circa 1932, of her interest in such young actors as Alexander Kirkland and Phillips Holmes. Meanwhile she exhibited a lioness's protectiveness toward her young son, Irving Thalberg, Jr., and later toward her daughter, Katherine. Journalists and columnists who liked and admired her adopted a protective attitude toward her, and were ready to overlook her dalliances.

After Thalberg's death at the age of thirty-seven, Norma found herself a widow at thirty-six. Her physical and emotional drives were approaching their height. Feeling she had done her duty to a man she had deeply loved but who had not

totally fulfilled her as a woman, she embarked, after a full
year of mourning, on a concentrated and intense pursuit of
love that was to bring her heartbreak and frustration with the
fourteen-years-younger bisexual Tyrone Power and to temporary consolations with George Raft, who was not free to
marry her because his wife of many years refused to give him
a divorce.

Finally, while on a trip to Sun Valley with her children in
1942, Norma met a young ski instructor, Martin Arrouge,
who was twenty-eight to her forty-two; he reminded her of a
robust and virile version of the frail, anemic Thalberg, and
she defied the Hollywood gossips by marrying him. Thus she
embarked on the totally fulfilled liaison that she had intently
pursued, and until then had never found, throughout the first
four decades of her life. And in this marriage to a young man
Norma Shearer finally reached the fulfillment and happiness
she had always sought.

Some years ago, film historians and commentators tended
to downgrade Norma Shearer's contribution to the star system
of the Golden Period of the 1920s to the 1940s. She was, for a
time, unfairly dismissed as "decorative," "cold," "pretty,"
and "effective at the projection of highly mannered surface
emotion." Unfair observations showed up in print concerning
her alleged "inside pull," for as the wife of Thalberg, who
from 1924 on with Louis B. Mayer built Metro-Goldwyn-
Mayer to its towering position among movie studios of the
1920s, she naturally enjoyed entrée of the first order.

But in my opinion, whatever breaks came Shearer's way
because she was Thalberg's wife, she amply deserved. She
was one of the hardest-working, most reliable actresses in
Hollywood, and it has been often overlooked that she had
struggled up through extra and bit parts to solid leads and
major attention *before* her marriage.

Of course Thalberg helped her more and more from 1923
on. He found her good roles; he made her work at technique;
he insisted on top lighting, the best costuming, the most flattering camera angles; and, especially after 1930, he got her

the strongest stories available, thus metamorphosing her into a superstar. But Irving Thalberg was too much of an objective professional not to recognize his wife's intrinsic quality. He knew what he had in her, and he turned her into a strong prestige asset and a box-office gold mine for Metro-Goldwyn-Mayer.

Norma Shearer was also a much finer actress than some latter-day commentators are willing to concede. Far from being "mannered," "surfacey," "cold," and "flighty," the emotions she projected from the nation's screens were powerful and arresting. Many of her admirers feel that *The Barretts of Wimpole Street* (1934) was her finest performance, and she was indeed moving as the poetess Elizabeth Barrett Browning, but to me, *Marie Antoinette* (1938) is her masterpiece. In this picture, for which she won one of her five Oscar nominations, she ran the gamut from innocent girlishness to disillusioned maturity. Her characterization was deeply feminine, fully realized, sincerely felt. She played with bravura, technical resource, and versatility, and with a consummate authority seldom duplicated on the screen. A true original, Shearer galvanized audiences in the more rousing scenes and reduced them to tears in the prison and guillotine sequences.

Shearer's Juliet is another fine performance. With Leslie Howard as Romeo, this Thalberg superspectacle was the big cinema event of 1936. Some thought thirty-five-year-old Shearer somewhat mature for the girlish rhapsodizings of Juliet, but aided by expert coaching from several Shakespearean actresses, and after much thought, study, and application, she gave a polished and professional rendition, all the more remarkable because she had never done Shakespeare in a full-length performance.

In *The Women* (1939) she was warm and wise and womanly. Indeed, in this screen version of Clare Boothe's trenchant Broadway play, Shearer performed solidly as the betrayed wife who returns to her errant but finally contrite husband at the fadeout with the oft-quoted words: "Pride is a luxury that a woman in love can't afford!" Joan Crawford

gave stiff competition as her bitchy love rival, and many felt
that Rosalind Russell, as the malicious gossip, stole the show,
but Shearer held her own and won fine critical notices.

It should be noted that such fine Shearer performances as
Marie Antoinette, The Women, and *Escape* came in the years
after Thalberg's death. Thrown back on her own, Shearer
demonstrated conclusively that consummate self-sufficiency,
personally and in her career, that had always been one of her
outstanding qualities. From her earliest days she had had only
herself, her will, her drive, to sustain her.

As a mother, she delivered admirably. Irving Thalberg, Jr.,
who was born in 1930 and who died in 1987, was a scholarly,
retiring man who shunned the Hollywood limelight and lifestyle and eventually became a university professor of philosophy after serving in the Korean War. Katherine, born in 1935,
a year before her father's death, also shunned publicity and
Hollywood, settling for a career as housewife and mother.
Among her husbands was the actor Richard Anderson. The
overall steady course of both children's lives attests to
Shearer's positive qualities as a parent.

Like Garbo, Shearer retired in 1942, at the age of forty-
two. She said she wanted the fans to remember her at the
height of her beauty. Certainly there was an element of vanity
in this, a touch of the Norma Desmond of *Sunset Boulevard.*
But basically Shearer had had her fill of career strivings and
pressures, and elected for personal happiness. Garbo had not
really meant to retire, but the failure of her weak comedy,
Two-Faced Woman, in 1941 had discouraged her, and when
the European market, where she had always been strongest,
collapsed with World War II, her box-office draw was im-
paired. Both Garbo and Shearer toyed with "comebacks" in
the late 1940s, but the fact that neither followed through seriously makes it obvious that they wanted out, permanently.

Other stars of their era, like Joan Crawford, went to other
studios and even greater success, with Crawford winning an
Oscar in 1945 for *Mildred Pierce* at Warners. Crawford, in
fact, continued in films for another twenty-five years, but after

1957 the quality of her roles steadily diminished and she wound up in horror spinoffs, growing old before the audience's eyes (she was sixty-six when her final film, *Trog,* was released).

Bette Davis was another who lingered too long. After 1953 her films slipped in quality and in the 1960s and 1970s she, also, found herself doing horror-style grotesqueries. She, too, grew old before her audiences, and her celebrated technique became a caricature of its former excellence. Barbara Stanwyck and Sylvia Sidney also aged before the camera, though their roles had more substance than Crawford's and Davis's and they eased into "character star" status. Others, like Rita Hayworth, Hedy Lamarr, and Lana Turner, who had depended on their beauty and sex appeal to put them over, faded out. The fates of these actresses indicate that Shearer's decision to retire while still "looking her best" might have been a wise move after all.

Norma Shearer is fondly recalled today by those remaining few who knew her when she was a reigning star, and she is winning fresh new audiences among subsequent generations, who enjoy her performances in movie revival houses and on videocassettes. "Nature broke the mold when it made *her,*" an old Metro-Goldwyn-Mayer associate said recently, "and when you play a *Marie Antoinette* against some of the weak, forgettable stuff today's female 'stars' are turning out, you realize that a light has gone out of Hollywood in more ways than one."

1

Love and Death
in Montreal

S HEARER was born Edith Norma Shearer on August
10, 1900 (not 1902, or 1904, as studio publicity later
claimed) in the then-affluent suburb of Westmount, a
part of Montreal, Canada. Her father, Andrew Shearer, of
Scottish descent, was at the time president of the Shearer,
Brown and Wills Construction Company. Her grandfather,
James Shearer, had founded the company and had been a
powerful force in Montreal business life, building some of the
city's prominent structures. Her mother, born Edith Fisher,
was of English descent, and had come from Islington, near
Toronto; *her* maternal grandfather had been a famous
Toronto minister who supposedly had preached the first ser-
mon in the region. The family included Norma's two-year-
younger sister, Athole (pronounced *ä thō le,* with accent on
all three syllables) and her two-years-older brother, Douglas.
She had been named Edith after her mother. Edith had seen
the names "Norma" and "Athole," which studio publicists
later called family-originated, in an old playbill. At the time
of Norma's birth, the family was financially well fixed, and
respected and admired in Montreal social circles.

Norma said in a 1936 interview:

> As a child, mine was a glorious life, one for which I have
> never ceased to be thankful. . . . My parents were decid-
> edly not the pampering type, which, whether or not they
> realized it at the time, was a substantial rock in the founda-
> tions they were building for us. We were given greater free-
> dom and more opportunities to show initiative than is the
> lot of most youngsters.
>
> Because I loved this freedom, I preferred to study at
> home rather than be confined to a schoolroom. In many
> ways this was an advantage, but then sometimes one is not
> so sure. Education, even the conventional kind, is a fortify-
> ing armor; but so is the spirit bred by freedom and finding
> out things for yourself. Who can tell?

The two-story brick house at 507 Grosvenor Street har-
bored a family replete with an unusual sense of well-being.
Norma recalled the special closeness she was to know with her
brother and sister, their one-for-all and all-for-one spirit. As
she remembered it, their interplay was singularly free of what
came to be known later as sibling rivalry. She recalls that they
were always there for each other, and that this was to hold
true for all their lives.

When they were each about 14, Norma and Athole entered
Westmount High School. Norma remembered being the ring-
leader in whatever adolescent mischief was perpetrated. Later
she stated that she was probably compensating in adolescence
for the long periods in childhood when she seemed to be per-
petually ill. The Canadian winters were harsh ones, and she
contracted colds easily. As this was especially true before she
was ten, her delicate health—as well as her and her parents'
ideas of "freedom"—was probably why she was schooled at
home.

As Canadians are children of the great outdoors ("There
was so much of it, too!" Norma later said, laughing), she and
her siblings were encouraged to participate in all manner of

sports, including riding, skiing, ice-skating, tobogganing, and in the summer such activities as swimming and canoeing. She remembered the period between fourteen and sixteen as "a pleasant dream."

Norma was particularly fond of their summer sojourns at the Shearer country place, Millwood, located near the Humber River. Her grandfather Shearer had bought the property as an investment decades before, and there had constructed a wonderful old mill, where she and her sister loved to retreat. "We would explore all its strange corners, and the things we came up with!" In later years she was to make a sentimental pilgrimage to that happy spot, and would there know a shocking disillusionment—the old mill had succumbed to the invasions of modern life, with the lulling sound of the falls overcome by cacophonous sounds from a nightclub on the opposite side of the river. She, Athole, and Douglas had loved swimming in that river—all were experts—but when a child drowned there, her parents prohibited unsupervised swimming. "That was my very first experience of death—it had a sobering effect," Norma remembered. "It was my first intimation that life had its darker side." She talked it over with her father. "Life is like a room filled with hanging wires," he counseled her gravely, "and you have to avoid jangling the wires if you want to reach the exit." It was advice she was never to forget.

As a child she was all things to all people. She could enjoy the rough-and-tumble companionship of her brother's pals, considered herself their physical equal, enjoyed besting them in snowball fights, and frightened her mother when she came home one February evening to report gaily that she had accepted a dare from the boys and had skated far out on a lake whose ice had not sufficiently hardened. "How I escaped disaster *that* time, I will never know!" she told me, laughing.

I always liked the company of boys, but I was never a tomboy. And even at an early age, long before twelve, I was aware of how attractive a boy could be, especially if he were strong and handsome and athletic. I had my share of "crushes" from the very beginning, but I guess it was my Scottish practicality, inherited from my father, that had me analyzing things while I felt them, and when a boy wanted me to go off in the woods with him, I always held back. So did my sister. Mother had warned me, as early as four or five, that boys liked to "play doctor" and that was a game to be avoided.

But that didn't discourage Norma's romantic feelings. (She had dropped the "Edith" early in life to avoid confusion with her mother; also she felt the name "Norma" was more glamorous, "just like an actress's."

Norma gave an interesting clue to her adult life when she recalled one of her earliest childhood memories. She often heard her mother refer to her father as "my husband." Five-year-old Norma, sitting on the front stoop of her house, was watching a new family moving in next door. When she saw the handsome young son, who must have been about nine years old at the time, she took in his blond hair, blue eyes, and stalwart young shoulders and told herself: "There he is . . . *my* husband. . . ." She began referring to the boy as "my husband" in confidences with her sister and her friends, and took a lot of teasing about it. Then, about two years later, had come a tragedy. The boy was killed when the bike he was riding was hit by a truck.

"I couldn't have been more than seven or eight," she remembered, "but I begged Mother to let me see him laid out in his coffin." She thought it a morbid wish, but as she was paying her respects anyway, Edith Shearer took Norma along.

It was awful—terrible! The parents were grief-stricken, with the mother loudly crying and the father gray. All these years and I can remember the scene with photographic clarity. And the boy I called "my husband"—he looked so beautiful in the coffin, with flowers all around him; he was in a black suit with a bow tie. Suddenly I knew I would never hear him shouting greetings across the fence to me again; I would never see him on his bicycle . . . My "husband" was dead. I burst into wild tears. My mother took me home and for many nights I cried over him.

"Childhood shows the man," the famous saying goes. Such a traumatic incident shows that in Shearer's case, "childhood showed the *woman,*" too. Shearer would later become one of our most sensitive actresses.

She remembered also having a gentling influence on the boys she palled around with. Once the boys had cornered a squirrel in a tree; as they grabbed it and began to torture it, Norma jumped on the boys' backs, then turned and faced them and pummeled them with her fists. Startled, the boys dropped the squirrel and fled. The squirrel raced for the safety of a tall tree.

"I liked boys and even loved them," she remembered, "but I knew how to stand my ground when it was necessary." Again a prophetic note had been sounded for the future star Norma Shearer, future consort of the MGM lion.

She always had a love for music, with a fine ear and perfect pitch and timing; her mother took note of it and started Norma on the piano at age eight. She practiced constantly, so eager was she to perfect her command of the instrument, and soon graduated to the less complicated pieces of Chopin, Brahms, and Schumann. "I was too precocious for my own good," she said, laughing, years later. "Not only at the piano but at dreaming of handsome boys when Chopin, especially, got to me. The term 'boy crazy' wasn't in fashion then, of course, but it would certainly have applied to me."

When the neighbors began stopping by the open music-room window to hear Norma play, and when a schoolteacher remarked on her evident talent, Edith Shearer decided that Norma would make a concert pianist. Young as she was, she was taken to the famous Blossom Connelly, a forlorn, little hunch-backed woman who, as Athole later recalled, "suddenly became the most beautiful lady you ever saw when she

got going on the keyboard. It was like she was transformed."
As Shearer remembered it: "Together we would sit before the
piano and plan that day when I would take the final examina-
tion of the Royal Academy of Music. Blossom was full of op-
timism. Passing it meant mounting the steps that would lead
to musical fame."

But again death interposed itself between Shearer's dream
and fulfillment. Death once had robbed her of a vision of
love; now it crushed her hopes for a concert pianist's career.
Blossom Connelly, always frail and beset with health problems, died suddenly. As Norma remembered it in a 1936 interview, "This fine dream castle crashed in ruins around my
feet. My future and Miss Connelly were so intertwined that it
was impossible to imagine continuing alone. Music seemed
suddenly wiped out of my existence. . . . Upon recovering
from the shock, I closed the piano and never took another
lesson. But this was not the last of pianos. They were to have
a greater influence on my life and career than I realized.
Three times a piano was responsible for turning my steps toward the acting profession."

One summer day she visited two graves—that of the young
neighbor boy and that of the frail music teacher who became
transformed when she began to play. When she went home,
she received another traumatic shock—one that was to affect
her for the rest of her life.

Her mother sat the children down and quietly explained
that they would have to move. As Norma remembered it: "At
first it was difficult to grasp. Move from the home of our
babyhood—the only home we had ever known? We bom-
barded Mother with questions. Finally she explained that Father's business had had serious reverses and we had to
retrench. And that was the first time I was conscious of the
word 'fail.' My father's business had 'failed temporarily,' they
said."

She remembered forming an instantaneous and permanent
dislike for the word "fail." Hardy Scottish people didn't fail.
They might trip and fall but they always picked themselves

right up again. A temporary reverse, yes. Failure—real failure, no. She recalled, "At that early date I formed a philosophy about failure. Perhaps an endeavor, like my father's business, could fail, but that didn't mean Father had failed." Norma likened it, in her mind, to the many games she had played with her siblings and her friends. More than once her efforts to come out on top had failed, but she could always play the same game again—and this time emerge the winner! But she came, in time, to feel that her father *had* failed, personally.

She remembered her feelings of depression when they moved into the new house. It was much smaller. It had an air of pinched poverty about it. The floors and walls looked hard-used and scruffy. Some of their furniture had come with them from the old house, and it looked inappropriate in the meaner surroundings. The rest had been sold to pay debts; so had the horses and carriages. The shiny new automobiles her father had planned to buy, and in which she and her pals would whirl merrily through the Montreal streets, were never to be. Two memories of that humiliating "comedown" period stayed especially: "The icebox in the kitchen did not have the fat, prosperous appearance that we had known, and the dining-room table looked small and a little bit forlorn."

Soon it became unbearable to see her father's beaten-down look, her mother's pinched features. Douglas went and got a job. Athole, too, made plans for employment. Norma's mind turned constantly on the matter of what *she* should do.

"Impossibly, romantically, impractically, and oh-so-foolishly," as she recalled it, her thoughts turned to acting. Ever since she was fifteen people had been telling her she had a special type of beauty. She didn't believe it herself, for her mirror had told her her eyes were small and "wall-eyed" and she detected a small cast in one that greatly embarrassed her. She set herself, nonetheless, to enter a beauty contest. Subtly applied makeup made her look a little older and the eyeliner disguised the cast. To her surprise, she received first prize. She then talked her mother, who was beginning to sense that

she just might have the makings of an actress in the family,
into letting her join a local amateur theater group. To be sure,
it didn't pay, but she had to start somewhere, she reasoned.
To impress the recruiting committee she recited such peren-
nial favorites as "Dangerous Dan McGrew" and "The Face
on the Bar-room Floor" written by her favorite author, Robert W. Service, a Canadian. She figured he would bring her
luck. The dramatic troupe accepted her. Among the "actors"
were several extremely handsome boys from Montreal's upper
crust, who proceeded to make a play for her. But feeling that
she couldn't invite them to her mean little house, Shearer refused all dates. "I won't have those rich boys looking down at
me," she told her brother. Athole later recalled that there
was one boy, blond and blue-eyed like Norma's childhood
love, whom she had particularly liked but had been too proud
to pursue, as he was the son of one of Montreal's richest en-
trepreneurs.

Years later, in looking back on that period of sudden and
stark penury, Norma Shearer told me: "In many ways it is
worse to have had money and then to lose it. The comedown,
the contrast is so terrible! If you have been poor from the
start you don't know what you lost, and don't know what you
missed." Her father, Andrew, once so hearty and confident,
seemed to have shrunk into himself. With his business failure
he seemed to have lost part of his manhood. And it broke
Norma's heart to see Douglas, her gifted, inventive brother,
forced to take jobs way below his potential.

At this point, guilt set in. The others were trying to earn
money; she would have to, also. If she didn't, she couldn't
live with herself. To her family's surprise, she started practic-
ing piano again; this time it was not the handsome baby grand
of the other home; it was a second-hand upright. And her aim
was practical.

She searched for jobs around Montreal while pretending to
be at the movies or the library. After a day of rejection at
various firms, she would sneak into the movies on the lunch
money her mother had given her. She remembered that Pearl

White was a particular favorite. She would sit for hours watching Pearl's hair-raising adventures, often seeing two shows for the price of one after hiding in the ladies' room of the Strand Theatre between screenings. She would also sit near the pianist, watching closely as he kept his inventive scorings timed to Pearl's stunts. She went around to other movie houses and left her name, saying she was an expert pianist and could accommodate her style to anything they wanted.

One of the big events of that time was Pearl White's special appearance at the Strand. When White, to the acclaim of Montreal movie enthusiasts lined up three deep around the block, got into her handsome limousine, Norma followed her on bicycle all the way back to her hotel. As she waited to see the popular star sweep through the lobby, someone stole her bicycle. Soon she was back walking to save carfare.

One of the boys at the amateur theatrical troupe told her that she was particularly enchanting when she smiled. To see if her smile might gain her a job, one day Norma entered a sheet music store near St. James Cathedral and gave the proprietor the biggest, widest smile she could summon.

She told him of her playing skills and soon had charmed him into letting her play. "If you can play those popular tunes from the sheet music fast and snappy, you'll have a job," he told her. She gave the tunes everything she had, and was hired for ten dollars a week. As she remembered it, "To say that was an elating experience would be to put my actual state of mind mildly. And so I went blithely from Mozart and Chopin to Tin Pan Alley's current musical whims."

Shearer proceeded to regale the customers with "snappy" and "fast" renditions of such popular fare as "On the Beach at Waikiki" and "They're Wearing Them Higher in Hawaii." Meanwhile Athole had secured work in an office as a clerk and Mrs. Shearer embarrassed her harried husband by becoming a saleslady in a department store. Douglas, who had long shown an interest in engineering, had gotten a job with a firm selling electrical apparatus. All the salaries were small,

however, and what with the debts and assorted expenses resulting from the business failure, there was never enough to
go around. "They say poverty is a state of mind, and certainly
we had every encouragement to *stay* in that state of mind,"
Norma remembered later.

Meanwhile her mother had decided that the middle-aged
and married proprietor of the sheet music store might be contemplating a seduction of his popular young pianist. "How do
you *know* that, Mother?" Norma asked. "Never you mind,
girl; I *know*" was the retort. One day when Norma was happily playing away surrounded by young men on their lunch
hour, her mother stalked into the store. "The expression in
her eyes was not one to be soon forgotten," Norma recalled.
"Then and there a budding career as a song-plugger ended.
The proprietor still owes me half a week's salary!"

At home that night, there was a special family conference.
Her father sat with the children, mute. His wife did all the
talking. She said that Andrew Shearer had to stay in Montreal
to try to recoup some of the heavy losses resulting from unfor-
tunate investments he had made after selling his share of the
company. Instead of handing the money to her, he had made
those bad investments without telling her, and now everything
was gone. That, Edith Shearer snapped, was what happened
when a man didn't consult with his wife on all important
moves. Under new ownership, the firm named for her grandfather was starting to prosper, but the Shearers were out of it
now, her mother said. No use trying to salvage the unsal-
vageable or cry after spilt milk. Norma shrank inwardly from
the expression of miserable defeat on her father's face and
realized that the family could never depend on him again.
She, her mother, her brother, and her sister were on their
own. If they were to escape from the poverty to which they
would never allow themselves to become accustomed, they
would have to follow their own counsel. Norma yet again experienced a profound disappointment in her father that would
never leave her. The trauma ran deep. It would influence her
in the direction, later, of older men who represented the suc-

cess and fatherly protection that Andrew Shearer had somehow abdicated.

After her father quietly left the room that night, the other
four began to discuss the future. Athole hated her clerkship;
the work was boring and the men were too fresh, she said.
Douglas said he wanted to stay in Montreal where he hoped
to advance in his firm.

Edith Shearer then came up with a plan. Why not try New
York? New York! Yes, Edith said. Her girls were both pretty.
Why not try becoming professional actresses, or models?
With her on hand there would be no dangers for them. "I'm
afraid my mother was an exponent of the all-men-are-beasts
school, old-fashioned as it was becoming even in 1920,"
Norma said later. "Two sisters alone in New York would be
their prey. But with *her* to watch over them, well—things
might work out differently!" Edith's brother had married an
actress, one Gertrude Ritchie. They had started several theater companies. Perhaps they could provide references in
New York. Norma suddenly recalled Aunt Gertrude's glamorous life. When visiting her aunt and uncle she would sometimes purloin Gertrude's makeup box and goo herself up to
the nines. She remembered talking theater shop with them,
and their encouragement. But there was a problem; they
didn't have the required "pull" in far-off New York; in the
world of Manhattan they were "small time." All they could
offer was an introduction to a friend of Gertrude's, a former
actress, who owned a small boardinghouse in New York; she
might put them up cheap. They solved the problem of trans-
portation and temporary expenses by selling the piano. In
Norma's words: "It was the money secured by its sale that
sent the three of us, Mother, Athole, and myself, on a great
adventure. . . ."

2

The Siege of
Big, Bad New York

NEW YORK in 1920 was an exciting—and frightening—place for three gently reared women who were
accustomed to Montreal's far slower, more muted
pace. Canada's biggest city it might be, but it went about its
business in a more relaxed, genteel style, as Norma remembered years later, when she tried to re-create the "culture
shock" of New York. "To come to Manhattan on vacation or
with plenty of money would have been shock enough—but to
come to it *poor*—that was really a toughening experience,"
she said.

World War I had ended only a year or so before, and in its
wake it had brought the social and cultural displacements and
disillusionments that led directly into the jazz age, the age
immortalized by F. Scott Fitzgerald, whose smash-hit first
novel, *This Side of Paradise,* would be the Manhattan vogue
of that year. Scott and Norma's paths were to cross later—
much later. In 1920 she had ventured into Manhattan poor,
unknown, not even an American citizen. He, on the other
hand, was the young novelist of the hour. Time was to bring a
strange reversal in their relative circumstances.

Everything in New York bewildered the Shearers—the lights, the fast pace of the traffic, the frenetically busy people on the street, too many of whom scorned to wait for the traffic lights they considered nuisances. The New York theaters were going full blast, with their glamorous stars showcased on garish billboards and brilliantly lit theater marquees. Movie houses were popping up everywhere, and Norma and Athole remembered sneaking into the handsome new Capitol to see the movie and stage show. At Broadway and 45th Street, the flourishing Loews, Inc., was about to build its handsome new sandstone edifice; the ground for it was already broken. Edith went on a walking tour their first day, from Central Park down to 40th Street, and declared the people vulgar, pushy, inconsiderate—in short, inhuman. The girls paid no attention. It was the vitality of New York they noted, its aura of success, upward mobility, get-up-and-go—its unlimited promise of new horizons, endless possibilities, fulfilled dreams, and the excitement of the unknown. Norma was to remember her first impression when they got off the train from Montreal—the feeling of how wonderful it was to be nineteen years old in the winter of 1920 and to feel she had her whole life before her and could—and *would*—make of it whatever she wished. Her wishes, she knew, were unlimited, boundless as the sea, and she could not, would not, be unduly disheartened by her more realistic mother's favorite and oft-repeated pronouncement: "If wishes were horses, beggars would ride."

As they walked along 42nd Street, Norma and Athole noticed the young men of New York—how much more masculine, enterprising, exciting, and dynamic they seemed. And even the older men had about them a look, a confidence, a purposefulness, a gleam in the eye that her own father's eye had lost. These men looked tough compared to her gentle father; they looked as if they could absorb anything the Big Town could dish out and come back slugging. Both girls felt the sexual pull of these men—it was something visceral, something strange and dynamic.

Edith had come to New York forearmed for all contingencies. She had gone to every theatrical manager and every movie house operator in Montreal, most of them absolute strangers, and had wheedled about a dozen introductions to prominent men in the New York theatrical and movie worlds. Among those introductions were letters to Florenz Ziegfeld, whose Follies and musical shows had made him the biggest man on Broadway, George M. Cohan, who was equally famous, and, on the movie side, Marcus Loew, Carl Laemmle—and James R. Quirk, editor of *Photoplay Magazine,* the most influential 1920 screen journal.

But first there was the matter of where to live. When they arrived at the ramshackle boardinghouse run by Aunt Gertrude's friend at Eighth Avenue and West 57th Street, their hearts sank.

Aunt Gertrude had said the proprietor, her former-actress pal, was "really an *angel*; she may even let you take rooms *for free* for a while," she had gushed, as it turned out unrealistically.

The lady of the house, surrounded by depressing grime, doors that looked none too secure, and down-and-out theatrical people slinking through the hallways, informed the Shearers that she wasn't running a charity flophouse and that the rent was $7.50 a week, take it or leave it. They took it.

The next day Edith Shearer went to four department stores and finally landed a salesclerk's job. The girls were sent out to hunt acting jobs.

As Norma later remembered the boardinghouse:

> The elevated trains roared past our windows like dragons, every dull, yellow light a blinking eye. Sleep, for the first few nights, was impossible. We cooked our coffee over a tin of solid alcohol and ate breakfast off the top of a trunk. It was all so strange! Somehow we weren't in the least discouraged, in spite of the fact that none of us knew the first thing about the theatrical profession.
>
> "The whole experience was new and thrilling, and we welcomed it. For one thing we had the glorious thrill of

being wide-eyed nonentities in the most invigorating city in the world. . . . At this time I was just at the age when young women get their own ideas about dress. New York shops fascinated me—one in particular, in which there was a hat that I felt I couldn't live without. I remember it so well. It was a strictly afternoon model, trimmed with a tiny pink ostrich feather. I bought it in spite of the fact that it didn't go at all well with my strictly sports coat."

Despite their efforts to keep up their spirits, the girls found the room depressing. Edith was out all day at her department store job and came home too tired to care much about her surroundings, but the girls were there for part of the day. The room had one double bed and a cot—without a mattress. The wardrobe trunk was their eating table and the stove was only a small gas jet where they made their skimpy breakfast, a monotonous round of coffee, marmalade, and hardened rolls. Juice was too expensive, so they skipped it. They went without lunch and, after much debate over costs, managed to eat a spartan meal, three nights a week, in one of the cheap restaurants nearby. Eggplant was a favorite, because it cost less. When they ate "dinner" at home, the meal came out of cans.

They had arrived in February (1920), the height of winter, and the room was not adequately heated; often they nearly froze, as the draft came in from the cracks in the window, and when the old radiator sputtered out, they bundled, all three of them, in the one bed to keep warm.

Despite the skimping and the steady dwindling of the money from the piano sale, Norma and Athole realized that they had to have presentable clothes with which to make their rounds. Norma's first "making-the-rounds dress" had been an unfashionable affair—a hobble skirt reaching to her ankles, a wide-brimmed, unfashionable hat with ribbon straggling down the back. She then went out looking for bargains in cheaper stores and came up with a mannish coat, man's hat and cane, with which she hoped to attract attention. Edith promptly vetoed the outfit as apt to cause the *wrong* kind of attention from the wrong men, and she bought materials with which to fashion for Norma what she considered appropriate "rounds" attire.

Father, in Montreal, wrote infrequently, and Edith's attitude was: "If he can't send good or encouraging news, what difference does it make?" Norma and Athole felt saddened when their mother complained of being on her feet all day; watching her soak her toes in a tub was always depressing.

Soon Edith announced that they would start bearding the theatrical and film men with letters of introduction.

3

Married Men, Wolves, and Movies

AS EDITH was busy days at the department store, Norma and Athole went on their rounds without her. They split up the introduction letters fifty-fifty, and Norma went downtown to the offices of *Photoplay Magazine*. A Montreal movie-house manager had told Edith that *Photoplay*'s editor, Jimmy Quirk, was widely influential in films and could help her.

At the time of their first face-to-face meeting, Norma was nineteen and Jimmy Quirk thirty-five. He was a dynamic Irishman with a quick wit and flashing blue eyes; married for eleven years, he was the father of two small daughters. He was noted for his kindnesses to actors and his admiration for creative people in general. In six years he had turned *Photoplay* from a seldom-read little journal featuring mainly movie plots into a prestige magazine with a wide film and theater audience. Jimmy was consulted by top producers on anything and everything, and his chief Hollywood writer, the flamboyant and vivacious Adela Rogers St. Johns, was already noted for her sparkling profiles of movie personalities.

Despite the fact that Jimmy's secretary told him that a shy, rather drab-looking young girl was waiting, without an appointment or phone call, in his outer office, armed only with a letter of introduction, he did not keep Norma waiting. Jimmy had met the letter writer in New York the year before, and read with interest what he had to say about Norma. Soon she was ushered into his office.

His practiced eye took immediate note of her liabilities. Her teeth needed some work, she had a slight cast in one eye, and her legs, he saw, were not among her prime assets. She was a petite five feet two, with brown hair and blue eyes. They talked awhile and she mentioned that she would be going over to see Ziegfeld with her next letter. Jimmy penned a quick note to Ziegfeld, whom he knew well, and mentioned to Norma that the famed stage entrepreneur would be casting his new edition of the Follies soon and that he might have something for her. Privately, Jimmy had reservations. He didn't think Norma would be Ziegfeld's type, but he didn't want to discourage her. When Ziegfeld gave her a few minutes, during a busy rehearsal at the New Amsterdam on 42nd Street, he immediately noted the cast in the eye, the teeth, and the legs. Also her height; she simply wasn't tall enough to be a Ziegfeld girl. In other departments he found Norma unexceptional. Trying to be nice, he read the letter from his Montreal acquaintance and gave her two tickets for his show. Then he sent her on her way with a noncommittal observation that she should stay in touch.

Later Ziegfeld phoned Jimmy Quirk. "Why did you send me *that* dog?" he asked. "I didn't send her; the Montreal guys sent her." Jimmy then proceeded to tell Ziggy that he was wrong, that he sensed potential there, however green and unformed. "There's an intensity, a determination about her," Jimmy said.

"Well, if you're so interested, start with that damned eye!" Ziggy snapped. Jimmy Quirk was to admit years later to my mother, Margaret Connery Quirk, who became his sister-in-law in 1922, that he had felt an instant attraction to Norma. Her vulnerability, along with her spunk, had impressed him.

But in 1920 Jimmy was still trying to make a success of his first marriage and he was in a husband-and-daddy phase. (He and Norma were to become close in the future.)

But he did phone her, he told my mother, shortly after their first meeting, and bluntly advised her to consult an eye specialist about the cast and to get her teeth capped at the first opportunity. She was later to follow his advice about the eye doctor, who performed a simple operation that disguised the cast almost completely; careful eye makeup took care of the rest. "Of course there was nothing I could do about my legs; they were my worst feature," Norma told me years later. Laughing, she added: "I was always grateful when the styles sent the hemlines plummeting toward the ankles." She also did slimming exercises that concentrated on her ankles and calves. ". . . I distracted attention from [my legs] every way I could!" she told Adela Rogers St. Johns, to whom Jimmy introduced her on Adela's next visit to New York from Hollywood. "She had the slowest rise of any star I ever knew," Adela told me years later. "Sheer grit made the difference; that little girl overcame many obstacles all along the way. There was steel under that sweetness and gentility, and she let everyone know it, in time."

In that same phone call, Jimmy told Norma he would keep an eye out for any opportunities for her, and took down her address. He was to make good on his promise several times over the next four years.

Norma and Athole continued to make the rounds. The other introductions turned into dry holes—holes as big as those in her shoes. Norma concealed these with artfully arranged pasteboards and made sure that when she sat in receptionists' offices she kept her feet flat on the floor. Jimmy Quirk had recommended a reputable film bureau, where Norma and Athole both registered. Some calls for extra work came their way. Once twelve girls were needed, but when Norma and Athole arrived, they found about sixty ahead of them. Norma seized on the strategy of coughing loudly to at-

tract the casting director's attention. She and Athole moved
to the top of the list, and started at five dollars a day.

If the sun shone, the picture was shot; if it was cloudy everyone sat around waiting for better weather—without pay.
The company then repaired to Mount Vernon—and a drafty
studio where both sisters caught colds. Too poor to afford
makeup, Norma and Athole borrowed it from the other girls.
Norma was later to remember the long narrow room in which
they dressed, the wind howling through the window cracks.
Sometimes they didn't get back to Eighth and 57th before
midnight. Much of their work landed on the cutting-room
floor.

Norma Shearer always listed her first official picture as *The
Flapper,* starring the lovely Olive Thomas, who would within
the year marry Jack Pickford and die mysteriously of barbiturate poisoning in Paris. Offered the usual five dollars a day,
Norma maneuvered to turn her extra work into her first bit
part, fleeting to be sure, but she did escape the cutter this
time out. Daring and enterprising as always, Norma also managed to get Athole into the picture as an extra, and, pulling a
colossal bluff, haughtily informed the assistant director that
she needed better clothes and needed one hundred dollars to
buy them. Her air of experience impressed the man, and she
got the money. She used it to get the eye operation that
Jimmy Quirk had recommended (one hundred dollars went a
lot farther in 1920 than in 1988).

The film was largely shot in Tarrytown-on-Hudson, and one
scene called for one hundred extra girls and bit players to go
sliding down a long hill on bobsleds. Several of the girls, including Athole, were seriously hurt in the stunt, and Athole
landed in the hospital for weeks, leaving Norma to carry on
alone.

Norma was never to forget the personal kindnesses that
Olive Thomas showed her and her sister at that time; she sent
Athole flowers, Norma remembered, and quietly defrayed the
hospital expenses while lending them a little money to tide
them over. Five years later, when Norma was Jack Pickford's

leading lady in a film, she remembered commenting how tragically brief Olive's life had been when she was such a lovely person who deserved so much to live. "Jack only frowned and turned away without a word." She added, "I wonder what *really* happened that tragic night in Paris? . . ."

As Norma remembered the weeks that followed: "They were pretty cheerless, especially for youth and ambition. Occasionally a day's work as an extra would appear at seven dollars and a half. Subtract from that amount five dollars for a rented costume, fifty cents for the agency procuring the job, street car and bus fares, and the remaining pennies looked sad indeed."

Jimmy Quirk came to the rescue and spoke to his friend William Randolph Hearst, whose flamboyant but affable mistress Marion Davies was making a picture called *The Restless Sex* at the Cosmopolitan studios. Hearst sent Norma to director Robert Z. Leonard, who was kind but disinterested. She got a few passing seconds in the film, mostly hidden behind others in the crowd scenes. Again pressured by Jimmy, who had done him and Marion a number of favors and featured her flatteringly in *Photoplay,* Hearst had Norma formally screen-tested. The publisher was unimpressed. Nothing came of it.

Unfazed, Jimmy Quirk next sent her over to the *Way Down East* location up in Mamaroneck. She arrived in time to see Lillian Gish get rescued by Richard Barthelmess in the famous ice-floes-approaching-the-falls scene. "I'm not so sure I want to be in that picture," she told Athole and Edith later. "If that's how they treat the *stars,* how in heaven will they treat the *extras*?" Griffith, who saw her only to please Jimmy, was also unimpressed with her. His advice was curt and to the point. Her eyes would not photograph well, she was on the short side, and he didn't think her cut out for the cinema. He urged her to go home to Montreal. But to please Jimmy, Griffith put Norma into a sleigh scene; she was left in the final cut but you have to look sharp—very sharp—to find her flashing by. Norma did not hold Griffith's indifference to her potential against him, and later expressed her admiration for his talent and dedication, recalling: "I always remember his amazing habit of disregarding time. We knocked off meals at any time, and the end of the day was just as likely to be twelve or one o'clock that night. But we didn't mind it because of the tremendous thrill of working for the great D.W."

With the cast in her eye ameliorated and with her increasing expertise with makeup, plus work on her teeth (they were later capped; for a time she wore a brace on them), Norma felt she was ready for modeling jobs. Jimmy Quirk put her in touch with his cover illustrator and introduced her to Rolf Armstrong, a famous illustrator and artist. He used her for a number of ads, and through Armstrong she met James Montgomery Flagg, who years later would do distinctive covers for *Photoplay*. Charles Dana Gibson, the illustrator, also gave her work, and then the Kelly-Springfield tire executives, who had seen her in an Armstrong pose, sent for her, tested her, and proceeded to plaster her face all over the billboards peeking out from a tire; dubbed "Miss Lotta Miles," these jobs helped make Norma's face familiar to the public. Next she was posing for toothpaste, housecoat, and rouge ads, meeting some creative photographers along the way. It was from these men, she later claimed, that she learned the mastery of facial expression that later served her well in her films.

Meanwhile Athole, now fully recovered physically from the accident on the *Flapper* location, decided to follow other pursuits. Eventually she settled for marriage, becoming in 1928 the first wife of the famous director Howard Hawks and the mother of his children. "I'm glad Athole got out of that rat race; she was sensitive and it could be abrasive in so many ways. And she lacked my driving ambition—perhaps she was luckier than I, who knows?" Norma said years later.

When the modeling jobs ran dry, Norma tried to play the piano in movie houses but she didn't play speedily or snappily enough and lacked the necessary union card.

Arnold Genthe's distinctive portraits of actresses, arrived

or aspiring, made him a much-sought-after photographer. Five years later his pictures of Garbo helped land her the serious attention that shortly led to top stardom. Edith, whose philosophy was always "Aim high!" took Norma to see him and persuaded him to take more than a hundred pictures "on spec," complete with pay-later plan. They were never used in her efforts to secure roles, as the breaks came soon after, but the pictures have popped up from time to time and showcase twenty-year-old Norma in a haunting, evocative manner.

Finally a talent agent, Eddie Small, later a well-known Hollywood producer (*The Count of Monte Cristo, The Last of the Mohicans,*) signed Norma on. He got her a lead in a two-reeler with Johnny Hines of which only a single still remains. In it she looks strained and unhappy, nor is she well photographed. Small later talked her into a thriller called *The Sign on the Door,* directed by Herbert Brenon. She got a week's worth of work but her scenes were later cut entirely. "I don't like the way she photographs," Brenon told Small. Neither film appeared until early 1921.

But Small had an instinct about his client, and he persuaded the producers to give her a good supporting role in *The Stealers,* directed by Christy Cabanne for Robertson-Cole Productions and filmed in Mount Vernon.

Before these breaks, the Shearers had made one final, humiliating retreat home to Montreal, because Athole was homesick. Brother Douglas financed the trip. But Norma and her mother were home only a short time when the condescension of former friends proved too much for her. Also, Small contacted her and said that she might be replacing another actress in a film called *Pink Tights.* The lead, Gladys Walton, didn't like the fact that she had to partially disrobe, and had feigned illness. Overjoyed, Norma and her mother rushed back to New York and put up at a good hotel, waiting for more news. Then Walton changed her mind and resumed her role. The Shearers had only a few dollars left, and again Norma found herself back behind a piano in an Eighth Avenue movie house, "a dingy little pit," as she recalled.

Despite Norma's substantial part, *The Stealers* did not do as much for her as she had hoped. But it did mean that before she had spent a full year in New York, she had a role that put her right up front on the screen and in the ads. It also attracted the notice of young Irving Thalberg, then the twenty-one-year-old studio manager of Carl Laemmle's Universal Films in Hollywood. He sent an offer of a contract but Small, to her extreme regret, vetoed it because he didn't think the money warranted her moving to California. Norma had the wit to write Thalberg a note of thanks, expressing her hope of a future involvement. While it would not come for over three years, it was to prove worth the wait.

Today the plot of *The Stealers* seems ridiculous, and the film has never appeared on the list of Great Silent Films. Though advertised as something really special and directed with great energy by William Christy Cabanne, *The Stealers* was a paltry, melodramatic film in which Shearer was supposed to be the sweet, nice, and innocent daughter of a corrupt minister. The minister winds up leading a fancy crew of embezzlers in a small town. Overblown ads for the film read: "Every day people waging a baffling fight to solve The Greatest Mystery until, through the storm clouds of life, there breaks understanding which leads the way to that happiness which should be the lot of all." Yet Norma received one of her first pats on the back for her performance from a film reviewer, with Edwin Schallert commenting in *The Los Angeles Times*: "The daughter is ably interpreted by Norma Shearer."

The Stealers came and went, but on the strength of it Eddie Small got Norma into the first two of a series of two-reel features starring Reginald Denny that ran from 1922 to 1924. (Denny was later replaced by Billy Sullivan.) In these shorts, Denny played a pugilist with social graces and the beginnings of cultural pretensions. They were produced by Carl Laemmle's Universal-Jewell productions and directed by Harry Pollard from the popular H. C. Witwer weekly stories in *Collier's* magazine. Out in Hollywood, Thalberg again took note of Norma, and he began to keep a small file on her. "An interesting girl who doesn't look or act like anyone else!" one of his notations read. In the file was her original letter to him, which he always kept. Shearer's name did not appear in the ads for the first segments, though there is a drawing of her and Denny in a love scene. She had little to do except look pretty and make eyes at Denny.

In her first leading role in *The Man Who Paid,* released early in 1922, she was cast opposite handsome Wilfred Lytell, brother of the more famous Bert, a well-known stage and movie actor. Lytell is a trapper in a Canadian settlement who is wrongly accused of embezzlement. Shearer plays his patient, long-suffering, and passive wife and the mother of his child. She gets kidnapped by her husband's rival, gets rescued, and her husband is vindicated. In the reviews young Lytell came out well, but Shearer came out even better. The trade paper *Exhibitor's Herald* (New York) stated: "Miss Shearer's good looks are shown to advantage, and she not only photographs extremely well but shows no small amount of talent in the portrayal of her part." *Moving Picture World* considered her "pretty, and in her emotional scenes, very vivid." *Motion Picture News* went all out, with its critic stating that Norma embraced her acting opportunities "with a poise and skill that stamps this newcomer to the screen as an actress of promise. The girl has beauty and screen personality and she can act. Even in the wild melodrama that many parts of the picture exhibit, she is able to make her work hold attention and her role seem real."

Norma received fifth billing in her next film, *The Bootleggers,* in which she is up to her ears in center-stage melodrama: She gets shanghaied by a rum-runner on his boat and gets rescued by her naval officer boyfriend. Directed by Roy Sheldon, the film features such actors as Walter Miller and Paul Panzer. *Photoplay* dismissed it with: "much rum-running, a sick sister, a working girl, a lover in the revenue service, and a pseudo-Spanish villain. The old formulae." The magazine added: "If all the bootleggers were as dull and uninteresting as the picture of the name, Volstead would be right." Mary Kelly in *Motion Picture World* singled Norma out for praise, however, writing: "[She] is a pleasing figure in the midst of this turmoil. She has beauty, charm and dramatic sincerity."

During this period Norma shunted from one small production company to another, coping with all kinds of conditions and all kinds of personalities. "It kept me on my toes and certainly sharpened my mind," she said later. "And always, always, I was gaining in acting experience as I adjusted, in turn, to one director's conceptions after another. Sometimes he *had* no conceptions, but I had learned enough by then to take care of myself in the scenes I was given." During 1921 and 1922 she worked for such companies as First National, Educational, Robertson-Cole, Universal-Jewel, Apfel Productions, Film Booking Offices, and Select.

In her final 1922 film, *Channing of the Northwest,* Norma was the leading lady of the handsome and popular Eugene O'Brien, whose off-screen eye for the ladies rivaled that of another Shearer leading man, Wilfred Lytell. The plot was nonsense about a London playboy transplanted to Canada where he becomes a Mountie; it seems his fiancée back in England had given him the heave-ho when she learned he would be disinherited. He finds love in the backwoods—with Shearer, of course. There was more scenery on display than action, with only a fifty-minute running time, but director Ralph Ince and photographer Jack Brown saw that Shearer was displayed to advantage. Two reviews were typical: "Norma Shearer's acting is exceptionally clever. Her personal charm is a factor that will be recognized, too," *Motion Picture World* declared, while Laurence Reid in *Motion Picture News* stated: "Norma Shearer lends a fragrant charm and emotional capabilities of a high order to the role of the heroine."

Meanwhile *Photoplay,* presided over by her original mentor and continuous booster Jimmy Quirk, was featuring her in flattering layouts and stories, along with piquant column items. She was variously described in the magazine as "charming," "womanly," "serene," "beautiful," "restfully lovely," and "replete with true womanly dignity."

Ralph Ince and Eugene O'Brien were soon "coming on" to her, and she spent a certain percentage of the off-screen time in *Channing of the Northwest* eluding their advances. Ince proved easy enough to handle—he "had the restraints of an innate gentleman," as watchful mother Edith said, but O'Brien proved tougher to deal with. A man whom women invariably pursued, the handsome Eugene, then a youthful forty, was unaccustomed to rejection, and one day, after taking Norma to lunch and having managed to avoid her mother's perpetual watchfulness, he took her for a wild spin in his big yellow roadster. He would speed up Broadway with her, wearing his Mountie uniform and frightening pedestrians and fellow drivers alike with his sudden turns, after which they would wind up at a side-street tearoom in the West Forties where, she remembered, a very nice lunch was to be had for 35 cents. Soon Norma was dating O'Brien steadily. One day the car broke down under the Sixth Avenue elevated and defied all of O'Brien's self-declared mechanical skill. Red-faced, he pushed it to the curb with a cop's help while onlookers grinned at the big guy in the Mountie garb who couldn't even fix his own auto. The couple were forced to grab a taxi while the studio sent for a repairman and a tow service. This humiliated O'Brien so thoroughly that he didn't ask her to lunch with him again. But he did suggest dinner, at his place, candlelight and all, and at this Edith Shearer put down her foot. She didn't get much argument from Norma, who said years later of this period:

"I was afraid of drinkers and womanizers always. I saw what happened to other young actresses when they let men get too familiar with them; they always got taken for granted; in time, the men lost respect for them, and they got dumped in short order."

Edith Shearer had drummed into Norma some injunctions that stuck. "Never let a man know you like him" was one. "If you do, he'll try to exploit what he thinks you feel." Another was: "Many men womanize every time they have a chance— they have picked up terrible social diseases (the popular 1922 term for VD) and they infect women with them and then the

babies are born defective." This 1922 variation on the "all
men are beasts" aphorism so popular in Victorian times made
an impression on both Norma and Athole. The loose manners
and mores of the free-wheeling 1920s were coming into full
ascendancy by 1922, and the film industry was rife with gossip
about promiscuous Fatty Arbuckle, who had allegedly raped a
girl with a Coke bottle, contributing to her death, and druggie
Wallace Reid, who was shortly to die of his addiction. The
industry had had to call in former Postmaster General Will
Hays to form a group dedicated to cleaning up movie plots
and situations. After consulting with Jimmy Quirk and the
major producers, Hays let it be known that moral turpitudes
of all kinds would be cracked down upon. According to
Edith, this might be true for the movies themselves, but the
movie people carried on in the same old way. "You can't leg-
islate human nature," as she put it.

With the likes of Mr. Ince and Mr. O'Brien disposed of,
Edith began to worry about Norma's growing involvement
with *Photoplay*'s Jimmy Quirk, whose marriage by 1922 was
starting to come apart. Betty North Quirk, Jimmy's wife, and
Norma were very friendly, and Norma was a frequent guest at
their West 81st Street apartment where interesting people
from the world of films, theater, and other arts could often be
found "at some of the best parties in town," as Norma's
friend, screenwriter Anita Loos recalled. My mother, Margaret Connery Quirk, newly wed to Andrew, Jimmy's
brother, a *Photoplay* staffer, recalled Jimmy's growing interest in Norma, which did not escape Betty's notice, either:
"I'm sure they saw each other at lunch and at dinner without
Betty, though Norma's cautious mother usually accompanied
them, and left them little time to be alone together." My
mother took Norma shopping, often without Edith. Norma
liked my mother's style sense and accepted her tips on
clothes. "Norma would talk about nothing but Jimmy,"
my mother recalled. "How kind he was, how understanding. Betty's name was conspicuously absent from the conversation."

Then in December 1922 tragedy struck Jimmy Quirk's family. His baby son Robert died suddenly of what is today labeled crib death. Robert had been his only son, after two daughters, and the death plunged Betty into grief and pulled Jimmy even further into Norma's company. "The marriage went to pieces shortly thereafter," my mother remembered. "I think Jimmy and Betty saw Robert's death as a bad omen. Of course they had been drifting apart for some time. Betty told me they had been far happier and far more united in Jimmy's early struggling newspaper days when they were poor and lived on crackers and milk."

Norma was deeply fond of Jimmy, knew he found her consoling, but she was worried. "What do *you* think of it, Mother?" she asked Edith. "Jimmy's a married man—what do *you* think of it?" Edith snapped back. Norma countered that Jimmy seemed headed for a divorce (it was to come within a year). "They *all* say that," Edith responded tartly.

The romance continued into early 1923. Then Norma departed for Hollywood to make films, and distance turned the relationship into a permanent friendship.

To my mother, it was obvious that Jimmy had felt more for Norma than she had felt for him. "When she saw that he really was divorcing and that his troubles with Betty had nothing to do with her, I think she even thought about marrying him for a while," my mother said. "I'm sure she was dazzled by his authority and charm, though he was pushing forty by then and she was only twenty-two or so."

But Norma's hard-headed caution prevailed in the end, backed up by her mother's disapproving observations.

In reminiscing about that time in her life many years later, Norma Shearer told me: "My own father had in many ways disappointed me, and Jimmy was fatherly, helpful, gave MGM many suggestions for improving my roles and image; I admired and respected him extravagantly, and I even deluded myself for a time that it would make for a secure and reliable relationship. But Jimmy's marital status (he was not yet divorced) and the age difference finally caused me to decide against it. Jimmy was wonderful about it—he continued to help me every way he could." By 1926, with his divorce long final and after numerous flings with such beauties as Renée Adorée, Phyllis Haver, and even the very young Joan Crawford, Jimmy was introduced by Adela Rogers St. Johns to the beautiful silent-film star May Allison, who had been in movies since 1914 and was one of the era's celebrated beauties. Jimmy and May were married in November 1926 and stayed married until his death in 1932.

Shearer made two more films in the East before moving to Hollywood in early 1923. In the first, *A Clouded Name,* opposite Gladden James, she finds herself the innocent victim of a complex family scandal, with the sudden disappearance and death of one of her parents. This was yet another of the cheapjack productions that proliferated at the time, often running less than an hour, and from which she by then longed to escape. Norma's sympathetic reviewer friend, Mary Kelly of *Motion Picture World,* wrote of this effort, produced by one "Playgoers Pictures, Inc.": "Somewhat lacking in action, this picture will appeal primarily to those who are sentimentally inclined. The story progresses slowly, with very little suspense. The picture's most attractive feature is Norma Shearer, who imbues familiar situations with considerable interest. She is appealing enough to make one forget at times the obvious trend of the story."

The second, and final, New York production was *Man and Wife,* from a company known as Arrow Film Corporation. In this, in which Norma was given third billing, she is the wife of Robert Elliott. After she is reported dead in a hotel fire, her supposed widower marries her sister, then learns that she is still alive. Eventually she perishes from brain surgery. While most critics felt there was too much plot for believability and audience interest, *Moving Picture World* damned it with faint praise, calling it: "Not a big picture but it is honest-to-goodness entertainment and a worthwhile program feature." Norma was generally neglected in the reviews.

Norma went to Hollywood in the winter of 1923 under contract to Louis B. Mayer. By this time Irving Thalberg was his production chief. These two men would be crucial henceforth in her career and in her personal life.

Louis B. Mayer had been born Lazar Mayer in Minsk, Russia, in 1885. Of humble laboring stock, as a child he emigrated with his parents to New York. Then the family set off for St. John, New Brunswick, Canada, where the elder Mayer started a junk business. Lazar, who renamed himself Louis, joined him when he reached manhood. From this he progressed into scrap metal, then in 1907 took over a rundown movie house in Haverhill, Massachusetts, emphasizing quality films. This led to his ownership of more theaters, and soon Mayer had the largest theater chain in New England.

By 1914 he was involved in film distribution, and he profited greatly from the New England release of *Birth of a Nation* the following year. Mayer then went into movie production, and in 1917 he founded Louis B. Mayer productions, which highlighted the pictures of his star, Anita Stewart.

The other man who was to loom large in Shearer's future was Irving Thalberg, who was born of German-Jewish parentage in Brooklyn, New York, in 1899, making him a year older than Shearer. A frail, sickly child, often bedridden, he developed a rheumatic heart condition that was to dog him all his life. Naturally artistic, he had educated himself via extensive and varied reading; too frail for college, he had taken a shorthand and speed-typing course, and at nineteen took a job in business. In 1918 he joined Carl Laemmle of Universal Pictures, who was a family friend, and finally became his secretary. Laemmle took a fatherly interest in the frail but creative young man. When Laemmle realized Thalberg's instinctive grasp of creative aspects of film, as well as its business end, he progressed rapidly and wound up in charge of Universal's West Coast production before he was twenty-one, winning from an admiring movie press the title of "The Boy Genius."

A firm and capable administrator, as demanding with himself as he was with his subordinates, Thalberg showed himself

a literate and intelligent entrepreneur with an intuitive understanding of quality story material that would please the public
while subtly and nonintrusively raising its cultural and esthetic
appreciation.

He was notable for his firm but understanding approach to
the temperamental and contrary genius, Erich von Stroheim.
He coddled the actor-director after a fashion but refused to
indulge him when von Stroheim's vaunted egoism and free-
wheeling got out of hand. By 1923 Thalberg had tired of
Laemmle's hiring of relatives who obstructed studio opera-
tions, and after an abortive arrangement with Hal Roach, he
joined up with Louis B. Mayer.

4

Hollywood—and the Boy Genius

T HE CONTRACT that Norma had signed with Mayer in
New York called for one hundred fifty dollars a week on
a six-month option. She and Athole and their mother
boarded the train in a buoyant, expectant mood, and found
the trip through the midwestern and western states exciting.
Athole recalled that when they changed trains in Chicago,
Norma decided to see all the main sights of the city during
the short wait, and they barely made the connecting train
West. She stared out the window and from the observation
platform at all the cities and towns, the prairies and deserts,
telling her mother, "How vast and wonderful and varied
America is!"

When the train pulled into the Los Angeles station, the
trio expected to be greeted by a studio representative, but
they found no one. Agent Eddie Small had gotten Mayer to
pay the family's expenses to California and had informed
him of the date of Norma's arrival, so she found the
absence of a welcoming committee a depressing disappointment.

As she later put it:

41

Having read reams of newspaper and magazine chatter
about the gorgeous reception tendered arriving actors and
actresses, Mother and I spent hours getting me ready for
the greeting which I felt sure would be waiting for me. But
there was no one there—not even a messenger boy from
the studios to direct us to our next move. We had to make
inquiries as to hotels and find our own way to our first Hollywood home, which was the famous Hollywood Hotel in
the heart of the movie city.

Norma found the Hollywood of 1923 hot, sunny (exces-
sively so; it bothered her delicate skin and she avoided the
sunlight as much as possible, wearing floppy hats and seeking
the shade), bewilderingly spread out, and, after the frenetic
vitality of New York, "oddly sleepy and even provincial. And
those spaces! They were so vast that one had better have a car
or develop speedily enough a condition I later labeled 'ma-
roon-paranoia.' Not being able to go where one wanted by
subway or bus presented such a contrast to Manhattan. Taxis
were expensive and certainly not available in the way they
were back east—not by miles—literally. 'Miles and miles and
miles that went nowhere,' that was my first impression of
spread-out Los Angeles!"
    When there was no sign of Mayer or Thalberg the next day
(they had been informed that the family had settled on the
Hollywood Hotel), Norma decided to take matters into her
own hands. An expensive taxi seemed to take forever to get
out to Mission Road in the northern portion of downtown Los
Angeles. In the outer office of The Mayer Company she ran
into what seemed a very young man. He seemed shy and at first
failed to heed her peremptory instructions to find Mr.
Thalberg's secretary and inform him that his new star, Miss
Shearer, had arrived. "I was irritated at the treatment I was
getting," Norma later recalled. She felt the term "new star"
("though I was anything but at that point") "had the imperious
ring that would bring one or both of my bosses running."
    Instead the young man quietly took her down a hall and

into an office (quite a big one for an office boy, she remembered thinking) and sat down behind the desk.

"I want to see Mr. Thalberg, boy," she said.

"Miss Shearer, *I* am Mr. Thalberg," he replied quietly.

She remembered later that she had been so surprised that she sat down heavily in the chair he indicated. "He was so *young*—why he looked about nineteen or twenty!" she remembered. (Thalberg was then twenty-four.) His grace and gentle courtesy won her over, and soon they were talking like old friends. But she was still somewhat on the defensive, and, still feeling put out about the lack of a station reception, she tried to impress him by telling him about offers she had had from other studios to come to California, mentioning one from Universal for $200 a week. "Miss Shearer," the man behind the desk replied, "I was at Universal then and *I* made you the offer—and it wasn't $200 a week."

"I knew I was licked then," she recalled. "This man had a way of putting one down in a courteous but definite way that made you almost like it!"

Thalberg proceeded to outline his plans for her. He and Mayer were impressed with her potential, he said, but it always helped to get added seasoning, and the Hollywood way of doing things was different from the brand of movie-making in the East. "You were with too many of those small films there that want to grind it out like sausage in a couple of weeks," he added, "and now we are going to get you polished up."

She remembered later thinking ironically that the Hollywood brand of polishing up certainly didn't apply to the first picture he lent her out for. "It will show you how we do things on location here," he told her. "And we will be lending you to other firms, yes, for a while, until we have the projects we want for you in a sufficient state of preparation."

That first Hollywood loanout was what she later termed "a rickety mess" called *The Devil's Partner,* produced by a small firm called Iroquois. A five-reeler directed by Caryl Fleming (of whom little was heard thereafter), it was supposed to take place in Northwest Canada. Shearer and her lover (Charles Delaney) were threatened by nefarious smuggler Edward Roseman. "I found it endurable only because it took a minute to shoot!" she said of it. "It is best described as unimportant," *Photoplay* stated, reflecting Jimmy Quirk's continuing concern over Norma's vehicles now that she had gone West. *Variety* consoled her with: "Norma Shearer is always charming."

Then Thalberg announced that *Pleasure Mad* would be her first picture for Mayer. She was not too crazy about the role— a girl who lived only for good times and a fast life after her family comes into money—and even less crazy about director Reginald Barker. He called her a greenhorn and told her the Hollywood way was more professional than the slapdash techniques of those pot boilers she had sashayed through back East and that she had better get her act together and stop mugging amateurishly. She for a time was too proud and, by her own later admission, "conceited and stuck up" to realize that he was being cruel only to be kind and wanted to jolt her in order to bring out the native talent that he and Thalberg knew lurked there.

Soon she and Barker were screaming at each other. Barker sent her to Thalberg's office where she was told in no uncertain terms that "pros" took directions, and she had better stop cutting up or her contract would be canceled. When she answered in kind, Thalberg stopped her cold by asking, "Is it too much for you? Are you *afraid* of the responsibility of giving a good performance?" "I'll show you who's afraid!" she shot back. She returned to the set, and after that she and Barker began to cooperate. She came out of *Pleasure Mad,* which also starred Huntley Gordon and Mary Alden, a better actress, with *Variety* noting: "Little Norma Shearer manages to put over another wallop for herself in this picture that shows that she can troupe!" When the picture was finished, Norma got a little card for Thalberg, wrote the words "Thanks, Boss!" on it, and left it against his inkstand. He kept that card for the rest of his life.

William Collier, Jr., son of the famous actor of the same name, appeared with Norma in *Pleasure Mad* and later told me: "She was such a *little* thing—but did she have big ideas, a big ego, and even then, obviously a big talent!"

But it was two steps forward with *Pleasure Mad* and three steps backward with her next, *The Wanters,* on loan to First National. John M. Stahl, the director, did not like Norma's first scenes and demoted her to a supporting role, with the more experienced Marie Prevost stepping into the lead. "How that itsy-bitsy girl with the big-big glare gave me the business!" Marie later recalled. "Did she have a good opinion of herself!" In the film Norma was saddled with the thankless role of a snooty society girl whose brother, Robert Ellis, falls in love with a domestic, Prevost, and commits the cardinal social sin of marrying her, with resultant flak from his family. Ellis (who had been married to May Allison before she divorced him and married Jimmy Quirk) noted that Norma sulked around the set a lot but pulled herself together to make the most of her relatively few scenes. *Motion Picture News* felt the plot was too familiar, and Jimmy Quirk wired Thalberg: "What are you guys trying to do to Norma!"

Next it was over to Warners on yet another loanout ("I'm Hollywood's wandering orphan girl!" Norma wrote Jimmy), and this time she found herself supporting Irene Rich and Monte Blue under Jack Conway's direction in a so-so drama called *Lucretia Lombard.* This is one of Norma Shearer's silent films seen most often in revival. The film has to do with an influential and wealthy widow who is suspected of the death of her much older invalid husband. Blue is a young attorney who falls in love with her, and after much illogical and forced emoting, the principals find themselves in a forest fire and flood in which Shearer dies. The picture is remembered, if at all, for the fact that its scenes were tinted a rather sickly red during the fire—an added gimmick that went over like a lead balloon with 1923 audiences. The witty Robert E. Sherwood, who confessed to having a "crush" on Norma, wrote in *Life*: "Lucretia Lombard, by the way, has an alternate title,

Flaming Passion, which is used in those districts where passion is popular." He added, "As a matter of fact, the title
doesn't make much difference. It isn't a good picture."

After that the ever-more-exasperated Norma was kicked
over to an independent firm with the modestly fetching name
of Biltmore-Producer's Security Corporation for a bit of out-
door juvenility called *The Trail of the Law.* Norma was to get
a reprimand from producer-director Oscar Apfel for tacking
on the back of his chair, in a backhanded reference to the title
of his firm: Abandon All Security, Ye Actors Who Enter
Here. In this she was a tomboy in the Maine backwoods who
protects herself by dressing in male attire because the environment is unsafe for girls. Her mother had been killed by a
marauder when she was a child, and it takes handsome city
boy Wilfred Lytell (in his second role with Norma) to make a
real woman out of her and get her back into pretty frocks.
Lytell, who had courted Norma in the East, made his pitch
yet again but was quickly put in his place. "I'm doomed to
pictures with silly plots and men with busy hands," she told
her mother, who counseled patience.

Irving Thalberg replied along the same lines when she complained to him yet again about the pictures she was getting.
"Trust us," he said. "We are building you up, seasoning you,
and we have big plans for you." Her growing admiration for
Thalberg triumphed again over her chronic impatience, and
after consoling herself with *Variety*'s reference to her as "undoubtedly a comer," (though she wondered to Athole "When
do I become an *arriver*?"), Norma went on a brief vacation.

She and Athole and her mother toured northern California
by car. "It was second-hand, it was always breaking down,
and we were forever being 'aided' by young men, some of
whom I would not have wanted to meet alone on a lonely
highway," she later remembered.

Edith kept both a long knife and a shotgun in the back of
the car for emergencies. Several of these arose, as she knew
they would. "The roads are bad and these men are worse than
bad," she stated, sitting in the backseat with gun and knife

close to hand. "Is that all men think of—women and love-making? What *children* they are!"

When their mother went into a store for food and supplies, Norma and Athole indulged in giggly speculations as to just what their mother's sex life with the hapless Andrew Shearer had amounted to. "Not much, probably" was Norma's verdict.

Norma and John Gilbert first met up at Fox during one of her loanouts. It was for a picture called *The Wolf Man*, a melodramatic tale about a young English aristocrat who flees to Canada after he thinks he has killed his fiancée's brother while drunk. His brother, who also wants to marry the girl he is in love with and engaged to, has encouraged the deception. In Canada he tries not to drink, but starts to go wild again when he learns that his fiancée has married his black-hearted, lying brother. Soon he is running wild in the Canadian woods (hence the title) and, while intoxicated, kidnaps the daughter of a railroad magnate, takes her to his cabin, and forces his attentions on her. The police come after him and, while escaping, he saves his prisoner from drowning in the rapids. She forgives him and he is eventually exonerated of the murder back in England, but not before his new love saves him from a lynch mob. Then they wind up in each other's arms. *The Wolf Man* got only mild reviews.

Photoplay's Jimmy Quirk was a good friend of Gilbert's (in 1926 he was to tender him the Photoplay Gold Medal for *The Big Parade*), and tried to be nice, stating: "John Gilbert is at his best in a Jekyll and Hyde sort of role," but *Variety* put the case more bluntly, calling *The Wolf Man* "just a little program production that seems to start off as though it was going to be a real tale, but does flop before the finish and ends rather abruptly. Judging from the characters programmed by the regular press sheet and those shown in the picture, the tale must have been changed materially from the original and re-vamped after the picture was made."

Whatever the quality of *The Wolf Man*, there is considerable evidence that Norma Shearer and John Gilbert were romantically involved during its making. In 1956 King Vidor mentioned to me that Norma had been one of Jack's many loves and that, as he recalled, "it went hot and heavy for a while, even though Jack was married to Leatrice Joy at the time."

According to Leatrice Gilbert Fountain, Leatrice Joy's daughter, by Jack Gilbert, King had told her that "Jack and Norma had been sweethearts before they came to MGM." In one of her letters to me, Leatrice added, "But Jack was married to Leatrice while he was at Fox, so it might not be true, except for the fact that my parents fought and separated and got back together again as regularly as sunrise and sunset. It was during their separations that he had his flings with Bebe Daniels, Barbara Lamarr, Lila Lee, and possibly Norma." Leatrice added that her mother, not to be outdone, went out with such swains as Tom Mix, John Farrow (later to be husband of Maureen O'Sullivan and father of Mia Farrow), and Thomas Meighan. Leatrice believes that Shearer and Gilbert were "close friends, perhaps more."

The Wolf Man was also what was known as an "overheat" film, meaning the intense physical action tended to be aphrodisiacal and the on-screen passions calculated to set forest fires going in two young and passionate people such as twenty-four-year-old Jack and twenty-three-year-old Norma.

Seventy-three-year-old Norma had written to Leatrice about an autobiography she was working on. Like so many stars, Norma wanted to gloss over any racy passions or career power struggles with the usual dismissive clichés. From these and other letters and from her somewhat more frank and unguarded statements to me, I got the distinct impression that Norma did not intend to tell all, as her intrinsic nature was ladylike, dignified, and reserved. Her philosophy about autobiographies was like that of Blanche Sweet, who told me she could have hurt a lot of people with a frank life story but did not choose to. "There's enough mischief in those tell-all bios like Gloria Swanson's," Blanche told me. "I won't add my share." Norma wasn't really out to settle old scores, however justified she might have been in doing so. To date the autobiography has never been published.

But Norma did tell Leatrice in one of her letters: "I have only the most enchanting recollection of Jack Gilbert for he was a glamorous personality, both on and off the screen . . . he held a great fascination for me. He was handsome and impudent with flashing brown eyes and a gift of sudden laughter which always seemed to hold a touch of sadness. This, in a strange way, gave him great appeal which could be called 'charisma' or is this too well worn a phrase?" Going on to discuss his later talkie débacles, Norma added:

> My impression is that he was a very fine and sensitive actor with great clarity of speech. This very precise diction, I remember, caused some criticism when talking pictures came along a few years later, although I feel this was terribly exaggerated at the time and later became a "fable" which in any language means "untrue." Jack was a man of great pride and I imagine this unkind criticism destroyed his confidence in himself, the ego which is so necessary to an actor. There is more than one way to break a man's heart. But I think of Jack Gilbert as a gentleman of great style and spirit, always with a certain flamboyance or sense of mischief which made him enchanting.

The seventy-three-year-old concluded: "It is wonderful to be remembered like that—never growing old."

To Norma's exasperation, a trivial little film she had made in late 1922, *Blue Waters,* about fishermen in the Bay of Fundy, got a limited-release in May of 1924. She thought herself very inadequate in it, as a girl who gets a sailor on the rebound from a girl who has deserted him. The company that made it reportedly went bankrupt, and no reviews of it can be found. When Norma learned that it had finally popped up on the States Rights circuit (a limited-release mechanism used with pictures known as ultimate fourth-rate losers), it did not help her already battered morale. It had been produced by a firm with the unwieldy name of New Brunswick Films Ltd. of St. John, New Brunswick, and it had been shot in two weeks or so. Shearer was always to consider it an embarrassment.

Mayer and Thalberg reportedly tried to buy it for her later, but were unable to trace it.

Norma was to get her best break yet in a 1924 film called *Broadway After Dark*. It was directed by Monta Bell, who was to guide her through several other films in which she appeared to advantage. Bell seemed to understand her image and chemistry better than anyone she had yet worked with. Again on loan to Warner Brothers, here she was teamed with the sophisticated Adolphe Menjou, who plays a socialite who helps a domestic ex-convict (Shearer) rise in the world and later marries her. Some of Menjou's polish rubbed off on her, and the production values were classier than usual. *Photoplay* seemed to echo Jimmy Quirk's obvious relief at Norma's upgrading when it commented: "Norma Shearer does her best work so far as the slavy who dons fine feathers," and *The New York Times* labeled her "sympathetic."

About this time (May, 1924) Mayer and Thalberg merged with the old Goldwyn Company, under the banner of Metro-Goldwyn. By 1926 the title would be Metro-Goldwyn-Mayer. The combination of Thalberg's inherent taste and ability to package quality films and Mayer's feel for what the public wanted and his ability to supervise a complex studio operation would result in a mammoth complex, sporting an impressive lion in the logo. MGM's parent company, in New York, was Loew's, Inc., headed until his death in 1927 by Marcus Loew, and later by Nicholas Schenck.

Shearer, John Gilbert, Lon Chaney, and others were to be the pioneer personalities in this new studio phenomenon, which was formally inaugurated with an opening ceremony in April 1924. Now Thalberg, who by then had developed an enduring faith in Norma's long-range potential, could really begin to groom her for her eventual position as the lion's consort. Leo the Lion was on his way to preeminence as the greatest, most prestigious studio in Hollywood, and with its parent company, Loew's, Inc., in a position to give it maximum exhibition and distribution clout, it would be leading the field within three years.

Meanwhile Norma had to do three more films while Metro-Goldwyn geared for truly ambitious programming. Comforted by Thalberg's assurances that it was onward and upward if she would just work her way through these three, she tackled her work with renewed enthusiasm.

Broken Barriers, the first film to carry the official Metro-Goldwyn imprimatur on its logo (though it was not the Metro-Goldwyn inaugural film) starred James Kirkwood with Norma. It was a soggy tale about a shopgirl (Shearer) involved with a wealthy man (Kirkwood) who cannot secure his marital freedom from a selfish wife (Winifred Bryson) until he is crippled in an accident and he is left to Shearer. Reginald Barker directed it and found Shearer's acting vastly improved. *Photoplay* also noted her "steady improvement." After a "guest star" appearance in Metro-Goldwyn's *Married Flirts,* a domestic drama starring Pauline Frederick as an ugly-duckling wife who turns swan, Norma went over for a quick loan to Paramount for *Empty Hands,* with Jack Holt, who plays a young engineer in northern Canada who cures her spoiled-rich-girl ways. The film was trite and trivial and so were the reviewers' reactions. "She seems to be a good swimmer when in the water," *The New York Times* commented, obviously at a loss for anything else to say.

However, during the shooting of this film, Norma developed a crush on her director, Victor Fleming. Part Cherokee Indian, Fleming was a man's man with a great ladies' appeal. He would later become Clark Gable's favorite director and would be responsible for directing *Gone With the Wind* (though George Cukor and Sam Wood were also involved in *GWTW,* Fleming was the "official" director).

Henry Hathaway, who was later to become a well-known director on his own, was an assistant director on *Empty Hands.* He told interviewer John Kobal years later: "I lived through that love affair [Shearer] had with Victor Fleming. Every dame he ever worked with fell on her ass for him."

Fleming was later to have wild affairs with such stars as Clara Bow and Ingrid Bergman. At the time of *Empty Hands,* he was a young-looking forty, well muscled and with a strong, well-proportioned body. Shearer let him know she found him attractive, and soon the pair were taking long "hikes" together in the woods where *Empty Hands* was on location (simulating the Canadian wilds). The watchful Edith Shearer was not on hand to supervise as usual.

George Cukor later said, "If she were going to 'go all the way' with anyone at that time, it probably would have been Victor. He was positively irresistible to women. He had an overwhelmingly male charisma, projecting what would be more vulgarly known today as 'penis impact.'"

Of course Norma, in what was becoming a habitual pattern, had chosen yet another married man to get involved with, and Fleming, who enjoyed being married though he did *not* enjoy the idea of fidelity, was certainly not going to disrupt his domestic arrangements for her sake. "*She* felt more than *he* did—it was the usual story," Helen Ferguson, an actress and later publicist who knew Shearer well, later said. "He played around with her, and she took it all much too seriously." Even in 1947, when he was in his sixties, Fleming was busily proving his manhood with Ingrid Bergman, whom he directed in *Joan of Arc*. Shearer always spoke well of Fleming, whom she was to know well socially in the 1930s at MGM.

He Who Gets Slapped (1924) was tabbed by the new Metro-Goldwyn company as a superspecial-prestige picture from the word go. It was to be their first official production, and they were determined to get off to a rousing start. A *succes d'estime* when the Theatre Guild produced it on Broadway in 1922, it was, according to Thalberg and Mayer, a perfect vehicle for the great Lon Chaney, who was then under contract to them after his singular triumphs in *Hunchback of Notre Dame* (1923) and *Phantom of the Opera*.

One of the more prestigious pictures of the early postamalgamation period at Metro-Goldwyn, *He Who Gets Slapped* has a compelling story. A once-brilliant scientist (Chaney) becomes disillusioned when he is cuckolded by a baron he thought was his friend; he joins a circus where he becomes a pathetic clown whose self-denigrating act depicts his inner disillusionment with mankind. He falls in love with a bareback rider, played by Shearer, who in turn is in love with her riding partner, Gilbert. The clown's slapping act, complete with another variation of the famed Chaney makeup, becomes a great success. Chaney hides his unrequited love for Shearer until his old nemesis, the baron, reveals his intention of marrying Shearer, who recoils from him. Her father, who seeks a life of ease, conspires with the baron to win her over. In a thrilling, grisly, and rousing denouement, the enraged clown unleashes a lion on the two miscreants, killing them both but sacrificing his own life when he is shot by the baron. He dies in Shearer's arms, and she and Gilbert are united.

The brilliant Swedish director Victor Seastrom, who at that time had only been in the United States for a year, was assigned to the film; he not only directed it, but cowrote the screenplay with Carey Wilson, who transcribed Seastrom's thoughts from Swedish into English.

Shearer and Gilbert were not all that satisfied with their parts, as they felt they were playing second-fiddle to the great Chaney. There was no denying that it was his picture; he dominated the proceedings throughout and didn't let anyone forget it.

Norma later remembered Chaney as grim, withdrawn, totally self-absorbed—and even a little frightening. He fussed endlessly with his makeup, went over scenes compulsively in advance, and seemed oblivious to most of the people around him.

Gilbert had not wanted to do the role of the bareback rider, feeling that his scenes were limited and that he was being consigned for romantic stud duty. Thalberg convinced him, however, that the picture would do a lot for him, and that he and Norma ought to sacrifice their prideful yens for center-stage and attach themselves, that once, to Chaney's prestigious kite and reap the benefits. This proved to be wise advice, for fan mail for both increased after the picture's release.

While reminiscing via letter with Leatrice Gilbert Fountain,

Norma wrote: "Jack and I played circus performers who were, of course, in love. This was easy to imagine, as we rode, standing in each other's arms, on the back of a prancing white horse. Fortunately my heart belonged to someone else or I might have lost my balance!" (The "someone else" of the particular moment remains a mystery. As Helen Ferguson put it: "There were so many infatuations for Norma then—they came and went revolving-door style.")

The critics went all out in their praise for *He Who Gets Slapped*. Mordaunt Hall of *The New York Times* wrote: "Mr. Seastrom has directed this dramatic story with all the genius of a Chaplin or a Lubitsch . . . Miss Shearer is charming as Consuelo and Mr. Gilbert is a sympathetic sweetheart."

The great Chaney, of course, dominated the reviews. *Theatre* magazine's critic pronounced: "Lon Chaney, the clown who accepts the kicks and jeers of the multitude, gives an interpretation of surpassing fineness. One of his tender moments with the little bareback rider whom he so hopelessly loves is memorable. Norma Shearer, too, is delightful in the freshness and gaiety of youth."

When I saw *He Who Gets Slapped* at Frank Rowley's Regency Revival House in New York sixty years later, the film retained every ounce of its original force and power, and deeply moved the 1984 audience. *Quirk's Reviews* associate editor and film critic William Schoell wrote: "Victor Seastrom's direction, far from being primitive, is most clever and imaginative, and the pace, for the most part, is faster than that of a lot of contemporary pictures. Performances (particularly Chaney's) are excellent."

Jimmy Quirk personally wrote the *Photoplay* review that ran, in part: "The acting is remarkably fine. Lon Chaney does the best work of his career. Here his performance has breadth, force and imagination. . . . Norma Shearer and Jack Gilbert, as the lovers, are delightful."

Despite the film's critical and popular success, Norma expressed no desire to work again with Chaney. Joan Crawford remembered that three years later, when she expressed her excitement to Norma over being cast in Chaney's *The Unknown,* Norma replied: "Don't get overjoyed too soon—you may get a letdown, like I did. There's something strange about the man. He makes you glad he's self-involved, as he usually is, because it would be goose-pimply to be the direct object of that man's attention or interest." When Joan asked Norma what she meant exactly, Norma merely replied, "You'll find out for yourself soon enough."

Right after completing this film, Shearer and Gilbert were reunited at Metro-Goldwyn for their third film together, *The Snob.* This time they were not in Chaney's shadow, and they gave rousing performances in a story of a social-climbing teacher (Gilbert) who fawns on the aristocracy and seeks to "marry up." He marries Shearer out of pity, not knowing that she is in reality an heiress, meanwhile setting his cap for another rich girl. Eventually Shearer recognizes his shallow, selfish nature and leaves him for the Bostonian of her own station who has long loved her (Conrad Nagel).

Gilbert had fought for the role of the ambitious climber, feeling it had depth and dimension that would reveal his character as a fully rounded human being. The fact that the fans perceived him to be an unmitigated cad in this film delighted him. As his daughter Leatrice has noted, he dreaded stereotyping as the great lover and wanted to prove he could handle a variety of roles. *The Snob,* as Leatrice told me, was another "in a series of 'anti-hero' roles that Jack delighted in." She added, "I suspect there was some kind of psychological reason why he so enjoyed playing bad or depraved people, when he was so far from that in his own character."

Shearer, too, found that her role added new dimensions to her film persona. She undergoes a transformation of sorts, evolving from innocent, trusting, loving young wife to a lady coldly determined to leave a husband who has profoundly disillusioned her.

The Snob was yet another indication of the faith Mayer and Thalberg had in their two promising young players. Monta Bell, who directed the film in his usual professional manner, later said: "The original story by Helen Martin was unusually adult and mature compared to the standard fare of 1924. Jack seemed to glory in his role, as did Norma, and they translated their enthusiasm into fine performances. I always felt that these two were forever trying to get their teeth into roles that stretched their talents, and *The Snob* certainly did that for them."

Fellow actor Conrad Nagel remembered the picture favorably. "Of course I was the rinso-white knight on the white charger who came galloping to the rescue after Norma had had enough of Jack, so I can't say the role gave me much range, but it was a first-class production, the mounting was good, and I always enjoyed working with good people."

Also on hand for the role of Shearer's love rival for Jack was Phyllis Haver, a beautiful blonde who had been involved with Jimmy Quirk and was rumored, during the shooting of the picture, to be involved with Jack. Whatever passionate interest Jack might have expressed in Norma a year before when they were cavorting through the wilds in *The Wolf Man* had obviously become a thing of the past.

But you'd never know it from some of the impassioned love scenes in the early part of the film, and *Photoplay* signaled its approval with: "Check a hit down to the promising Monta Bell, who first revealed his possibilities in *Broadway After Dark*. Bell has developed his dramatic story with fine freshness and individuality. . . . John Gilbert is excellent as the professor and the cast is admirable, particularly Norma Shearer as his wife."

Leatrice Fountain has quoted her father on *The Snob*: "The part provided an opportunity for real characterization. He is likable in many ways for all his selfishness and conceit, and the character with its changes of emotions and poses gives a chance for a real psychological study of a complex personality."

In 1925 Shearer's brother Douglas, who had become a full-fledged engineer, came to Hollywood, ostensibly to pay his family a visit. Shearer introduced him to people at Metro, and

Louis B. Mayer was impressed with the young man's grasp of technical matters when he talked with him at a party.

Douglas knew that sound would eventually come to films, and, he told his sister and others, he wanted to get in on the ground floor. At the time Mayer and Thalberg were not particularly interested in the possibilities of sound for films, and Mayer told Douglas so. Douglas, however, refused to be discouraged, and went to the trouble of preparing an extensive treatise, carefully typed and technically expert, which he left at Mayer's office. Mayer looked it over one day, and because Douglas had made his language clear and accessible, he found himself intrigued. He wrote Douglas a note of commendation and said he would keep him and his ideas in mind. "Your brother's a real comer," he told Shearer. "One of these days we'll take him in with us. But I've got to find the right slot for him. Right now he's obsessed with this sound thing."

By 1927, with the success of the part talkie, *The Jazz Singer,* and the news that Paramount was experimenting seriously with sound and had even hired technicians to explore it fully, Mayer asked Shearer to dig up her smart brother. Douglas came to see him and the two men made earnest plans.

Mayer sent Douglas Shearer to Bell Laboratories in the East with instructions to learn the business of sound apparatus and related techniques from the ground up. Later that year Douglas pioneered a sound department for Metro-Goldwyn-Mayer. By 1929 Douglas was head sound recorder. For the next forty years he was to enhance the product of his sister's studio with soundtracks and dialogue treatments that were to be the envy of other studios and would win him his share of Oscars.

5

The Men
Who Got Away

EXCUSE ME, (1925) a rollicking farce by Rupert Hughes (uncle of Howard), a writer who had been dubbed by his close pal Jimmy Quirk "the wittiest man in Hollywood," was designed to be a change of pace for Norma. It gave her a chance to strut her stuff in comedy, a genre in which she had not gotten too much of a workout. Hughes had staged it as a play some years before, and had refurbished it for the screen when Thalberg told him he was looking for something with laughs for Norma. "When she rolls her eyes to the heavens in attitudes of despair," Hughes told Thalberg, "I can just imagine her as straight woman to the comical goings-on in *my* story."

As it turned out, Norma was far more than a "straight woman" and revealed a delightful comedy sense under the direction of Alf Goulding. Cameraman John Boyle was instructed to make her look as lovely as possible, but art director Cedric Gibbons went around the lot complaining because the train-compartment set was a background for so much of the acting.

The story concerned a naval lieutenant (Conrad Nagel) and

a society girl (Shearer) who undergo many tribulations on a cross-country train while trying to find a minister to marry them so they can honeymoon in the Philippines. The ostensible "other woman," ravishing Renée Adorée, is trying to use Nagel to protect herself and her child from her ex-husband, and gets thoroughly misunderstood by Shearer in the process. Nagel rescues the passengers from a threatened train wreck, and a minister on vacation refuses to marry the impatient pair. Everything is eventually straightened out, but the love-birds have to transfer to a plane to make San Francisco and their boat for the islands.

According to Helen Ferguson, Norma was "in love with love, and she worked up steam over one handsome actor after another. I think her mother was keeping her on too tight a leash and she was rebelling; after all, by then she was a grown woman of twenty-four, for heaven's sake!"

According to Helen, the young man elected for Norma's crush of the moment was handsome John Boles, who was later to become a popular leading man in the talkies but who in 1925 was doing small parts in films while singing in Broadway musicals—the latter being, in his view, his true calling. Two years later Gloria Swanson, after seeing him wow a theater audience in a piece called *Kitty's Kisses,* drafted Boles for her first independent film, *The Love of Sunya,* which really launched his film career.

Boles told me in the late 1950s:

Excuse Me was only my second movie and I was really green about picture technique. I felt I would never make a movie actor and couldn't wait to get back to the stage. Norma was wonderful; we spent a lot of time together at the studio and even went out a couple of times. But I was romantically involved elsewhere and I was a one-woman dog by nature, so it never came to anything. But she did talk movies with me by the hour, and told me she really believed I had a future in them. While it was Gloria who really got me launched, it was Norma who got me thinking positively about films.

Had Norma been in love with him, as others claimed? "You'd have to ask *her*," he replied, suddenly formal and withdrawn. "I don't discuss a lady when it comes to such matters." But the blush on his face indicated that there had indeed been some sort of fire behind the gossipy smoke.

As Helen Ferguson recalled it, Norma had even called Boles's talents and looks to the attention of Mayer himself; though he promised to look into it, he let Boles's option drop. "When Boles left the lot at the film's completion, I remember that Norma came over to my house and cried. "Now I'll never see him again," she said. "I thought it was rather sad—here was a girl that a number of men chased, but she couldn't nail down the ones *she* seemed to want."

Conrad Nagel, too, remembered the Boles matter, when I talked with him. "I know Norma liked him—he was very handsome at the time, and very charming, and a gentleman, and quiet, unlike so many of the men she knew; he had her level of breeding, and doubtless that was some kind of bond. But as to how deep her feelings went, I wouldn't presume to speculate."

Excuse Me went in for a lot of special effects to keep the train rumbling, starting, and stopping. On one occasion the "spec boys," as they were dubbed, overdid things a bit, and Norma was hurtled across the set and out of it straight into the arms of John Boles, who, as "Lieutenant Shaw," was not on call and was watching the proceedings. That seems to have been the only time she got close to this man she had obviously been most attracted to.

Norma's fine comedy instincts won the commendation of Rupert Hughes, who told Mayer, "That little lady can do anything she sets her mind to." Harriette Underhill of *Movie Weekly* seemed to agree with him, writing "Norma Shearer is a charming and beautiful comedienne. We prophesy big things for Norma, for her rise has been very marked and rapid."

Motion Picture News declared: "Rupert Hughes' rollicking farce, *Excuse Me,* reaches the screen as one of the funniest films of the season." After commending the "high-spirited" performances of Norma and her coworkers, the publication called it "neatly staged, and certain of responsive laughs."

Thalberg, always sensitive to the moods of his performers, and aware, along with Mayer, that a deeper chord than usual had been sounded in Norma by her unrequited feeling for John Boles, began casting around for a picture that would showcase the pretty actress's evident capacity for feeling and sentiment. Adela Rogers St. Johns was drafted to supply the requisite emotional depth, and her original story, *Lady of the Night,* was purchased for Norma, with special instructions given to adaptor Alice D. G. Miller to retain all the emotional stops that Adela had pulled out in her original.

Lady of the Night was no comedy but rather a poignant study of unrequited love, with Norma in a dual role. As Molly, she is a reform school alumnus who makes up and dresses garishly and cheaply. As Florence, she is a refined, high-toned society girl. Molly is cheap and rough-edged. Florence is the soul of ladylike gentility and breeding. Malcolm McGregor is the young inventor they both love. Molly gets him first; he is her neighbor and offers her gang a safe-opening device he has. She feels he is cut out for better things and suggests he take it to a legitimate manufacturer. He meets the tycoon's daughter, Florence, and falls in love with her. Molly, who has rescued her hero from a peripheral involvement with crime circles, realizes he loves Florence and sadly withdraws from his life.

Lady of the Night gave Norma her best acting opportunity to date. Her depictions of two women from radically disparate backgrounds who have in common only their love for one young man whose welfare is paramount to them show great contrast. When in the same frame, the two Normas are wonderfully striking. Since the public had associated her primarily with genteel lasses who reacted to events rather than caused them, it was pleasantly surprised by the versatility and range Norma displayed here; she was as convincing as the criminal-with-the-golden-heart as she was in her more accustomed guise, the sweet-Miss-with-heart-on-her-sleeve who loves purely and honestly.

Monta Bell, whose feelings for Shearer were not one of Hollywood's best-kept secrets, recalled later that he found her peculiarly touching while making this film. "She seemed to be in a sort of trance most of the time," he remembered. The trance, as Helen Ferguson related, was occasioned by handsome Malcolm McGregor, and Helen felt that Norma had waltzed out of the Boles frying pan into the fire when she got up against Malcolm. "I believe she was really in love with *him*," she said. "But again she ran into bad luck; his primary emotions were engaged elsewhere—it was another John Boles–style disaster for her, but worse this time," Helen said.

Malcolm, who was one of the handsomest leading men in 1920s Hollywood, seemed fated throughout his career to be the focal point of unreciprocated feminine passions. He lacked the polish and breeding of John Boles, but he made up for it in forthright all-American-boy masculine appeal. "He was like Ralph Graves in that," Helen remembered. "Ralph was another wholesome all-American type who became the girls' collective dream prince in Griffith's *Dream Street* in 1921, and as late as 1930 with Barbara Stanwyck in *Ladies of Leisure*. After that he got burnout as an actor and turned to writing. Malcolm burned out, too. But oh, what a lovely masculine light he gave while he lasted!"

Malcolm seems to have lacked John Boles's gentle tact when he realized Norma had fallen for him hook, line, and sinker. "John was a let-them-down-lightly-and-gently boy," Anita Loos, Norma's screenwriter pal, said, "while Malcolm was blunt and direct, and if he wasn't interested he'd make it plain. Maybe he thought he was being cruel only to be kind, who knows?" (Also, McGregor was married and a father, which may have given him pause, though it didn't stop Norma.)

Helen Ferguson remembered Norma, after a frustrating day of love scenes that *she* felt and Malcolm *didn't,* saying: "Why does it have to be like that so often—the ones who want *us* we don't want and the ones *we* want don't want us."

"C'est la vie, honey," Helen remembered replying. "It was scant consolation, but what else could I say? I was a friend of hers and certainly wasn't going to build up her hopes about Malcolm."

Since McGregor was an actor and a good one, he made sure that his love scenes with both of Norma's contrasting characters were thoroughly convincing. George K. Arthur, the light comedian who played Norma's companion in crime, said years later that he felt Norma took a terrible beating playing those complicated love scenes with a man she knew was not turned on by her. "I think she ended that picture with a big sigh of relief," he said.

Monta Bell remembered being deeply impressed with what came off the screen. "Whatever it was, it worked!" was his verdict. Mayer and Thalberg saw the picture together in a screening room and were impressed with Norma's new depth, subtlety, and virtuosity.

The critics, too, were impressed with the depth and range of Norma's performance in *Lady of the Night*. Since Hollywood scuttlebutt had spread the underground word of Norma's torch for McGregor, critics like Edwin Schallert in *The Los Angeles Times* couldn't help picking up on it. Shearer "has imbued this character [of the dance hall girl and criminal] with a great deal of sympathy," he wrote, "and particularly unforgettable is that scene where she visits the man she loves the same evening that he is escorting the other girl to a dance and offering her proof of his devotion." Mordaunt Hall of *The New York Times* said Shearer did "the best acting she has ever done," while *Motion Picture* commented on her "really inspired acting," adding, "It is an intelligent performance, one marked by real understanding and authority."

Norma suffered from a brief spell of depression after *Lady of the Night* was finished. Reportedly she was loaned out at this time to get her away from her surroundings and the memory of McGregor. Also there were rumors that she was making unrealistic salary demands—and hence had to be disciplined.

6

More Wolves

NORMA COULD not help but feel that she was being chastised for her impatience when she was peremptorily ordered to report to United Artists in 1925. "They didn't even ask me what I thought of the picture I was being loaned out for," she complained to her mother, Athole, and anyone else who would listen.

She had no idea what she was in for when she reported on the set of what she was told was to be a Jack Pickford film. It was called *Waking Up the Town,* but a reviewer was later to comment unkindly that it put the town to sleep wherever it was played.

Jack Pickford was the famous Mary's younger brother. He was then twenty-nine, had already failed several times at matrimony, and in 1920 had been involved in a sinister scandal when his new bride, the lovely actress Olive Thomas, had died of barbiturate poisoning while they were in Paris. Jack, always emotionally unstable, was regarded warily in Hollywood; it was felt that he was shamelessly trading on his sister's fame, and his career never really took off. Jack was a neurotic, Sybaritic, self-destructive fellow. He was a heavy drinker and a compulsive womanizer, to his wives' distress; there were also rumors that he took drugs and that he was not averse to the attentions of various male admirers. Will Hays looked askance at him, for he had the aura of reckless scandal about him, and *that* the Watchdog of Hollywood Morals could with certainty do without.

Waking Up the Town was a silly and highly forgettable film about a young inventor (Pickford) in a small town who cannot interest the town banker in his electric power project. An eccentric old codger (Alec B. Francis), who is an astrology nut, prophesies that the world is about to come to an end and gives him his life savings, eighteen thousand dollars, big money in 1925, to do with as he wishes. Now that he is moneyed, Jack wins the backing he needs for the invention that he is confident will improve the fortunes of the town. Meanwhile he is carrying on a romance of sorts with the nice out-of-towner (Shearer) who is visiting her grandparents. The film ends with an improbable dream sequence, with Jack imagining that the world has, after all, come to an end. He wakes with Shearer beside him; it appears that it is a good and safe world after all.

Jack, who codirected the film with Vernon Keyes, spent a lot of the time clowning. "He's a Peter Pan who will never ever grow up," actress Claire McDowell told Shearer. Soon it was evident that Jack's attentions toward Norma were more than those of a well-wishing coworker. A nervous Norma told McDowell that she was frankly afraid of Jack, whom she considered "sinister," and didn't want to be alone with him when they were not working. "I knew they sent me over here to punish me," she said, "but I didn't realize the extent of the punishment."

Jack started showing up in unexpected places and asking her out. Actress Lilyan Tashman, who called him, uncharitably but it appears accurately, "Mr. Syphilis," told Norma that Jack would be dead by forty. She was a better prophet than she realized; he died when he was thirty-six in 1933.

Like many women, Shearer was nervous when around men

who represented those more sinister aspects of life. She tried to discourage her persistent suitor by any means possible. "I even ate garlic one morning—the leavings of dinner—to give him a good whiff during a love scene we were about to play," she told Vernon Keyes, who reported it later to Jack. Jack got drunk and the liquor fumes nearly bowled her over in their next scene. That was Jack's idea of retaliation. *Waking Up the Town* was finally, mercifully completed, and Shearer headed back to Metro-Goldwyn, where Jack's letters and phone calls followed her.

"I can't get rid of him," she told friends. "And he honestly frightens me." "He's just trying to prove something—probably his manhood—I don't think he's too sure of it to start with," King Vidor told her. "Ignore him—he'll go away." Finally Jack got the message, and when she met him at parties he was polite, remote, and brief. "Just the way I want it," she told Vidor.

Back at Metro-Goldwyn, Norma was assigned to a film called *A Slave of Fashion*. Now she faced problems with sophisticated thirty-eight-year-old Lew Cody. Cody was a notorious bon vivant and womanizer who kept meticulous scores on every woman he got into bed. According to director Mickey Neilan, Lew suffered from a first-class case of satyriasis, and all the venereal diseases that went with it. He also had a weak heart, which finished him off in 1934 at age forty-seven. Sometimes Lew married the woman, but not often. The ill-fated Mabel Normand (whose career was ruined in the William Desmond Taylor 1922 murder scandal, and who died young of TB in 1930) was one of his wives. Earlier he had wed actress Dorothy Dalton twice—and divorced her twice. According to Mickey, Mabel followed Lew to his assignations more than once, and when she found him in bed with a floozie (he alternated between "nice girls" and prostitutes) she pulled back the bedclothes and hit him solidly in the groin. "They could hear Lew howling all the way to Santa Monica," Mickey recalled gleefully.

Mickey's then wife, Blanche Sweet, told me Lew Cody was

a racy guy. "They called him a 'he-vamp' and a 'butterfly man,' neither term complimentary," she added. "That's why he and Mickey so enjoyed each other—they were birds of a feather." Blanche added that she felt Mabel Normand never should have married Lew. "He knew she was sick with tuberculosis and that she was emotionally out of it, especially after the William Desmond Taylor murder, in which she was implicated back in 1922 (she was among the suspects), and by his lights he tried to be kind, but Lew was not the kind of guy who should have been married to anybody. He had only one real love, himself. And if he'd confined his lovemaking to himself he'd have saved many a woman a lot of grief."

When I asked Blanche what she thought had gone on between Lew and Shearer, with whom he was to make several films in the mid-1920s, she replied crisply: "Oh, Norma teased and flirted and drove him crazy, I'm sure. Whatever trouble he caused her she deserved." Asked if she thought they had gone to bed together, Blanche's reply was enigmatic. "Only God and they knew that—but Mickey claimed they did. Of course," she added, "Mickey always thought the worst of every situation; the only feminine streak in Mickey that I ever saw was that he loved to dish about others."

From what is known about Norma's previous involvements, there is good reason to believe that she played it cautious. Her mother and sister knew Lew's reputation and warned her about him. "Suddenly Mrs. Shearer was a regular visitor to her daughter's set, but that didn't stop Lew," screenwriter Frances Marion, a close friend of Norma's, told me. "He flattered the mother, disarmed her, and managed to be alone plenty of times with Norma."

A Slave of Fashion was directed by the hack-ish Hobart Henley and was a silly, inconsequential affair about an ambitious girl from Iowa who sets out to conquer New York. Her train to the Big City is wrecked and she purloins a letter from a dead passenger who had been given permission to stay at a man's posh New York apartment while he is abroad. Shearer brazenly moves in, begins living the high life, and blossoms into a champion girl-about-society; of course the millionaire returns, and there are misunderstandings complicated by a visit from her parents, but it all clears up and she gets the millionaire.

Jimmy Quirk, who knew Cody well, tried to warn Norma about him, but she said she could handle it. Jimmy may not have liked the Cody involvement but he did like the picture, with *Photoplay* commenting "The outlandish comedy is so gaily and adroitly played by Miss Shearer and Lew Cody that it becomes first-rate entertainment." *Photoplay* added, though: "Not much fun for the children."

It did not turn out to be all that much fun for satyr Cody either, who found, as men before and since had, that the little Shearer girl could be a first-class tease. "She had set her sights higher than Lew and she wasn't cheapening herself by getting too intimate with him," Anita Loos felt. "I think Lew stayed hot on her as long as he did because he loved the chase— especially when the lady held out." Mickey Neilan stated that Lew had the most generous endowment, where it counted, of any man in Hollywood. "Oddly enough little Willie Haines could hold his own with him in that department, but no *woman* would ever get to see it!" Mickey said, laughing. (Some years later Norma would prove Mickey Neilan wrong on Haines.)

Norma did accept dates with Lew; he could be amusing and he had an interesting personal history. His standard line to females during his periods of matrimony was "My wife and I have an understanding." "The hoariest line in all creation, but it worked most times," according to Mickey Neilan.

Cody had been born Louis Joseph Coté of French-Canadian parentage in Waterville, Maine. He had first wanted to be a doctor, then quit medical studies for the stage. Vaudeville and stock led to his first movie, aptly titled *The Mating*, in 1915. After that he found himself for the next twenty years, until his death, in demand as assorted charmers, seducers, heels, and diabolical defilers of women. Adela Rogers St. Johns said of him, "Lew put his heart and soul into his roles.

After all, he was playing a part of himself—the most important part."

Norma's mother thought Lew outrageously unsuitable as a swain and told her daughter so in no uncertain terms. "I believe men and women can be *friends,*" Norma insisted. "And that's what we are." "Lew was as 'friendly' with a pretty woman as a boa constrictor," Frances Marion said.

Heel and satyr he might have been, but Lew Cody and Norma Shearer had a good on-screen chemistry, and in the several pictures they made together, they got a good fan reaction. William Haines, who was in *A Slave of Fashion* and who never cared for Lew, thought him a vain stuffed shirt. "As if I care what that queer thinks," Lew told Neilan, and retaliated, reportedly, by briefing L. B. Mayer on Haines's latest gay highjinks at a particular bordello for men only on Wilshire Boulevard. "Willie got called on the carpet for *that,*" Anita Loos recalled, "and Mayer pulled strings to get the gay whorehouse closed by the police, especially when he learned that Haines had taken Ramon Novarro there. If powerful friends had not interceded at that point, William Haines's career at the studio might have ended then and there, but one of his rescuers, according to Anita Loos, was William Randolph Hearst. "Marion is fond of Willie," he told Mayer.

Cody squired Shearer all over town that summer and fall of 1925. They went to sporting events, movie premieres, and parties. "It was evident that Norma didn't take the man seriously," Frances Marion said. "About as seriously as she took Billy Haines. Actually she liked Billy better than Lew." There was much laughter around town when one columnist began linking Shearer and Haines romantically. Her mother liked him, however. "He was amusing *and safe,*" Anita Loos said. (At *that* point [1925] Loos was right about Haines.)

Another Shearer squire at the time was director Harry d'Abbadie D'Arrast. D'Arrast, then about twenty-nine, had been born in Argentina of French Basque descent, and had been wounded in World War I. Brought to Hollywood by a friend, director George Fitzmaurice, he assisted Charlie

Chaplin in various capacities as researcher and technician on such movies as *A Woman of Paris* and *The Gold Rush*; between 1927 and 1933 he directed a half-dozen Hollywood films, both silent and talkie. They were distinguished for their wit, pacing, good photography, and general charm. A maverick, and independent in his thinking, D'Arrast eventually had to find work in Europe, as studio bosses outlawed him. He had a devastating wit, which he applied against the wrong people, King Vidor later reported.

D'Arrast amused Shearer just as Cody had, but it is doubtful that anything more serious developed. "Harry just didn't turn Norma on," Frances Marion said. "The chemistry wasn't there. I think Harry took it hard. He had the idea he wasn't successful enough for her, as he wasn't in that early period. He told me once he was sure Norma intended to 'marry up.'"

Shearer wasn't keen on the next film she did after getting away from Cody. But she was a contract player, and Mayer and Thalberg told her it was a striking cameo role (though cameo wasn't the word they used in 1925) that would help dress up the picture, and would she please be a good sport and do it. The film was *Pretty Ladies*.

ZaSu Pitts and Tom Moore were the leads in a backstage story about a wallflower type (Pitts) who falls in love with a drummer (Moore) who also writes songs. They marry, he becomes a success as a composer, a vamp tries to break them up but they are eventually reconciled. That's the sum total of the plot, but the picture featured personal appearances by such as Ann Pennington, a popular musical star of the 1920s, and the background color, modeled on Ziegfeld shows and their atmosphere, is fetching.

Impersonating Frances White, a popular musical comedy star of the day, Norma was "heavily made up and wearing an unusually large chapeau that was flat and round, under which she wore a curved hair-do around the side of her face, and daintily holding a thin walking stick that rested on her half-bare shoulders and body. [She] was a stunning sight to behold," according to Jack Jacobs and Myron Braum in *The Films of Norma Shearer.*

Lucille LeSueur, later to be known as Joan Crawford, had a small part as one of the chorus girls; she had also doubled for Shearer in another film. But this was the first movie together for a duo who were to come to grips years later in a far more prestigious film and whose running "feud," whether actual or publicity-inspired, was to generate a wealth of news copy. In *Pretty Ladies* their paths crossed only fleetingly, and there is good reason to believe that Shearer was hardly aware of the slightly hefty, dark-haired girl with the French name who in time would become one of the great stars of Metro-Goldwyn-Mayer—and no bosom buddy of Norma Shearer Thalberg.

Thalberg doubtless felt he was giving Norma a real break when he assigned her to yet another Lon Chaney vehicle, *The Tower of Lies.* This was a heavygoing film, based on the Selma Lagerlof novel, *The Emperor of Portugallia,* and it was drenched in Scandinavian moodiness and atmospherics, courtesy of director Victor Seastrom. Agnes Christine Johnston and Max Marcin were responsible for the scenario, and Seastrom, determined to keep what he called "Hollywoodisms" out of it, went to the other extreme and created a mood piece that was long on the philosophical ruminations and characterizational subtleties and short on the romance and suspense that American audiences responded to.

It concerns a farmer (Chaney) who dotes on his lovely daughter (Shearer). When his farm is in danger of being foreclosed, she takes off for the big city to make money to save it, and of course winds up on the primrose path, which in her case pays off big. When she returns with the money for her family, the townspeople suspect that she is a high-priced courtesan and outlaw her. The lecherous new landlord (Ian Keith) pursues her, her father goes crazy and imagines himself the emperor of a foreign country (hence the novel's title, later changed to the more phallic *Tower of Lies*), and after both eventually die she returns to the simple life and the simple suitor who had loved her from childhood.

The role of the country girl who goes wrong should have afforded Norma an opportunity for some fancy histrionics, but as more than one reviewer noted, she seemed the same woman after her "fall" as before, with wide eyes and simple ways. Shearer later blamed her failure to develop her character on Victor Seastrom who, she said, "was more concerned with the moods he was creating than with the shadings he should have injected into my performance." Chaney did not receive his usual rave reviews. The critics commented negatively on his fake whiskers, and one critic called Chaney "stiff and exaggerated." Young William Haines came off well as the long-languishing suitor, but Keith overacted as her nemesis. Claire McDowell came off best as Chaney's wife, with one reviewer commenting that she seemed to *be* the character rather than play it.

The Tower of Lies was yet another of those Metro-Goldwyn movies in which an attempt was made to duplicate the moody realism and fatalism of the Swedish movies then so popular, and who better than Victor Seastrom to guide it, since he was a native Swede. But in shortchanging the romance in favor of heavy symbolisms and human commentaries, Seastrom & Co., and for that matter the producers, forgot that the final arbiters on such fare were the paying customers.

Variety, in its September 30, 1925, review, summed up the reaction of most critics when it stated: "Notwithstanding that *The Tower of Lies* is a sincerely made picture and excellent from the artistic and literary viewpoints, it is too heavy for the picture audiences. When finished, the impression is left that one more prostitute has been reformed and been forgiven."

Metro-Goldwyn for a time had big hopes for stage actor Ian Keith, but his performance in this and other films eventually relegated him to character roles in the talkies, where his intensity and unglamorous glowering turned into assets rather than liabilities. Thalberg liked William Haines and protected him from Mayer, who did not cotton to his gay lifestyle. Haines served as escort for Thalberg's sister Sylvia, and even went with Thalberg and other family members on vacations.

A witty, charming young man, Haines enjoyed serving as a sort of "court jester"; feeling vulnerable, he used humor as a shield; for a time, it worked.

That year Shearer was reunited with Lew Cody for yet another trifle, *His Secretary*, directed by Hobart Henley from a story by Carey Wilson. The plot, rather timeworn even then, had Shearer a plain-Jane stenographer whose lack of sex appeal and spinsterish ways keep men looking straight past her. She is secretly in love with one of the partners of her firm (Cody), whose wife punishes him for fooling around with his blond secretary (Gwen Lee) by insisting that he hire Shearer in her stead. When Shearer overhears the man she loves say that he wouldn't want to kiss her even if he got paid, she dolls herself up, gets a new wardrobe, and wins him after some rather tiresome maneuverings.

Norma managed to wade through and, on occasion, overcome the clichés to the extent that *Photoplay* wrote: "Norma Shearer gives a splendid performance as Ruth Lawrence, the kind of secretary that only the boss's wife could love. Cotton stockings, sensible shoes, pince-nez and all. Without any exaggerated makeup, beautiful Miss Shearer looks plain enough to be a movie critic."

Mordaunt Hall in *The New York Times* felt Shearer had handled her part "with a good deal of thought and earnestness," but added, "at times she overdoes the pantomime in her gestures . . . rattling off long speeches with accompanying expressions." Cody, who never could be sure of critical approval, got off with "acceptable as the insincere but plausible man about town."

Cody continued his persistent attentions to Norma during their second film together, and while she admitted to friends that she liked him, the spark wasn't there, and she had to tell him so honestly. As an experienced wolf, Cody wasn't easily discouraged, and there were many feintings and maneuverings during the shooting. To accommodate Norma and her mother, who had again taken to visiting and staying on the set, director Henley started scheduling Cody's scenes for a later hour than Shearer's, with the result that she and her mother were often able to disappear before he finished work—to his great annoyance.

In a *Motion Picture* interview while shooting this film, Shearer gave her views on the acting expertise she was steadily developing. "I just try to be as natural as I can, and as sincere. When I'm playing a part in which I have to be something that is not quite my own natural self, I use my imagination and try to imagine the kind of girl she might be. I think back among my friends and associates and try to put into her some of the characteristics that I feel are right for her."

On the subject of romance, Shearer told the same interviewer:

> I know it's a cliché to say so but I would have to feel it, instinctively, all the way before committing myself permanently to a man. As for marriage, it is a serious step; I'm twenty-five now, and that is supposed to be getting on for a woman who wants a husband and children, but I won't rush into things. If I don't think the man is right for me, for the long haul, then I won't encourage it.
>
> Of course I see various men; some are developing into very good friends; the value of friendship must never be underestimated, and in many cases it lasts so much longer than love. If a man feels more than I can, I try to let him know how things stand; I don't want to lead someone on and then after he has gotten in too deep emotionally, cut him off. If I am honest with him from the beginning, then he won't blame me if things don't work out as he would wish.

Asked for her definition of "true love," Norma stated: "She should see the man as someone she really likes to be with; someone whose success and happiness really interest her; someone she should see as a life partner; and it is important to be able to laugh with him—and then there's that spark that cannot be defined—if it's there, it's wonderful, and if it isn't, one must either walk away or try to salvage the man as a friend."

If Lew Cody had read that interview during the making of *His Secretary,* it would doubtless have caused him to down some stiff drinks.

For her first film released in 1926, Thalberg had promised Norma something unusual. "You've wanted different, more unusual film fare, and this ought to be it," he told her. It seemed that he had decided to bring to Hollywood the Danish director Benjamin Christensen (he spelled it Christiansen in the States), who had made a reputation for creatively macabre films in his native land, especially one called *Witchcraft through the Ages,* in which he had appeared as no less than Lucifer. According to one commentator, "The film, made in Sweden, [was] a masterpiece of the horror genre, a horrifyingly vivid record in striking lights and shades, of diabolism and satanic practices from the Middle Ages to the Twentieth Century."

The film acquired an international reputation, and soon Christiansen was working for UFA (Universum Film Aktien Gesellschaft), the German film production combine. At times he acted, most notably in the lead role in Carl Dreyer's *Chained* (1924), known in Europe as *Mikael.* Coming to Hollywood under Thalberg's auspices (the producer was always looking for unusual talents who would give excitement and variety to MGM products), Christiansen was to specialize in mysteries and unusual dramas with a macabre twist. He later returned to Denmark, where his career petered out.

The film Thalberg had in mind for the Danish director's Hollywood debut was called *The Devil's Circus,* and it was a story suggested to him by Christiansen himself, who proceeded to write the scenario.

"This is something unusual, of the kind you have been hoping for," Thalberg told Norma. "I have an instinct about it, so trust me and go along with it."

Christiansen had dreamed up a macabre tale about a destitute waif (the Shearer role) who is awaiting the release of her convict lover and who joins a circus where a married lion tamer takes a shine to her. His jealous wife cuts the rope of Shearer's trapeze act and she falls into a cage of lions below, breaking both legs (though she escapes the lions' jaws). Crippled and again destitute, Shearer becomes a vendor of dolls and wanders the streets hawking them. She is eventually reunited with her convict lover, and learns that the lion tamer is now also destitute. Eventually she walks again and happiness is presaged for her.

The plot seemed murky to Norma, but she saw possibilities for strong drama in it; the picture, as she told Anita Loos, also seemed macabre in the Danish manner, but Christiansen's poor command of English was not much help, either. They communicated in sign language plus the few Danish and English words that she and Christiansen regularly inflicted on each other. Charles Emmett Mack, Carnel Myers, and John Miljan were also in the film.

Christiansen was an intense fellow with a European approach to matters great and small, professional *and* personal. Soon Norma became aware of his growing interest in her, and again she found herself fending off a man in his forties. At first Christiansen interpreted her reserve as coyness and hard-to-get game-playing. It was only after Norma appealed to Thalberg personally and he in turn made the truth of her disinterest clear to the designing Dane that matters settled down and they all concentrated on the picture, which Christiansen, poor English and all, managed to deliver at decent cost within schedule (no von Stroheim was he).

The critics thought the film strange and questioned whether Americans as a whole would cotton to it. *Variety* said: "Miss Shearer does not convince as the country girl become a circus aerialist. The four-year jump in the continuity which picks her up as the cripple shows her face as clear and fresh as before the accident and the hardships of the war, a fault on somebody's part if realism were the objective." Passing verdict on Christiansen and his concepts, Delight Evans in *Screenland* stated: "Altogether, Mr. Satan's circus wasn't as much fun as some I've been to."

The Waning Sex (1926), her next film, showcased Shearer in a story by Ray and Fanny Hatton, directed by Robert Z. Leonard. Opposite her were two actors who the gossips numbered among her allegedly unrequited admirers, Conrad Nagel and George K. Arthur.

Photoplay nailed down the plot of *The Waning Sex* in its review:

> Is woman's place in the home or in business? The young district attorney thinks babies are the thing. The pretty lady lawyer thinks different. Since Norma Shearer is the fair Portia the problem becomes darned acute to us, particularly as Miss Shearer demonstrates gracefully that the modern woman's place is in the one-piece bathing suit. This is pleasant entertainment, proving again Miss Shearer's aptitude for character comedy. Conrad Nagel is the D.A.

Conrad Nagel told me years later:

> Norma was always delightful to work with, but even in her early career was she a scene-stealer? You can bet on it! We had a photographer, Ben Reynolds, on *The Waning Sex,* and you know that 1926 was rather early in her MGM period, and darned if she and he didn't have their heads together before and after every shot. We looked at rushes one time and I was completely in shadow! "It's my *skin,* Conrad," she hastened to tell me. "My skin has an unusual transparency and I have to ensure the lights are right!" Her skin didn't seem that unusual to me, but I went along with it. It was true that the ladies' whiter skin usually got more attention than the men's, but it seemed to me that she and Reynolds were overdoing it a bit.

Had he been in love with Shearer? Nagel was tactfully evasive, but in his usual gentlemanly manner he said, "Every man who knew or worked with her was in love with her. She had an unusual grace and tact, and she was very sensitive to other people's feelings. And she always went out of her way to make the older character actors feel comfortable and truly a part of the proceedings."

Shearer is particularly effective in a courtroom scene. Dressed in a severely tailored black costume with "sensible" shoes and a severe hairdo, she keeps the jury so spellbound that they are all leaning forward. Leonard remembered that in this scene she worked herself up to such a lather with her impassioned pleading that two "jurors" almost fell over the railing at her feet. "She seemed to enjoy that," he said. "After I called 'cut' she even pushed two of the younger ones back into their seats. Later they were following her around the set and she turned and said 'Court's out now, and I have things to do.'"

Leonard recalled:

> She was very hardworking and so ambitious it was frightening. That was a year or so before she married Thalberg [1926], and she saw the sensation Greta Garbo had made after doing only a couple of Hollywood pictures, and here she had been plugging along in so-so roles, some of them almost bits, and she wanted to make faster progress and it was really frustrating her.
>
> She was a great one for retakes, and I had to remind her that we could only do just so many of them as Mayer didn't like unnecessary costs. I remember her quoting the old saw, "Anything worth doing at all is worth doing well."

And her male admirers? "She had a clever way of handling them," Leonard said. "She was direct and honest but tried to be nice, and if they interested her enough, she'd aim for a friendship. If that didn't work and the guy went on carrying the torch and getting sour about it, she'd just shrug it off and walk away from it."

Typical of the good personal reviews she was getting in

1926 was *Variety*'s: "A nice picture comedy, *The Waning Sex,* made nicer and nicer by Norma Shearer. This fresh-looking girl who plays with charm, does a great deal for a picture that has its laugh punches. The film might not stand up so well without this girl, despite the excellent direction by Robert Z. Leonard." Conrad Nagel, her rumored admirer, did not come off so well: "[He] gives a lukewarm performance in a wavering characterization."

While the last of her 1926 releases, *Upstage,* was no world-beater, Norma did benefit from the photography of Tony Gaudio (at that time credited as Gaetano Gaudio.) Gaudio, who was later to film Bette Davis and other top stars with impressive results, gave Shearer the "star" treatment, and other aspects of the film were well mounted, especially the art direction of Cedric Gibbons. Shearer's wardrobe in this was particularly scintillating, though some critics felt director Monta Bell had let Shearer, Oscar Shaw, and Tenen Holtz, down.

Confronted with *Upstage,* Mordaunt Hall in *The New York Times* stated:

> The unevenness of this photoplay is surprising for it was directed by Monta Bell, who, in the unfurling of screen narratives, has matched his wits against the best producers, and curiously enough, it is occasionally the skipping of unnecessary detail that excuses an episode to be almost ridiculous. As Norma Shearer and Oscar Shaw render an excellent account of themselves, the falsity of some of the doings of the characters they impersonate falls upon Mr. Bell's shoulders.

Gladys Hall of *Motion Picture,* who had always liked Norma and who rooted for her at every turn, wrote: "Oscar Shaw is human, appealing, convincing. And we all know Norma. She is particularly good in these impersonations of a stage, circus or vaudeville girl. There is considerable drama, a great many deft touches, reality and compassion. You will have an enjoyable hour or so, guaranteed."

Part of Gladys's steady enthusiasm for Shearer and her works might have been due to Norma's facility as an interviewee. "She always sent me away with sparkling quotes," Gladys later recalled. "She had a natural bent for self-publicizing; she could outdo MGM publicist Howard Strickling or any of them—in fact, she herself wrote at least the first drafts of a lot of stuff Howard put out on her."

In 1926 Shearer was telling Gladys: "MGM is giving me some variety in my roles and for that I'm truly grateful. They give me a chance to stretch my imagination and enlarge my capacities."

The story of *Upstage* dealt with a small-town girl, Dolly Haven, who has a business degree and goes to New York with office work in mind; she lands in show business through an accidental meeting with vaudevillian Oscar Shaw. She likes the stage but recognizes that her talent is not of the first order, and after taking a woman's place during a knife act (the woman's child falls off the balcony), Shearer decides that love and marriage are more important than her career.

While the material, based on an original story and scenario by one Lorna Moon, was slight, Norma makes it seem more important than it is with some lively acting and saving humor. Oscar Shaw, a recruit from Broadway, was her leading man and proceeded to join the ranks of her admirers. Monta Bell recalled that Shearer dealt with him "in her usual manner, half joshing, half sympathetic, and one-hundred-percent wary."

Of the Norma Shearer of late 1926, Louella Parsons wrote in the *San Francisco Examiner*: "She's a girl on the prowl—she wants the right picture, the right kind of money, the right friends—and, obviously, the right man, as Heaven knows she's taking her time settling on him. That's her Scottish practicality for you. Nothing will throw this girl. She's game for anything they throw at her."

Parsons added, rather naïvely: "Whatever man eventually gets her—and she's had her pick of the best in Hollywood—will be a lucky guy. She'll stick with him to the end—this girl's code doesn't allow for divorce or straying, or casual romance either. It is nice to see such a beautiful girl so level-headed, and fundamentally so decent and balanced."

It was back to Lew Cody in the new year, 1927 . . . as co-star. Robert Z. Leonard was again the director, with story and continuity by F. Hugh Herbert and Florence Ryerson. The picture was *The Demi-Bride,* naughty as all get out in what Hollywood conceived of as the French manner, whatever *that* was. Here Norma is a student in a decorous convent school who goes chasing pell-mell after wealthy boulevardier-and-roué Lew Cody. What this aggressive little girl *doesn't* know is that Lecherous Lew (as he was known off-screen) is actually her mother's paramour—she's one of many, of course.

Leonard later told me that Lew Cody was never more impassioned than in his scenes with Norma in this film—at first he is indifferent to her budding charms, even impatient and annoyed by her attention, but then she begins to grow on him and "Romance: 1927 style" is soon explored.

In an interview with Gladys Hall during the shooting, Lew went overboard in his rhapsodizings on Shearer: "She's such a wonderful girl—I always come off a scene with her feeling braced for the rest of the day. Her very presence is a tonic—it is so wonderful always to play with her." Was he in love with Norma? Gladys asked. "More and more every day," Lew stated. "And when they tell me I'm going to be cast with her, it sets me up for the week." Gladys mischievously asked him if current wives ever objected to his feelings for his leading ladies. Responding like a genuine Parisian boulevardier, Lew replied, "My wives have always known that my primary devotion to them never has, and never will, preclude my admiration for feminine beauty wherever I encounter it. I am only human, and lovely women affect me strongly."

Whatever Mabel Normand's reactions to words like these might have been, she did not choose to share them with the public—at that moment, anyway.

Notwithstanding Mr. Cody's unrestrained enthusiasm for

Norma, *Variety* dismissed *The Demi-Bride* forthwith, and with
a minimum of words: "Despite the box-office draft of the star,
Norma Shearer, *The Demi-Bride* is a tedious picture, and all-
told, just fair."

Norma must have had more than a few friends at *Motion
Picture,* notably the loyal Gladys Hall, for its review stated:

> A very lively French farce has been directed by Robert Z.
> Leonard with a sure hand, and a humorous eye, which rests
> not only on each separate scene, but always sees straight
> through to the end of the picture. Which is no ordinary
> achievement in the handling of these flippant complexities.
> Each scene is very nicely turned, and the whole is original,
> utterly ridiculous, and highly entertaining. . . . [Shearer's]
> performance is clever, consistent and delightful. Lew
> Cody's version of the ultra sophisticated Frenchman is
> rather apathetic, but he gets his effect. It's worth seeing.

Shearer won particular commendation for early scenes in
which she convincingly got across the yearnings and mischievous schemings of a teenage girl. Though she was pushing
twenty-seven, Shearer assured Adela Rogers St. Johns, chief
writer for Jimmy Quirk's *Photoplay,* that memory and imagination were the keys to recapturing the ardors of the teen
years. "You let your memory roam back to that time—to
what you were thinking and feeling, to the boy you might
have had an innocent crush on, to the lavish, overblown ex-
pectations all teenagers feel. Also, I had an old diary from my
teen years; just re-reading parts of it helped me create the
effect I wanted. After all, are we not the sum total of everything we have ever felt and known and observed and taken
in?" When Adela expressed a desire to see what she felt
would be a fascinating insight into Shearer-as-teenager, the
star demurred. "It's too personal." She laughed. "That was
my make-a-fool-of-myself time." And the status of l'affaire
Cody? Adela queried in parting. "Lew and I understand each
other" was the enigmatic reply.

After Midnight, Norma's second 1927 film, brought her back together with director Monta Bell who, rumor had it, had joined the list of her unrequited admirers. Handsome leading man Lawrence Gray played his love scenes with such impassioned sincerity that the Gray-Shearer rumor mill got grinding. Lest there be misunderstandings, Norma told Adela St. Johns that "Mr. Gray and I have a professional association, nothing more. Mr. Gray is a very handsome man, and a good actor, and he is a professional, so he knows he has to play love scenes in a convincing manner. I can assure you that his and my emotional interests lie definitely elsewhere."

In *After Midnight,* Shearer is a nightclub cigarette girl who is almost robbed by petty criminal Gray. After she hits him over the head with the lead pipe she has been pressured into "purchasing" from him, she worries that she may have killed him and takes him home to nurse. Good-looking and intelligent, Gray is redeemed by his love for her and decides to save money via honest work and buy a cab.

Meanwhile Norma is being demoralized by her racy sister, Gwen Lee, who is a chorus girl in the club where Norma languishes behind the cigarette counter. When she sees the easy life her more attractive sister has, what with the men who subsidize her, her desire for the straight and narrow palls briefly. After Lee is killed in an auto accident, Shearer decides that she and Gray will walk the straight and narrow after all. Drab it may be, but they'll have their self-respect and each other, and so on. Such is the plot of *After Midnight,* from an original story by director Bell, with scenario by Lorna Moon.

The real hit of the picture was Gwen Lee, who frequently worked with Shearer in the 1920s, usually as a comedienne. Lee, a very pretty blonde with a distinctively tart personality, almost stole the picture from Shearer in a role that was more dramatic and dimensional than the talented Gwen was usually handed. Off-screen Norma and Gwen were good friends, and when Gwen ran into trouble with men and money, as she tended to more often than not, Norma was always there with a helping hand.

Despite Gwen's fine work, and sincere playing by Norma and Gray, *After Midnight* came through as a rather mediocre film with few redeeming qualities. Mordaunt Hall of *The New York Times* made fun of what appeared to be Monta Bell's efforts to copy the style of a controversial director. "In some of the intimate scenes of the two sisters, Mr. Bell manifests a tendency to emulate Erich von Stroheim and you are constantly made aware that cabaret girls *must* have silk stockings."

He added: "Norma Shearer takes her role seriously and gives a really fine performance. Lawrence Gray does the best work of his screen career as Joe and Gwen Lee is capital as the dizzy Maisie. This all means that a lot of talent is wasted on a childish yarn."

Photoplay, usually eager to find something good to say of a Norma Shearer picture, was thrown for a loop with this one. The magazine stated: "Monta Bell wrote this [about] a real cigarette girl in a Hollywood restaurant. Then he directed it with Norma Shearer as the young woman. The story, however, is the old yarn of the heroine who, dazzled by money, is about to slip from the straight and narrow path. This time her sister is killed after a drunken party. Not worthy of Miss Shearer and Mr. Bell. Mediocre stuff."

7

Marriage and
the Mother-in-Law

B Y 1927 NORMA was definitely considered a star, though of the second rank, in the studio that proudly advertised itself as the home of "all the stars that are in the heavens." Greta Garbo had won first-class stardom that year in *Flesh and The Devil* with John Gilbert. A newer actress, Joan Crawford, whose dancing feet and endless vitality had begun to impress audiences, was on the verge of stardom, and on the contract roster were such luminaries as Mae Murray (who was shortly to depart), Lon Chaney, Marie Dressler (who would later go on to great stardom), Ramon Novarro, Lionel Barrymore, William Haines, Renée Adorée, and a dozen others.

By this time Norma was drawing a thousand dollars a week. She asked Mayer for a revised contract that would gradually increase her salary, over the next five years, to five thousand a week. Mayer went along with her plans but intended eventually to let her go before her salary got too high. But Thalberg, whose personal interest in her was by now evident to all, persuaded Mayer to let her stay. He was planning, he said, to build her into a superstar, truly the lion's consort. Her refinement, grace, poise, authority, he said, made her the actress most fit not only for the title of First Lady of the Screen but First Lady of Metro-Goldwyn-Mayer.

Shearer turned twenty-seven in 1927. Thalberg knew she had a way to go before she could lay full claim to the position he visualized for her. One way he would clinch it would be to make her Mrs. Irving Thalberg, for by summer of that year he had fallen in love with her.

Irving's feeling for Norma had grown gradually. At first she had interested him as an actress who could be molded into a star, his own, special star, truly a product of his planning and imagination. But over the years she had gradually come to cast a spell over him. Frail in health, more comfortable with his men friends, Thalberg had escorted a number of Hollywood beauties, including the much-married playgirl and sometime actress Peggy Hopkins Joyce and flighty, fickle Constance Talmadge, who with her sister Norma Talmadge (Norma went in for drama, Connie for comedy) had become one of the most popular of film stars. From about 1925, Irving had begun to date Norma, usually when he wanted to relax at a preview or just wanted to talk to someone over dinner. He did not carry the relationship into the personal realm at the time. Norma called herself Irving's "spare tire." "He falls back on me when the heavygoing romance with the other girls got *too* heavy," she said with a laugh.

Thalberg's mother, Henrietta, preferred Norma to Thalberg's other involvements. Norma put herself out to be nice to the older woman, who with her husband, William, had followed Irving to Hollywood and through a succession of ever-more-handsome homes. Irving's health was a constant concern to his mother. She wanted him married, wanted him to know the fullness of life, but she felt it had to be a woman of quiet poise, dignity, and essential maternalism, one mature and womanly enough to cope with Irving's uncertain health, to make sure he got proper rest and recreation, and who could provide him with a calm and orderly domestic existence.

Billy Grady, MGM casting director, told me: "Connie Talmadge would have been poison for Irving; she was a good-time gal who was a hell-raiser and she'd have killed him in no time. But Norma was warm, motherly, maternal, and supportive." Billy felt *that* was why she became the one and only Mrs. Thalberg, staying with him to the end.

Joan Crawford told me years later:

> Norma was a conservative when it came to men. She didn't want any hell-raising playboys and girl-chasers. She hated drinkers and men who didn't have their lives in order. Good looks and charm went only so far with her. She was always looking underneath. That's why she chose Thalberg—he was a mama's boy if ever there was one, and his frail health brought out Norma's maternal instincts. Also, he was practically a virgin when they married, and his mother thought it would be a great match. But oh what she had to put up with from her in-laws! I wouldn't have wished them on my worst enemy!

Henrietta Thalberg was not really the witchy mother-in-law of legend, and Irving's health gave her real cause for alarm. Louis B. Mayer, who loved Irving like a son, refused to encourage his daughters' evident romantic interest in him because, he said, a doctor had told him that Irving's heart was so weak that he might not live to age thirty. Rosabelle Laemmle, daughter of Thalberg's original mentor, Carl Laemmle of Universal, had been involved with Irving for a while but she proved an independent young woman who disliked Hollywood, and, according to movieland scuttlebutt, had no desire to find herself a young widow.

Just how experienced Irving Thalberg was sexually prior to his marriage is a subject of speculation. He lived with his parents, and Henrietta fussed over him, freed him of all domestic concerns, and ran the household with a firm and efficient hand. As one writer said of her: "A warm meal was always ready for him when he came home late from the studio. She sometimes chided him for working too hard, and she did everything possible to guard his strength. If he appeared pale, she made him remain in bed all morning before reporting to the studio. At the slightest sign of a cold, she began filling him with home remedies. He took her and his father along on most social occasions, and Henrietta would glower if Irving danced more than two numbers in a row."

Publicist-writer Jerry Asher felt that Irving dated various beauties only to keep up a front. He was undeniably heterosexual, but his health concerns had doubtless dimmed his sexual interests and capabilities, and he was more concerned with appearing to play the game; he didn't want to seem "slow" among his more healthy and more robustly virile friends.

Norma's refinement, sound sense, level-headedness, and relatively good moral reputation doubtless impressed Henrietta. She began to push Norma as a possible wife for Irving. True, Norma was a gentile—a Protestant—but that could be corrected, if Norma were willing. As it turned out, Henrietta didn't have to play matchmaker. By mid-1927 Irving was definitely in love. The engagement was announced in August. On September 29, 1927, they were married.

The ceremony was very simple. It was held in the Thalberg garden with only family members and close friends present. Rabbi Edgar F. Magnin presided. Norma had shed her Anglicanism for the Jewish faith. She said later of her conversion: "When I began to go with Irving, I began to associate with his people. His family were Orthodox Jews and I saw that they found peace and contentment in their religion. I wanted peace and contentment in our marriage. I decided that I had no particular religious conviction—that I could find it in the Jewish faith. I loved Irving so much that I wanted our children brought up in the same way he had been."

Louis B. Mayer served as best man at the wedding. His daughters, Irene and Edith, were bridesmaids. Marion Davies was also a bridesmaid, as was Bernice Ferns, a friend of Norma's from the old days in Montreal. Irving's sister Sylvia was maid of honor, and Andrew Shearer's estrangement from his family was evident in the choice of her brother Douglas to give the bride away.

Louella Parsons gushed about the wedding in the Hearst press nationwide. She rhapsodized:

> Never has Norma Shearer looked lovelier. Many, many times she has been called upon to play the role of a bride, but yesterday she gave her most realistic performance. Her gown of soft ivory velvet was particularly becoming. The severity of the plain white was relieved by a yoke of hand-made rose point lace studded with pearls and an occasional rhinestone. Her veil, edged with lace, was thrown back from her face in soft, gathered folds instead of the conventional bridal cap. She carried a bridal bouquet of white and tinted lavender orchids with pale yellow roses. Pinned to the bodice of her dress was a diamond pin—the gift of the bridegroom.

Over the decades since that wedding the question of how much in love with Irving was Norma when she married him has been asked many times.

Certainly she respected his character and the great position he had achieved through talent and hard work. Certainly she was grateful for what he had done for her own career; because of him she was a star in the MGM firmament, and the future promised to set her star still higher. Her warm maternal concern for him equaled that of his mother. His relative lack of sexual experience was probably, at the time, a reassurance to her; mother Edith had said, the night before the wedding: "Irving is a clean man; your children will have clean blood." Everything promised a full and happy life together. She doubtless pushed into the back of her mind her lack of genuine physical passion for him, the kind she had felt for other men with whom she had been fated, for one reason or another, never to unite. "Love is *caring about* someone," her mother had said. "Romance and sex are treacherous—they tarry but awhile. But that other feeling lasts forever." Norma had sighed and determined to make do with what those words indicated.

After their honeymoon at Del Monte on the Monterey peninsula, Norma and Irving went back to the house on Sunset Boulevard, where they lived with mother Henrietta and the other Thalbergs. Norma had made it definite that she would continue with her career. She had worked too hard for it, she and Irving had made too much of an investment in it over the years to stop now. She wanted to make her husband proud, to fulfill all his dreams of making her truly the lion's consort, the First Lady of the Screen.

Henrietta had no objections. She was the one who sat at the head of the dining table, who greeted guests, ordered the food, supervised the servants, did the shopping. She could have it both ways—see Irving happy with a beautiful wife, yet keep as firm an eye on him as ever. Norma did not come into her home as a rival but as another daughter. Norma was relieved to be rid of household duties; that way she could concentrate on her career aims. Children could be postponed until later. There was Irving's health to consider; his routine must continue to be supervised carefully. She and Henrietta were to be partners in a common purpose—for a while.

Louis B. Mayer was delighted with the marriage and pleased with Norma's conversion to Judaism. He felt that Irving might live longer now, with a calm, self-possessed, womanly wife like Norma. Now he and Irving could continue the furtherance of the studio's aims, the collection of more stars for their Metro-Goldwyn-Mayer heaven, the strivings for quality and prestige in which he fully concurred. Louis Burt Mayer had come a long way from the Lazar Mayer of Minsk, from junk dealer Louie Mayer of long-ago New Brunswick. He would be truly an entrepreneur extraordinaire, a man to be reckoned with in American business. Life promised even brighter horizons for the Mayer-Thalberg team. And when, in 1926, Mayer's name was honored as the third addition to the MGM logo (colleagues felt it was his due) he was truly a man content.

Phyllis Haver later said: "There was Norma, loving, but not, I suspect, really in love. She had substituted warm maternalism and loyalty for that combination of passion and romantic fulfillment of which she knew herself to be capable. Like Henrietta, she felt good about things. Her world was orderly and solid and right. But she was *fulfilled*? Hardly. *That* fulfillment still lay in the far future. . . ."

In *The Student Prince,* released September 1927, the month of her marriage to Thalberg, Shearer found herself surrounded by all the trappings of an "A" production. Wilhelm Meyer Forster's popular piece, *Old Heidelberg,* had been transformed into the popular musical, *The Student Prince,* with Sigmund Romberg providing the music. Thalberg had assigned Hans Kräly to do a screenplay that would stress the nostalgic and romantic values of the beloved story. John Mescall was assigned to the photography and told to make Shearer as lovely as possible while not stinting on the requisite pictorial effects. Marian Ainslee and Ruth Cummings were told to come up with particularly scintillating titles, and Cedric Gibbons and Richard Day went all out on the art direction for a picture that was to eventually run two hours and would moreover benefit from a specialized-exhibition approach (only two showings a day, at higher prices) that was followed in all major cities. David Mendoza and William Axt were told to write a musical score that would catch the flavor of the original operetta while gearing itself to the symphony orchestra approach of major film houses.

After much thought, Thalberg chose as director Ernst Lubitsch, who was German-born and understood the ambience of the University of Heidelberg, where the main action occurred, very well. *The Student Prince* is a tender romance of a royal crown prince who is sent to the university because of his desire to mingle with his fellows and escape the strictures of his position. He falls in love with the barmaid at the students' inn, and she with him, wins the comradeship of his fellow students, and then is catapulted back into his former life when he succeeds to the throne. He returns to Heidelberg as king, but the students salute formally at his approach; only his former love accepts him as in the past, but they recognize the disparity in their stations in life and part sadly.

In some ways, Lubitsch was a strange choice for the tender romanticizings of *The Student Prince*. It was not that he was incapable of injecting deep feeling into scenes when he was so minded. It was rather that he had come to be associated with the brittle studies of high society and the sophisticated, ironic marital dramas that had earned him his greatest fame since he had come from Germany to America after triumphs with Pola Negri and other German stars. In such films as *Forbidden Paradise* and *Lady Windermere's Fan* and *The Marriage Circle*, he had depicted sex as frivolous, cynical, and manipulative. Audiences identified, sometimes to their surprised annoyance, with his piercing insights into their less admirable selves. When Lubitsch had tried to direct Mary Pickford in *Rosita,* the result had been disastrous, as affirmative, upbeat Mary and downbeat, realistic Ernst mixed like oil and water.

Now he was to direct *The Student Prince*. According to Anita Loos he had been chosen primarily not only because he understood the teutonic milieu but because his films had come to symbolize prestigious high style.

While this Metro-Goldwyn-Mayer "special" did show elements of high style, especially in Lubitsch's handling of the supporting characters and his little ironic commentaries on human nature scattered here and there, he was not really suited to handling the likes of Norma Shearer (the barmaid) and Ramon Novarro (the prince).

As shooting progressed it became obvious that neither star cottoned to the Lubitsch approach. Novarro, who was doing his first picture with Shearer, took top billing over her because he was by that time a major star, having won the allegiance of many fans in *Ben-Hur* and subsequent pictures. A shy, sensitive young man of Mexican origin, he had a beautiful tenor voice (which he would use to good effect later in the talkies). He felt frustrated that he could not use his singing skills in the picture, which of course would be silent with musical accompaniment by an orchestra. Shearer, too, felt as the filming progressed that the barmaid's role was one-dimensional and Lubitsch's well-meant but ill-advised efforts to combine the innocent romancing with inappropriate sophisticated undercurrents were disconcerting. "I'm supposed to be an innocent young girl in love, not a slutty courtesan; she is *in love* with the prince, innocently and openly; she has no designs on him sexually or monetarily," she told King Vidor, who visited her on the set while doing another picture nearby, "yet Ernst keeps trying to get subtleties into my expressions and behavior that my own instincts tell me are inappropriate."

Many years later, in telling me of this, King Vidor remarked: "I think Norma had gotten perhaps a little paranoid about Ernst; she had started confusing him in her mind with Erich von Stroheim, who was decidedly of a different, and darker, feather. After all, it was not as if Ernst proposed to turn the students' inn into a bordello or something!"

Novarro's problems with Lubitsch were of another kind. Ramon was a homosexual whose love affairs with various males, including Valentino, were well known in the film colony, though unknown to the general public, which thrilled to his romantic attentions to various screen heroines. Valentino had presented him with a gold-plated dildo (which, forty-one years later, in 1968, was to be rammed down his throat by a hustler whom he had picked up on the highway, suffocating him). He combined his homosexual proclivities, oddly, with a fervent Roman Catholicism and had contemplated at one time becoming a monk. He had even converted Jimmy Quirk's charming young writer Herb Howe, who wrote often of Ramon in *Photoplay,* to Roman Catholicism. Louis B. Mayer found Ramon and William Haines's homosexual problems a collective nuisance, and Howard Strickling's publicity department was kept busy hushing up their sometimes indiscreet encounters. Both Thalberg and Jimmy Quirk had several times pleaded with Mayer on their behalf; they made Will Hays nervous, too, as they were forever skirting the technicalities of the moral turpitude clauses in their studio contracts.

Lubitsch, who loved gossip and intrigue, knew of all this; he was quite familiar with the German homosexual scene, which was well represented in the film industry there, and he found the Americans' puritanism and head-in-the-sand approach amusing. Despite himself he began injecting homosexual overtones into Ramon's scenes with other actors; they were subtle but definite, nonetheless, and they upset Ramon, who understood what he was doing only too well.

George Cukor, who later took over *The Women* from Lubitsch and who was himself gay, albeit highly closeted and cautious, told me once that he wished *he* had directed *The Student Prince*. "Poor Ramon," he said. "He was a very unhappy and sensitive fellow, and a rather lost one. I would have guided him through that with more gentleness and tact even if it *was* a silent."

Shearer, too, knew of Novarro's private life, as did Alice Terry and other ladies who had worked with him. Norma's attitude toward gays was always a sympathetic and tolerant one; she felt that their lives were difficult and complicated and that the emotional pressures were fierce. Thalberg, who had worked with many sensitive gay actors (and a few lesbians, too), shared this view.

But it taxed Norma's abilities to make love with an exclusively gay actor under the tutelage of a continental ironist who couldn't resist his penchant for mischief—creative mischief, but mischief all the same. She found herself, more often than not, the peacemaker when things got too tense between the director and his male star. In one scene involving boisterous student camaraderie, Lubitsch singled out, according to King Vidor, an obviously gay young bit player for Novarro to place his arm around and laugh and sing with. He kept demanding take after take of the laughing-singing-holding scene; it was Shearer who provided the distraction to the goings-on, in which Lubitsch was taking obvious pleasure. "She simply pulled a fainting spell," King Vidor related, "and damned if it wasn't a better performance than she was giving in the picture!" Thalberg later ordered the scene cut.

Charming and colorful as the film turned out to be, the critics, if not the audience, sensed the tensions that had gone on while the picture was shooting.

Mordaunt Hall in *The New York Times,* for instance, wrote: "Mr. Novarro is natural and earnest, but a little too Latin in appearance for the role. Norma Shearer is attractive . . . [but] does not seem to put her soul into the part. She, too, acts very well, but like Mr. Novarro she does not respond as other players have done to Mr. Lubitsch's direction." Robert E. Sherwood wrote for *Life*: "Norma Shearer as the girl gives a performance that is excellent at times, and at other times, a trifle laborious." And *Photoplay,* despite its editor-publisher's longtime affection for Norma and admiration for Thalberg, was forced to call a spade a spade, remarking, "Unfortunately, Norma Shearer is miscast and Lubitsch isn't completely in his element," but adding "Very much worth seeing, nevertheless."

When I talked with Ramon Novarro in 1960 (he was then past sixty), his face darkened when the subject of Lubitsch and *The Student Prince* came up. "It was not one of my favorite films," he snapped, "and Lubitsch certainly wasn't my kind of director. I know he did well with others, but he was wrong for me. We just didn't have *simpatico,* and I was glad when it was over with."

Thalberg realized that he had been guilty of a lapse of judgment in casting Norma in *The Student Prince.* True, the film, lavishly produced and heavily promoted, had turned out to be a hit, but he belatedly realized that the attempt to meld the respective Lubitsch-Novarro-Shearer mystiques had been a miscalculation. King Vidor felt that Thalberg's prime consideration at that time was to rush Norma into the first prestige production available, so as to announce to all the world that she had graduated to real stardom. "If he had thought about it more, he would probably have starred her alone in something more sophisticated," Vidor said.

The new Mrs. Thalberg started off 1928 in rousing fashion in a sparkling comedy *The Latest from Paris,* directed by Sam Wood in the best tongue-in-cheek style. Ralph Forbes, a rather stiff and dour young actor who had not been used well in much of his previous fare, came alive in this and matched Norma's comedic inspirations all the way.

Thalberg made a real effort to showcase his wife in a quality production here, and the original story and scenario by A. P. Younger was expressly tailored to her requirements. William Daniels, who was to win a reputation as one of MGM's best all-time cameramen (his work later with Garbo was particularly celebrated) was given orders from above to make Mrs. Thalberg as beautiful as possible, which he proceeded to do. To *make* sure he did, Norma had frequent conferences with him, and was even seen checking the camera.

In this, Norma is a traveling saleslady engaged to her sales rival (Forbes), whom she consistently manages to outsell. Far from minding these defeats, he is spurred to pursue her further, all the while pressing for marriage. But there is a problem in the person of her young brother (William Bakewell), whose college education she is furthering. Forbes resents the fact that she must continue to work because of this obligation, and for a time they break off while he involves himself with another woman. When Bakewell tells her that it is time for him to be a man and announces his independence and marriage plans, Norma and Forbes get back together again.

This relatively simple plot is, however, dressed up with a lot of high fashion and sumptuous production mounting, and Cedric Gibbons again came through with some distinctive artwork.

The Los Angeles Times said: "Norma Shearer is ideally cast as Mary Dolan, imparting to the role much sparkle and zest. She appears to advantage, too, in smart, tailored clothes." Forbes came in for his share of approval from the same publication: "[He] is excellent as the rival salesman and lover. It is a new type of role for him, appearing as a typical American go-getter. He displays a good sense of comedy."

In an interview with *Motion Picture,* Ralph Forbes said of Norma:

I was very struck during the making of [*The Latest from Paris*] with her intense concentration on her part. I'm sure she studies everyone else's role along with her own because when she got into a scene with several of us, she carried us along in a splendid teamwork. It's a nice little picture, but her presence and authority have added to its effect greatly. I haven't done too much comedy, but Norma made me feel wonderfully at ease. Everything went along so smoothly and spontaneously because of her, and Sam Wood worked well with all of us. I feel she opened new avenues of acting work for me with this.

The young actor William Bakewell, later to play a German soldier in the famed *All Quiet on the Western Front,* always spoke well of Norma. "I was young and green and not a little frightened when I made [*The Latest from Paris*], and she was wonderfully calm and reassuring and helped me give a relaxed performance—or it seemed that way when I saw it at a screening room later. I did not have too high an opinion of my acting potential then, and thanks to her I made a fresh start. She said to me: '*Live* the part! *Become* that person! Then the acting part will almost take care of itself, though you must watch everything, of course.'"

Sam Wood always greatly admired Norma. He had worked with such top glamour queens of the screen as Gloria Swanson and he knew his screen personalities. Over the years he was among those who claimed that Shearer would have made it to top stardom with or without Thalberg. "That drive, combined with that talent, and her wonderful capacity for discipline—she was a winner from the start," he said. "Some called her perfectionist—well, isn't genius the capacity for taking infinite pains?"

Of her next film, *The Actress,* based on Sir Arthur Wing Pinero's 1898 play *Trelawney of the Wells, Photoplay* wrote: "After a series of pert, modern stories, it is good to see Norma Shearer return to her old-fashioned charm."

The popular play, considered delightful in its time, was a

shade out of date for 1928 audiences, but Thalberg felt that it would showcase his wife in a period picture and would demonstrate her versatility and range. While it was moderately well received by the critics and the public, and while it contained one of Shearer's more ingratiating and vital performances, it might not have been the wisest choice for audiences at the height of the jazzy roaring twenties.

The story deals with one Rose Trelawney (Shearer), an actress who does leads at the Wells Theater. The period is the 1860s. The place, London. Rose falls in love with aristocratic Arthur Gower (Ralph Forbes). Though his family look down on her as a commoner, they wed, and she retires to private life. Soon she finds the aristocratic life depressing and dull, as she has little in common with her snobbish, condescending new in-laws. When some of her theatrical friends call on her, she is revitalized by their joie de vivre, leaves her husband, and returns to the stage. There she finds that Tom Wench (Owen Moore), one of her company of actors, has written a comedy in which he wishes Rose to star. Her husband comes after her and even joins the production as an actor, and her mellowed father-in-law supplies the capital. The venture is successful, and all ends happily.

The Victorian unrealities of such a wish-fulfillment caprice might have sold well in 1898 London, but thirty years later they creaked rather noisily. Norma did her best to liven things up, but it was not one of her best roles.

Even though by this time she had been Mrs. Irving Thalberg for more than six months, the usual silly rumors surfaced about her alleged interest in, first, Ralph Forbes, her leading man yet again, and then Owen Moore, who had been Mary Pickford's first husband and was a bon vivant noted for his heavy drinking. By now Norma recognized the rumors as the usual foolish scuttlebutt and had Howard Strickling issue a statement, which she largely wrote, saying that "Miss Shearer is a married woman now, and any rumors that she has a more than professional interest in Mr. Forbes or Mr. Moore are totally false and are to be totally discounted."

Forbes, an intense, emotionally high-powered young man who had first come to notice in the 1926 *Beau Geste* and then had supported Lillian Gish in *The Enemy,* had, however, added fuel to the gossip by engaging Norma in lengthy conversations between shots, bringing her ice cream, asking her advice on his interpretation, and so on. Louis B. Mayer himself had to call Forbes into his office and warn him that his attentions were exceeding dignified limits. English gentleman that he was, Forbes apologized to both Shearer and Thalberg, and there was peace on the set from then on. The rumors ceased due to Strickling's insistence and backed by threats of noncooperation by other MGM personalities whom the publicists and writers were always trying to get at.

Owen Moore proceeded to tell one and all that *his* interest lay elsewhere; that he found Shearer a delightful associate professionally but that all rumors of his interest were damnably cheeky and he resented them. Louella Parsons, in one of her rare shafts of inventive wit, ran a "travesty" item in her column that had them chuckling in Strickling's office. It stated that the rather venerable (for Hollywood) character actor O. P. Heggie, who played the father-in-law, was "running a temperature" over Norma. Louella had her laugh, and no harm was done. Meanwhile Mordaunt Hall dismissed *The Actress* as "a pleasant little dream . . . a bit sentimental" and informed his *Times* readers that Norma "plays her part acceptably" but had "a tendency to overact."

Feeling that his wife's excursion into costume via *The Actress* had been perhaps premature, Thalberg then rushed her into theaters in a modern story, *A Lady of Chance,* released in December 1928. This was Norma's last silent film. It was to be synchronized (sound timed to coincide with a specific image), and some talking sequences were tacked on, but she herself did not speak. Shearer fans would have to wait for her first 1929 picture to gauge the quality of her voice. Meanwhile, in the opinion of more than a few reviewers, she was languishing in a trivial film unworthy of her talents.

A Lady of Chance is the old story of the crooked confidence woman who fleeces rich men, only to fall in love with an honest but poor young man whom she had mistakenly believed was rich. Johnny Mack Brown, the handsome, muscular ex-football hero who had made his first film in 1927, was the love interest here, and in his innocent, ingenuous way fell hard for his leading lady, off-screen as well as on.

Johnny, as Joan Crawford told me, never lost a fundamental clean-cut innocence, and his romantic attentions to Norma were so platonically guileless that she refused to take alarm, accepting the flowers and the little boxes of candy with gracious aplomb while telling him he really shouldn't bother. Thalberg found twenty-five-year-old Johnny's "crush" more amusing than anything else, and according to Eddie Mannix, Johnny escaped being hauled into Mayer's office for a warning lecture. "Johnny's boyish niceness stood out all over him," Eddie said. "If Johnny found himself in a parked car with a broad in a desolate area, he'd probably bore her to death talking football, their only physical contact coming when he put his coat around her to protect her from the evening breezes!"

But Johnny's evident adoration for Norma did come through well on screen, as the rushes indicated, and though Thalberg felt for a while that they might make a good team for a few more rounds, nothing came of it. "Johnny just wasn't a good enough actor," Mannix said. "He eventually landed in westerns, where he more or less remained."

Also in the film were Lowell Sherman, in another of his smarmy, odious incarnations as Norma's cohort in crime (no "romance" rumors circulated about *them,* for sure), along with Shearer's old supporting standby from other films, Gwen Lee, the third member of the crook triumvirate. As in all Hays-influenced little films, Shearer repents of her sins and goes to prison, but Johnny blithely promises to wait for her.

The critics dismissed the film. Mordaunt Hall in *The New York Times* wrote: "Considering her luckless part, Miss Shearer does exceedingly well," adding "as her type of beauty is essentially classical, it cannot be said that she is suitably cast." The lovelorn Johnny Mack Brown was written off by Hall as "acceptable" while Sherman got the nod as "capital."

Variety let the hapless Johnny have it, snapping: "Brown fits on appearance, wearing a gold football for those who remember, but isn't a heavyweight on histrionics here" and adding "Picture hasn't any action, but extracts some good moments from Miss Shearer, who is backed by the smooth-working Sherman in a role that is a pushover for him."

Photoplay tried to cover its disappointment with flippancy: "Norma Shearer in a drama of a gold-digger who reforms. If they only would in real life!"

Howard Strickling later recalled that some fleeting thought had been given to making *A Lady of Chance* Norma's first full talkie. Shearer vetoed the idea, maintaining, quite correctly, that her talkie debut should showcase her in a stronger story. Thalberg agreed, and a major hunt was initiated, with the help of the story department and all volunteers, for the right talkie for Mrs. Thalberg. Soon they found it.

8

Conquering the Talkies

WHEN IT CAME to Norma's first talkie, Thalberg was taking no chances. A recent Broadway stage hit, *The Trial of Mary Dugan,* had been suggested; an advantage: most of it could be shot in a single courtroom set—a boon to the still-immobile cameras. Even so, there were formidable technical problems. *The Trial of Mary Dugan* was MGM's second all-talkie release (the first being *The Broadway Melody*), and sound methods were still primitive; in fact, the recording posed serious problems, since traffic noises from the streets outside the studio kept intruding. Among the experiments that proved successful: a half-dozen cameras were nailed down on the set in long, coffinlike boxes. The scenes in those days ran as long as ten minutes because sound-film intercutting (synchronizing of sound and film) had not yet been perfected. This meant that the actors had to make long speeches, theater-fashion, and they often got nervous and forgot their lines, especially by the eighth or ninth minute. Then scenes had to be reshot *and* rerecorded.

The sound technicians who had been brought especially

from New York, where technological development was more advanced, often interposed their own approaches on the cameraman and crew, which led to some confusion and not a few high-decibel quarrels.

Thalberg was also worried. Should his wife make her talkie debut as a tough, brassy showgirl who has been the kept woman of several wealthy men and who proceeds to murder one of them? The bulk of the action is taken up with her trial. Her original defense lawyer backs out, and his place is taken by her young lawyer brother, whose studies she had financed as a courtesan. In the end the earlier defense lawyer is exposed as the real murderer and the showgirl is vindicated. Thalberg would have preferred that Norma appear as a more refined character in her first talkie; he had always (and always would) prefer her in genteel roles, though he recognized that the harsher portrayals demonstrated her versatility and range, thus widening the basis of her audience appeal.

Shearer wanted to play Mary Dugan, however, as she saw its strong dramatic possibilities. She had already prepared carefully for the momentous talkie debut on which her entire future in films depended. She had even gone to the trouble of having her voice analyzed extensively at the University of Southern California. The results showed a voice that was extremely pleasant, though high-pitched and lilting. Her voice tested well, and later Norma became involved in the university's sound testings for other players, whom she helped with advice, including praise and/or commiseration, depending on what was needed.

In 1929 all of the silent stars were nervous. Recognizing their concern, one *Photoplay* cover had Norma Talmadge staring intently at an ominously overhanging microphone. Since at that time the cameras were immobile, mikes had to be installed in flowerpots, lamps, and behind pillows—anywhere convenient to the star's vocalizing. As a result, the first talkies were flat, awkward, and stagy. Many of these transported stage plays, complete with Broadway stars arriving on every train, proved stagebound and deadly. It was another year before the cameras became fully mobile and before sound techniques matured. Norma Talmadge, William Haines, Ramon Novarro, and especially John Gilbert were among those to suffer at the hands of the primitive recording system. After two films Talmadge decided to retire; Novarro and Haines hung on into the mid-1930s, after a fashion, but it was Gilbert who really took the beating. His light baritone and precise diction did not record well; there were rumors that Mayer, who disliked him and found his expensive contract onerous, had had the recording devices tampered with to make Gilbert sound effeminate, high, and fluty; others blame the primitive sound mixers. Whatever the reason, Gilbert has gone down in film history as the first great casualty of sound. Oddly enough, his voice sounds fine in the 1933 *Queen Christina,* with Garbo, but by that time it was too late for him to recover the ground he had lost.

Shearer, however, was a triumph in *The Trial of Mary Dugan.* Thalberg had taken the precaution of rehearsing her with her fellow actors for two solid weeks; then he ordered a run-through. Satisfied with what he saw *and* heard, he gave her the part. Bayard Veiller, the play's author, was assigned as director. He felt Norma was ideal for the role, and coached her carefully. H. B. Warner was the prosecuting attorney, Lewis Stone (also in his talkie debut) her first defense lawyer, and Raymond Hackett her lawyer brother. All had stage experience and helped her at every turn. An interesting sidenote: To gain "local color" for the prison sequences, Shearer asked the studio to "book" her at the Los Angeles County jail; she was escorted through the women's quarters by special police, had her fingerprints taken, and even spoke to some of the inmates in order to catch their speech inflections.

When the picture opened at New York's Embassy Theater, audiences were delighted by Norma's distinctive, haunting, well-pitched voice (several voice coaches had drilled her carefully), and her emotional scenes were carried off most effectively. Thalberg's worries over his wife's future were at an end. She was destined to be a leading star in the sound era. Mordaunt Hall in *The New York Times* wrote: "She reveals herself quite able to meet the requirements of that temperamental device—the microphone"; and Norbert Lusk of *The Los Angeles Times* referred to her "vindication and triumph," adding "She emerges as a definitely compelling actress of greater individuality than she has ever revealed in silent pictures."

For her second talkie, Norma chose *The Last of Mrs. Cheyney,* a scintillating Frederick Lonsdale comedy that had been very popular on Broadway. In it she is a skillful lady thief (jewelry is one of her specialties) who poses as a wealthy Australian widow and proceeds to disarm the idle rich on the Riviera with her charm and social finesse. Things hit a snag when she falls in love with an English lord whose aunt she plans to rob. After a series of complications, she foregoes her light-fingered past and prepares to marry her aristocrat.

Basil Rathbone, the popular star of the New York and London stage, was drafted as her leading man. His portrayal of Lord Dilling impressed audiences greatly, though it did not lead him into romantic starring parts, as he had hoped. His delivery was too incisive, his profile too sharp, his aura too menacing and authoritative compared with other leading men at this time. In the 1930s he worked in character roles mostly, and achieved lasting fame.

Rathbone and Shearer became good friends, and she was to become a regular guest at the brilliant parties he and his wife, Ouida Bergere, hosted.

One of my longer visits with Basil Rathbone occurred in Boston in 1954 where he was doing a summer stock production of *The Winslow Boy*. He spoke of Norma at length and in glowing terms. He said:

> I was deeply impressed by her voice and her general bearing in *The Last of Mrs. Cheyney*. I remember telling her at the time that she would have had a fine career on the stage if fate had turned her initially in that direction, since she

was disciplined, hardworking, totally dedicated, and had a
distinctive, very intriguing voice—unlike any I had ever
heard. I added that if she ever elected to appear in the theater, I would gladly champion her, and would consider it an
honor to appear with her. She was very anxious to please
Irving, wanted him to be proud of her. I think she had a
great deal of determination—a tremendous will to succeed,
and that is particularly important in acting.

I got tired of hearing that she was Galatea to Irving's
Pygmalion; she was a very strong character on her own,
very much of a self-starter, with true self-sufficiency. I was
Tybalt in her *Romeo and Juliet* film at MGM years later,
and her command of the Shakespearean rhythms and ca-
dences astonished me—she spoke Shakespeare so naturally.
And I was not at all surprised when some of her finest performances came in the years after her husband's death,
when she was very much on her own.

Sidney Franklin, one of Shearer's all-time favorite directors, guided her through *The Last of Mrs. Cheyney*. Many
years later he told me of *Cheyney*:

Basil Rathbone was a great help to her in that picture; I
remember that she went out of her way to ask him to discuss without hesitancy anything he felt was out of key in her
performance or her inflections, vocally, and he took her at
her word, and she was happy to get whatever advice he
chose to impart. Basil got very impatient with the mikes
hidden in flowerpots and the stationary camera in its lined
case that stood stock still and prevented him from roaming
around the soundstage as he did in the theater. So they sort
of consoled each other—that first year of sound was rough
on actors—*and* directors. I greeted the new camera mobility of 1930 or so gratefully.

Delight Evans's review of *Cheyney* in *Screenland* was typical of the general praise: "A praiseworthy entertainment.

Norma Shearer is superb—as for Mr. Rathbone, I hope he is here to stay." Mordaunt Hall of *The New York Times* stated: "Miss Shearer's work is remarkably good. She talks charmingly."

Norma provided her fans with a startling novelty—of sorts—that year, 1929.

She and John Gilbert did the balcony scene from *Romeo and Juliet* in *The Hollywood Revue of 1929,* first as a serious Shakespearean rendition of the famed love sequence and then as a jape couched in modern slang. One reviewer called Shearer "charming" but said nothing about Gilbert. Another, Frederick James Smith, in *Liberty* magazine, let both stars have it in no uncertain terms. Commenting on their brief appearance in this all-star musical and talking extravaganza, Smith wrote: "The biggest fall-down among the screen stars is contributed by Norma Shearer and Jack Gilbert in the balcony scene from *Romeo and Juliet.* They are terrible when they tackle Shakespeare and they are nearly as bad when they try a modern flip version of the love tragedy."

Over the years film historians have debated the quality of Jack Gilbert's voice in *The Hollywood Revue.* Some felt he had made a fool of himself, while others thought him "pleasing" and "adequate." In my opinion, Gilbert came through pleasantly enough considering that halfway through, he and Shearer had to resort to such 1929 lovebird slang as "Julie, baby, you're the cream in my java, the berries in my pie." I always felt Jack Gilbert's voice sounded like Ronald Colman's, as it certainly does here. The film's primitive Technicolor plus Shearer and Gilbert's relatively brief appearance helped distract audience attention from Gilbert's voice. Some months later, when Gilbert's first full-length talkie, *His Glorious Night,* appeared, his vocal problems were clearly noticeable.

Shearer was charming in her more serious sequence, and good-humoredly got into the later clowning in *The Hollywood Review.* Jack and Norma's warm feeling for each other, their joy in their collaboration, was obvious.

The Hollywood Revue was an entertaining hodgepodge of star turns, with many MGM stars represented in singing, dancing, and thespian skits (Garbo was absent, being in Sweden at the time). For instance, a very young Jack Benny and Conrad Nagel were MCs; Nagel sang "You Were Meant for Me" to Anita Page; Joan Crawford sang "I've Got a Feelin' for You"; Laurel and Hardy did a magic skit; Marie Dressler and Polly Moran sang an amusing number called "I'm the Queen"; and so forth. *Photoplay*'s verdict was typical: "A great big merry girl and music show."

For Shearer, her final picture for 1929, *Their Own Desire,* was a step back. It was a trivial bit of pseudodramatic froth in which her diction won another round of admiration, but the role of a cynical society girl disillusioned by her father's philandering offered her few opportunities, and E. Mason Hopper's direction failed to highlight her more attractive qualities. Flatteringly photographed by William Daniels, the sound supporting cast included Belle Bennett, the original Stella Dallas of the 1925 Goldwyn film, whose career was starting to go downhill at that point, as the mother; and Lewis Stone, sterling as always, as her womanizing father:

The picture was more notable for introducing Robert Montgomery in his first costarring role opposite Shearer; they were to do four more films together. The plot requires Montgomery to restore Shearer's faith in love. After initial success he finds himself stymied when it turns out that his mother is her father's mistress. They decide to part, then get caught in a storm and are reported missing. Their contrite parents seek them out, and after the rescue her father rejoins her mother and all ends happily.

Montgomery told me in later years that Norma had helped him immeasurably in his early film career. He said:

> I was only twenty-five and I was still green in films, and she was the soul of kindness and helpfulness. But she was very strong-minded and wanted her way in certain things. I remember she was always arguing with Bill Daniels about

camera setups and she told me privately that she thought the script was terrible and that actors could only manage to be as good as script and direction allowed. She didn't care for our director, either, considered him a hack, said he didn't understand the new sound medium.

My chief impression of Norma was that she was a very ambitious woman with a definite plan for her career, and she wasn't letting anything or anybody get in the way of it. To give her credit, she did help me to look good; I can't say she wasn't generous to other players, but I felt her attention was always on herself. She didn't seem so much vain as worried. I got the distinct feeling that career success was an obsession with her—certainly she had the industry and discipline to bring *that* off, all right.

Unlike other stars I worked with, she was not a flirtatious type. She didn't seem to feel it necessary to prove her attractiveness to men—her happy marriage had a great deal to do with that, I'm sure. Whenever I saw her and Irving together, their mutual devotion was obvious; she had eyes for no man but him. I guess I had been spoiled by women up to then; I was attractive and didn't mind admitting it, and when a woman didn't play up, I took it as a personal insult, I guess. But I didn't feel that way with Norma. She was a lady. She had character. But boy, could she play passionate love scenes. I felt she was "selling" herself in those scenes, that she was telling herself, "I'm supposed to be madly in love with this fellow and suffering over him, and I'm going to make it convincing!"

Well, convincing it was, but as soon as Hopper called "cut," she'd switch it off so fast my head would swim. She'd go off by herself with her script and tell everyone she needed time to compose herself and work up to the next scene's mood.

The critics didn't think much of *Their Own Desire*. *Photoplay* led off the chorus of disappointment: "With just a little restraint, this effort at an emotional epic might have been

more than a vain attempt. Due to poor direction, the
principals emote until both themselves and the audience
are exhausted. As a climax, there is a stupendous studio
storm and a tailored-to-box-office ending. Norma Shearer is
badly miscast. A little hard to take after *The Last of Mrs.
Cheyney*."

Other serious critics agreed. When Jimmy Quirk made one
of his periodic visits to Hollywood with his wife, May Allison,
Norma asked his advice. "You've got to change your type,
Norma—you've got to vary your roles, go for something more
exciting," he said. Allison, who knew movies and movie players, took her aside. "Irving has you on a pedestal," she told
her. "He sees you as some kind of madonna. Look at that
sentimentalized ending in *Their Own Desire*. You need a
change of pace."

Frances Marion, Anita Loos, and other close friends told
her the same thing. Marion told me years later: "Norma
was a really first-class talent. I was afraid Irving would
overprotect her. But I needn't really have worried. Norma
was a very strong-minded woman. And when she wanted
things her way she got them. She saw the danger, and acted
upon it."

Norma began casting about for a picture that would showcase her in a new, refreshing incarnation that would get the
fans and critics stirred up. She had taken a shine to a novel by
Ursula Parrott, *Ex-Wife*, in which she would play a disillusioned divorcée who elected for sexual freedom, lots of romance, and no commitments. Of course she was still in love
with her ex-husband, and the ending was preordained, but not
before a bevy of sophisticated scenes and daring situations
that would permit her to display her new grasp on dramatic
complexities.

For an opening salvo, Norma went secretly to the studio
photographer and posed for him for several nights, hour after
hour, while they worked up some sexy, sophisticated photographs of her. She had her hairstylist and her dress designer

whip up some fetching creations in advance. When she was satisfied with the resulting shots, she laid them before her husband at breakfast one morning. Thalberg was electrified by what he saw.

"Now do you believe I can play a femme fatale and have them crying for more?" she asked. He nodded mutely.

9

Oscar Time

W HILE THALBERG agreed that Shearer could succeed in the starring role in *Ex-Wife,* he wasn't satisfied with the title. Norma came up with another: *The Divorcee.*

Robert Z. Leonard was selected as director of this 1930 release, the budget was shifted upward, Chester Morris, Conrad Nagel, and Robert Montgomery were the leading men. Four people were put to work on the scenario and dialogue: Nick Grinde, Zelda Sears, and John Meehan, with Frances Marion lending a hand as an unbilled fourth, as she told me. "I knew what Norma needed, and I added some touches here and there. They wanted me to take billing, but I said no. I wasn't usually so modest, but I decided to let the others have the credit."

Adrian was assigned to design some knockout clothes, and Cedric Gibbons cut loose with some ritzy and elaborate sets. "There was a new feeling on *The Divorcee,*" Robert Montgomery told me. "The project screamed *success* from the word go. Everyone was feeling positive. I knew Norma was happy with her role; they had given her something she could really get her teeth into, and I could sense her elation."

"She worked very hard on it," Leonard said. "I wasn't at all surprised when it won her the Academy Award for 1930. She went over her dialogue again and again—she drove us all crazy wanting rehearsals, then endless takes. She would sit with me in the cutting room muttering to herself. Knowing her anxiety, I would order even more takes to reassure her. Then she'd slap me playfully and hiss 'Slave-driver!'"

Florence Eldridge, who with her husband Fredric March was to become close friends with the Thalbergs, recalled that it was during the making of *The Divorcee* that Norma conceived her first child. (Irving Thalberg, Jr., was born on August 25, 1930.)

"Motherhood suited her," Leonard said. "And she put all of herself into *that,* too! She approached it with the same perfectionist zeal that she applied to a new film project. But later in the shooting she was starting to show—not much but enough—so we draped fans around her (Gilbert Adrian was very inventive) and got her behind furniture. But actually, as a mother-to-be she had a newfound glow that showed on the screen."

Shearer exhibited a broader range in *The Divorcee,* and critics and fans took note of it. The Oscar that Norma received made Thalberg deeply proud; his faith in his wife was now confirmed solidly, and for all the world to see.

Jimmy Quirk led the chorus of priase. "Now you're on your way," he told Shearer. He did the *Photoplay* review himself, writing in part:

> They banned the book *Ex-Wife* from the screen. But it was quite all right to film *The Divorcee,* and the strange thing is that whereas the book, although it sold hugely, was not what you might call a classic, the picture is.
>
> This has turned out to be a problem piece, as neat an essay on marital unfaithfulness as has been made in Hollywood. It sets Norma Shearer at the very top of the acting class. It gives Chester Morris a chance for another swell performance. The direction is as subtle as the scent of orchids and the clothes

are gorgeous. You won't forget this picture and you'll undoubtedly go home and have a good long talk with your spouse. But more important, you'll be amused and held spellbound until the last reel. Don't miss it.

Now Norma was taken with a new seriousness in Hollywood; as Louella Parsons told me in 1953: "She had joined Garbo as one of the collective celluloid dream princesses. Motherhood came, too, around the time of her award, and the two events seemed to change her status, the impression she made on people personally as well as before the cameras. When they spoke of The New Norma, the evidence was there for all to see."

Ambitious as always, Norma decided to sandwich in yet another film before her child was due. In a rush schedule, she tore through *Let Us Be Gay* in six weeks. The Rachel Crothers play had been well received on Broadway, and Thalberg had felt it would be a good vehicle for his wife, since he and director Robert Z. Leonard could stage it in a succession of quick scenes, many of them constructed on the same soundstage, which conserved Shearer's energies and stepped up the production pace.

For all its sparkle, smart dialogue, and snappy pacing, *Let Us Be Gay* was yet another story about the drab, colorless wife whose husband leaves her for more lively surroundings—and women—and who goes from ugly duckling to swan and collects her own share of admirers of the opposite sex. In the end, of course, the errant husband sees what a sophisticated, sexy lady his little wren has become, and they are reunited.

Hedda Hopper, an actress then, played Shearer's love rival for straying hubby Rob La Rocque, and Marie Dressler, who had shot to prominence as a character star after playing with Garbo in *Anna Christie,* played a society dowager who aids Shearer in becoming svelte, chic, and wise in the ways of the sex chase.

When we talked in 1964, Hopper dismissed *Let Us Be Gay.*

"It was just another of those thankless roles I was given at the time, though I was surprised to find myself Norma's love rival; they usually had me presiding at a tea table and asking 'Milk? Sugar?'" Hedda found herself amazed at Shearer's ability to conceal her rapidly advancing pregnancy. "The child was due in August, I believe, and the picture got released the same month!" she recalled. "I asked Norma why in hell she wanted to cope with morning sickness and other pregnancy discomforts on a movie set when she could have been home taking it easy, and she said pregnancy made her bored and restless and she'd rather keep busy. Also, she was afraid the fans would forget her if she stayed off the screen for many months. Now that is what I call cold-blooded!"

As in *The Divorcee,* Shearer hid her figure behind tables and chairs and drapes. When she had to wear anything of a more revealing nature, she got into stiff corsets and pored for hours over fitting designs. "It took a miracle to keep her svelte," Adrian later said, "but we performed that miracle and Irving later said it floored him."

Thalberg's mother disapproved mightily and let the family know that her son's wife was jeopardizing the child, but Shearer told Frances Marion, who had crafted the action to keep Shearer's physical movements at a minimum, that she was past caring what Mother Thalberg thought. She was a grown woman of twenty-nine and would use her own judgment.

Another problem for Norma and Thalberg during the shooting of *Let Us Be Gay* was Rod La Rocque, who had unwisely been cast as the erring husband. La Rocque had been a prominent silent star, and his 1927 marriage to the beautiful Vilma Banky, a Valentino costar in The Sheik's last two films, had been one of the events of the year. The Thalbergs liked Rod and wanted to help him repeat his earlier success, but his voice and diction defied the best efforts of Thalberg's speech coaches. Handsome and appealing, Rod was typical of the silent personalities whose voices failed to match their looks. Critic Richard Dana Skinner in *The Com-*

monwealth confirmed everyone's worst fears later when he wrote: "Mr. Rod La Rocque talks in the fashion of a traveling salesman who has about half-finished a course in elocution. His diction is deliberately monotonous and marred by a strong [regional accent] . . . he gives one the impression of being a hastily rehearsed amateur."

After the picture's release, Thalberg ceased his attempted revival of Rod La Rocque, and Rod, a sensible, realistic man, accepted with good grace the increasingly minor parts that came his way. In 1941 he retired altogether and wound up a real estate broker, where he prospered mightily.

"These silent stars who fall victim to the mike," Thalberg lamented to his wife. "The 'love of mike' turns to the 'hate of mike,' unfortunately!" But they had no such problems with Marie Dressler, who after decades on the stage understood the spoken word better than anyone. Her friend Frances Marion wrote some crackerjack dialogue for her as the society dame who teaches Shearer a few tricks in handling men and life, and Marie almost stole the show. (Marion had gotten Marie reinstated in movies after Marie's fight for actors' rights evoked producers' wrath.)

"That Norma is the most ambitious woman I ever met in my life," Dressler commented to Marion. "I can't accuse her of stealing scenes; she's gracious enough about giving other players their head, but does she pay attention to herself— mirrors, lighting, fittings, makeup, cosmetics, the whole kaboodle! I don't know where she finds the time to get in there and act, but she manages that, too. And pregnant, too!"

According to Frances Marion, a warm affection built up between Shearer and Dressler, who was to become one of the screen's great stars in the next four years before her untimely death, and Shearer was happy to be on hand for warm congratulations when Marie succeeded her as Oscar winner for 1931, winning for *Min and Bill*. She also gave Marie some shrewd financial advice, which helped her salt away more than she would have otherwise. Marie, Marion said, was a scatterbrain with money and a chronic soft touch.

The trade paper *Exhibitor's Herald-World,* based in New York, said of the picture: "Norma Shearer and Marie Dressler share the honors in this delightfully entertaining version of Rachel Crothers' stage play. Miss Dressler is no doubt laugh insurance for any picture. But the role of a belligerent, blustering society dame here allotted her is a perfect vehicle for her brand of humor." *The Commonwealth* critic who had blasted La Rocque's diction wrote of Shearer: "Her voice matches her personality and records with smoothness and effect. Her scenes . . . have the lightness, vivacity and naturalness of life itself."

The birth of Irving Thalberg, Jr., in August signaled a drastic change in the Thalbergs' domestic arrangements. Then thirty, Norma had a difficult time of it, and her doctors, after a birth described as "risky" and "chancy," insisted that she curb her career drives for a time and rest. Her common sense told her to take their advice. But on another matter she was to prove adamant.

She and her husband had been living with his parents for three years, and now Norma felt it was time they went their own way and take full charge of their personal lives. Privacy was a keynote in such an arrangement. She was a wife and mother now, a matriarch, and she told Thalberg that she wanted her own home, away from Henrietta and her fussings and assorted strictures. "My mother thinks only of me; she wants the best for me!" Irving told her. "And *I'm* your *wife,* and *I* want only the best for you!" Then, as she told Frances Marion, her impatience got the better of her and she shouted, "For God's sake, Irving, we're in our thirties now, with a little boy! It's time to cut loose! Now!" When he attempted to remonstrate, she repeated, "Now, Irving! *Now!*" When he said he didn't want to hurt Henrietta's feelings, she replied: "She'll have to accept it—life goes on and people grow up!" "When Norma made up her mind on something, that was *it*— no changing her!" Marion added.

"Norma was the kindest person in the world if she liked you," Marion said. "When my husband died a year or so before, Norma was the one there for me, at all times. But once she had made up her mind that her prerogatives were not to be interfered with, she was cold as steel. They called Jeanette MacDonald and Loretta Young 'steel butterflies'—it could have been just as easily applied to Norma."

Thalberg said he didn't have the heart to tell his mother, so Norma did. She firmly stated that she, her husband, and baby would be looking for a home of their own. Henrietta protested vigorously. Norma replied that a husband's welfare was his wife's responsibility, not his mother's; they would build themselves a house, and Norma planned to take Irving to Europe in the interests of that very well-being his mother dwelt upon. Henrietta was informed that in the new house she and other members of the family would be received as honored guests—but only at stated, prearranged times, and at the pleasure and/or convenience of the mistress of the household.

Norma began looking around for nannies, maids, housekeepers, butlers, all the conceivable aides she thought necessary. She consulted Frances Marion, Vilma Banky, her sister Athole, and Helen Ferguson. She did not ask Henrietta's opinion. "She's had her own way with Irving long enough," she told Helen Ferguson.

The house they designed was at the foot of the palisades at Santa Monica. On the same beach lived other film luminaries, including Marion Davies, who was also drafted for advice, as her beach house, where she presided under Hearst's aegis, was the most celebrated home in the area. Louis B. Mayer also lived on that beach; that didn't appeal to Norma so much. "He'll be in and out all the time," she told Ferguson. "Irving won't get any rest and quiet." But Thalberg felt it would be convenient to be able to hold spur-of-the-moment discussions with his partner, so Norma's reservations went by the board.

"I want nothing show-offish," Shearer told Ferguson. "I want it comfortable and homey—something Irving will look forward to at the end of a hard day at the studio." The house was designed tastefully but sensibly in French provincial style.

It sat on the beach only a few yards from the Pacific Ocean. Everything was designed for the master's comfort. Thalberg was a near insomniac, and slept so lightly that double windows were put in as well as soundproofing, to shut out the surf noises. Since ocean air was considered bad for his heart ailment, a primitive air-conditioning system was installed that featured air blown by a specially designed mechanism over cakes of ice. "If ocean air is bad for his health, what have you got him *there* for?" Henrietta screamed at Norma over the phone one night. "We are taking all precautions," was the icy answer, "and it is really none of your affair now."

Norma decided that a swimming pool would be in order; she used it regularly, but her husband never went near it. "What if he got a sudden heart attack in it and drowned alone? I'd never hear the end of it from the Thalbergs," Norma told Helen Ferguson. "Accordingly I forbade him the pool." "All of which reinforced my awareness," Ferguson told me, "that the great Thalberg was a studio lion but a lamb on the domestic front. But with the poor man's health being what it was, he had to relax somewhere! Certainly he was never allowed to over at Culver City!"

Mayer, as predicted, began "dropping by" on his way to his own home—a shade too often for Norma's taste. Tactfully but firmly she informed L.B. that Irving had to rest—and needed insulation from the outside world once he crossed his threshold.

There was also the new baby to consider. Norma loved her son and enjoyed cuddling and playing with him; she also intended to resume her career as quickly as possible. "I can't let any grass grow under my feet *there*," she told Frances Marion. "There's too much competition, too many ambitious women waiting to step into my shoes if I leave them empty too long." As a first step in her career renaissance, she negotiated a new contract with Metro-Goldwyn-Mayer for $6,000 per week, a phenomenal sum for the time, and had a number of perks built into it. Irving Jr. was consigned to the care of nannies and later governesses, and Norma prepared to return to the filmic wars.

But neither Irving Senior or Junior were ever to find themselves neglected. Norma always relegated certain hours to her son, and she organized the house around Senior's comings and goings. She did away with normal dinner hours, for instance, because Irving liked to stay late looking at rushes. Since she got home earlier than he did, she was on hand to greet him with the watered-down scotch the doctor had prescribed—no more than one. She was always on hand to hear his daily problems. "It was a really solid marriage, a real partnership, and a true friendship," Frances Marion told me. And their sex life? "Way down the priority list, from what she told *me*." Marion laughed. "I don't think they found all that much time for it. But with all those pressures, that was understandable enough."

Hedda Hopper and Helen Ferguson both felt that Norma became the classic sex-starved wife. "There was Irving's fragile health, his many pressures; she was more mother and nursemaid than bed partner," Ferguson told me. "If Irving said he was 'too tired' for sex, that was one husband who meant it. I am positive they were faithful to each other, really loved each other. Their marriage was held up as a model for all Hollywood. But let's face it, Irving's sex drive was not strong, what with his health problems and his many tensions." Hedda Hopper told me that she felt it must have been very difficult for Norma to play opposite sex dynamos like Gable and seductively charming lotharios like Montgomery, to be held and kissed by them, and then go home to the anemic Irving and his variegated concerns.

"She was romantically in love with Irving by then," Hopper added. "She told me once that he was too handsome to be a producer, and that he was the most gentle and tender and sweet man ever, but I don't know that all that translated into good old-fashioned lust." Other friends admired her willpower and her special brand of fortitude, but felt that she conducted discreet affairs to ease her tensions, then felt guilty.

"In a gossipy town that thrives on scandal of all kinds, Norma Shearer Thalberg is a wonder of wifely dignity and decency," Louella Parsons gushed in a 1931 story. "She knows the many ways of love, and she is mistress of them all. That special quality of grace, refinement, womanliness has made Norma the ideal mate for this complex genius. And her love for her little son is so touching. I went over to the new house and sat watching her cuddling and cooing with him, and it brought tears to my eyes."

"I think, for all the success and the money and the 'ideal' husband and the lovely little son and all the rest of it, she was a lonely and frustrated woman," Blanche Sweet told me. "If you ask me, her career was her real love, always had been, always would be. The husband and kid came with the territory, sure. It was all part and parcel of being a woman, and she used it all in her performances. But my husband Raymond Hackett said he felt she was not entirely fulfilled, either emotionally or sexually—not at that time, anyway." Quick sex might relieve tension, yes, but she longed, as always, for a perfect synthesis of sex *and* love.

Shearer knew that she had been able to ram through her salary demands (and this in a depression year) because her films were paying off at the box office. When Loew's president Nick Schenck, out from New York, was visiting the house and remarked, "Your films are a gold mine for us, Norma!" she had jumped right on him with her demand.

So when she had her domestic situation straightened out, Norma began poring over scripts for her next film. "It's my comeback and it's got to be socko!" she told producer Hunt Stromberg. "But Norma, when it comes out you'll only have been off the screen for eight months or so!" Hunt remonstrated. "In Hollywood, my friend, eight months is an eternity," he remembered her replying. "And boy, you should have seen the steely glint in her eye when she said it!"

"So she has the husband and she has the baby and she has the money and she has the fame," Henrietta Thalberg told Mayer. "What more can she possibly want?" He replied pithily, "The world!"

"She must have gone through two hundred scripts," MGM

casting director Billy Grady told me, "before she got one that passed muster. That was one fussy, choosy broad!" The story elected was *Strangers May Kiss,* based on yet another of those steamy, sexy Ursula Parrott novels that titillated the bored housewives and shopgirls with hurting feet across the face of 1931 America. Feeling there was no reason to walk away from a winning formula, Norma had chosen a story about a lady who gets consistently neglected by a globe-trotting hot-shot journalist who romances her when he's in town and in the mood, which isn't as often as she'd like, not by a long shot. Robert Montgomery is on hand again as the insouciant playboy who tries to fill in the gaps in her life, but in the end it's the journalist who gets her back. Costar Neil Hamilton, who, like Billy Grady, hailed from my hometown of Lynn, Massachusetts, shared with me many memories of Shearer in that film.

She was supposed to be a woman of loose morals, one step above a courtesan, traveling around Europe with many men in her life. And God, did she play the part to the hilt! Her love scenes positively sizzled, and she would get so passionate with me—before the camera's eye, of course—that I used to wonder if she was getting enough at home. But she always walked off by herself after the scene, never hung around me, never made even the hint of a pass.

I always felt there was something missing in her life, something she hadn't found, something she was waiting for. And this was the woman they said had everything!

Thalberg would come on the set sometimes, to have a word with George Fitzmaurice, who directed us, and he'd stay to watch the scene. It didn't seem to make the slightest difference to her. She'd kiss and hug and love me up like crazy—it got to be *very* arousing—and as soon as Fitzmaurice called "Cut!" she'd walk away from me and treat me as if I didn't exist. Oh, I don't mean she wasn't always courteous and ladylike, but she "turned it off" away from the camera. I think it was some kind of inner discipline she had, some kind of sense of the fitness of things.

Robert Montgomery felt that after the birth of her first child, Norma changed.

In *Strangers May Kiss* I sensed a new restlessness in her. Her career ambitions were as high as ever, but I felt she was compensating for something. It was nothing against the Thalberg marriage—it was a wonderful marriage—everyone thought them the ideal couple—but she seemed to be somehow taking charge on her own, while remaining always very solicitous of Irving in every respect. I was not the only one who felt Norma had such a strong inner drive, such a fierce discipline, she would have made it to all-out stardom no matter what the circumstances of her life.

George Fitzmaurice showcased Norma to maximum advantage in *Strangers May Kiss,* and John Meehan concocted some witty lines and situations for her in the screenplay that, with many amendations, she finally approved. She huddled endlessly with cameraman William Daniels, who later reported: "She worried about her figure and her complexion and we dickered a lot about the lighting. I had to assure her several times that her figure was as svelte and shapely as it was before her pregnancy. 'I don't want the fans to see any difference,' she said nervously. 'I did my exercises, watched my diet, and I *deserve* to look good in this. I've earned the right!'"

But while Daniels felt she looked wonderful, with no bulges that *he* could see, he went along with her fans and furbelows and retreats behind tables. Adrian complained that he had whipped up some really startling creations for Norma in *Kiss,* but that she insisted on covering them up. "She was obsessed with the idea that the pregnancy had left her pudgy, that the audience would be able to see through the fabric and undies straight to the stretch marks—it was ridiculous," Hunt Stromberg said. "In fact, she never looked better. Motherhood had given her a new bloom."

In the film Shearer was surrounded with a fine supporting cast, including Marjorie Rambeau, Irene Rich, and Hale Hamilton. The critics were generally kind when the picture was released in April 1931. *Photoplay* as usual led the pack with: "This is Norma's first picture since she became a mother and it's her finest picture to date. That's going some, as *The Divorcee* won many of the honors that were floating around last year, but Ursula Parrott develops her characters more logically and Norma's work in some scenes is superb. Rarely has one been as gorgeous as our Norma while treading the primrose path." Other critics referred to her "customary charm and intelligence," with her "sufferings" "cannily calculated to enthrall the feminine movie audience."

10

Gable and Glamour

NORMA had read a novel by Adela Rogers St. Johns, *A Free Soul,* had been mightily intrigued by it, and pushed it on Thalberg as her next film in 1931. Thalberg at first had his doubts, considering it a gamy, sexy story that might cause problems with Will Hays. "But, Irving, I want to set them on their ears," Norma pleaded. "The story is so strong it will top anything I've done yet!" Still, Thalberg continued to have his doubts. Shearer drafted Frances Marion into the cause, and Marion had her own private reasons for aiding Norma—she had an actor she was building up, and there was a role in it that would be perfect for him. The actor was Clark Gable. When Marion wrote *The Secret Six* earlier in 1931, she had built up Gable's part. After that, Joan Crawford took a shine to him, privately as well as professionally, and he appeared with her in a couple of pictures. Gable's fan mail increased astonishingly, and Thalberg, who had at first considered him nothing but a big-eared mug with bad teeth, began to have second thoughts.

Gable was primed for every break. He started by getting his teeth capped. Then he began exercising religiously to harden his already tough muscles. He emphasized his assertiveness at every opportunity, and his masculine charms were not lost on Norma.

Adela Rogers St. Johns told me in 1960: "I had written that novel from my heart, and I wanted it on the screen. Jimmy Quirk, who had gotten me started writing fiction after I wrote *Photoplay* stories for him for years, wanted the picture on the screen, too. He thought it had a tough realism about it that would be a tonic for 1931 movies that were overcoddling their women stars in a somewhat gooey manner. 'The fans are getting diabetes from all that sugar,' Jimmy said. 'They need a change.'" St. Johns recalled that Shearer was enthusiastic about the story and fought tooth and nail for it.

A Free Soul had a strong autobiographical element, as St. Johns's father, Earl Rogers, had been a free-wheeling, colorful criminal lawyer who drank heavily and conducted theatrical trials that often won juries over to his client. St. Johns had concocted a tale about a criminal lawyer who encouraged his daughter, as in her own case, to live her own life according to her own rules, and to hell with propriety and what other people thought. The daughter takes up with a ruthless gambler, a former client of her father's, whose virility excites her. At first bedazzled by what she conceives of as his Robin Hoodish individualism, she eventually becomes disenchanted, sees him for the criminal punk he is, and tries to break away—whereupon he pushes her around. Her father scorns him and her erstwhile fiancé kills him. At the trial, the father defends the spurned fiancé, puts his daughter on the stand, tells the court he regrets his freewheeling parenting, gets the defendant acquitted, and then dies dramatically in full view of all.

Thalberg knuckled under from all the pressure and bought the novel. John Meehan wrote the scenario, with instructions to follow the original closely and make it red hot. There were to be no punches pulled; Thalberg further instructed Meehan to make it as racy as possible and still get it by Will Hays. It did get by—by a hair.

Then Frances Marion made her move. She proposed Clark Gable for the role of Ace Wilfong, the gangster. Thalberg decided to take a chance on him, a decision that was to make Gable a star. The resultant picture, directed by Clarence Brown in a trenchant, hard-hitting, well-paced style, was a big hit and won Lionel Barrymore, as the father, the 1931 Academy Award for his courtroom-scene theatrics. Adrian dressed up Norma in some of the most daring creations she had ever worn, and she raised the hairs on Will Hays's head by sporting a satin negligee that exposes her legs and thighs (very racy stuff for 1931) in a scene in which her outraged father discovers her in the den of her lover, Ace Wilfong. But it was Gable who got all the fan mail; he was an overnight sensation, and shot to stardom in lavish productions opposite Joan Crawford and Greta Garbo (*Possessed* and *Susan Lenox* respectively.) Gable's pièce-de-résistance scene in *A Free Soul* was one in which he expressed his disgust with Shearer's attitude, pushed her roughly into a chair, and recited the immortal line (imitated by countless admiring American men): "You're an idiot—a spoiled silly brat that needs a hairbrush now and then!"

American women went wild for this forthright, individualistic, roughie-toughie who called the shots as he saw them and put the dame in her place if he felt she was out of line. In one fell swoop, Gable had made the romantic, tender-spirited film heroes of the recent past look old hat.

In the November 1931 issue of *Photoplay*, Jimmy Quirk wrote a story, "Why Women Go Crazy About Clark Gable." Jimmy opened up by tacking a cover line on it that read: "On the screen Clark Gable meets every woman with a challenge in his eyes, a mocking grin culminating in a laughing dimple, an aloofness that is not far distant and a skillful parry for every attempt to throw him off his guard. An adroit opponent in a duel of sex." In the story Jimmy wrote: "It is that uncertainty about him, that self-assuredness, that indifference that interests women. He is like a magnet that both attracts and repels. That complex mystery, woman, is baffled by a

greater mystery than her own—a man she cannot understand."

Norma, however, was not overshadowed. Her suggestive
costumes, the aura of uninhibited sexuality she exuded in the
film, the way she burned up the celluloid when she turned on
the come-hither eyes and invited Gable to come and put his
he-man arms around her, surprised audiences who had known
she could be sophisticated but tended to pigeonhole her as
naughty but nice; this time there were no such contradictory
phrases applied. Shearer could simmer, seethe, and scintillate
as kinetically as any dame on the screen.

In its July 1931 issue, *Photoplay* declared: "Norma Shearer
is excellent and handles the part of [the] daughter perfectly.
Her clothes are breathtaking in their daring. But you couldn't
get away with them in your drawing room." *Motion Picture*
followed suit with: "Norma Shearer covers white-hot emotions with the brittle manner of the modern girl in a way that
leaves no doubt of her ability as a dramatic actress." In
a publication called *Outlook,* one Creighton Peet didn't
like the film but seemed to have been attracted to Norma despite himself, when he wrote: "Some people may think they
have had their money's worth when they have seen Norma
Shearer silhouetted in a doorway, wrapped in a skin-tight gold
lamé negligee, her knee archly kinked, her hair coyly fluffed
and her chin in her palm—but I don't." (He didn't? Wanna
bet?)

The inevitable rumors started up about Shearer and Gable,
and they were a lot hotter than the stories and speculations
about her and the jaunty but relatively genteel Robert
Montgomery. As Howard Strickling told me, Thalberg had
mixed feelings about it—it made for good box office (Shearer
and Gable were to make two more films together; in one he
would get her pregnant and in the other he would romance
her while bombs fell all around them)—but this was his *wife*
they were talking about; his masculine honor was at stake.
Still, there is reason to believe that Thalberg enjoyed the hub-
bub—the man who, according to Lillian Gish, had tried to

arrange a juicy scandal for her back in the 1920s to hike up
her box office (Gish had refused the offer) would surely not
hesitate to throw his wife to the lions, if it helped make
money—especially when he knew there was nothing to it—or
was there?

According to Frances Marion, Gable had made Norma's
hormones jump. "After some extra-heavy kissing scenes, she
wandered off toward her dressing room looking flushed and
faint," Marion recalled. "Gable had that effect on all of them.
Joan Crawford was hellbent on bedding him down, and she
was still married to Doug Fairbanks, Jr., at the time! Gable
himself was married, but that didn't seem to bother anybody."

Frances Marion, a delightful woman given to self-deprecat-
ing humor that was not devoid of truth, admitted that she
herself would have had a hard time saying no. And Adela
Rogers St. Johns in later years dumbfounded a talk-show host
who asked if she had had a child by Gable in the 1930s by
replying that any woman would have been honored to be the
mother of Clark Gable's child—an ambiguous rejoinder if
ever there was one.

"I must confess that Norma surprised me in *A Free Soul,*"
Ruth Waterbury, one of my uncle's *Photoplay* writers, told
me. "Everyone up to that time thought that it was Crawford
who burned up the screen with Gable, but Norma revealed a
new side to her." Ruth was yet another one to tell me that she
suspected Norma wasn't sexually fulfilled at home.

What did Gable think of Norma? "Damn, the dame doesn't
wear any underwear in her scenes," he told Eddie Mannix
and others. "Is she doing that in the interests of realism or
what?" "She must be one hot lay if she can behave like that
with the cameras turning," he told Clarence Brown, who told
me that if Norma hadn't been married and, as Gable's boss's
wife "beyond the pale," she probably would have joined
Crawford in bed with Gable "but not in a threesome, of
course!" Brown hastily added as I laughed at his gaffe. Publicly, Gable was telling Louella Parsons in solemn and digni-

fied words: "Miss Shearer is a wonderful actress, and I am very grateful to have had the honor of appearing with her. It has been a great break for me and I shall always be grateful." Thus in public at least, the august Mrs. Thalberg was getting the respect from Womankiller Gable that he, aware of his place in the MGM pecking order of 1931, knew she was entitled to.

Norma next got her chance at high comedy, Coward-style.

Noel Coward, Gertrude Lawrence, and the young Laurence Olivier had made a solid hit out of the Broadway comedy in which they starred, *Private Lives* (1931), which was written, of course, by Coward, and MGM had hastened to option it for the screen. The story was some fluff about a couple who divorce and remarry and meet each other, with their respective new mates, on their second honeymoon. They proceed to run away with each other again, leaving their dull, pedestrian "seconds" to make their own peace—or possibly, mutual excitement. While the dialogue was scintillating, a lot depended on the performances, and Coward and Lawrence had given their renditions of "Eliot" and "Amanda" a verve and a bite that only the most expert comediennes could duplicate.

When Coward heard that Norma Shearer and Robert Montgomery had been assigned to the leads of the film version, he expressed to friends his reservations concerning their skills, both comic and athletic, as one of the highlights of the play (and the film) is a knock-down-drag-out fight between the reunited pair.

Norma assured everyone that she was more than up to the subtle horseplay and romantic tomfoolery. Informed of Coward's attitude, she said, "I don't care what he thinks—he thinks in theater terms—*I* think in film terms. It doesn't seem to occur to Mr. Coward that we both may turn out all right!" She requested Sidney Franklin, whom she greatly respected, as director, and Robert Montgomery for costar yet again. Adrian was drafted for the costumes, as always, to which he did his usual justice, and Hans Kräly, Richard Schayer, and

Claudine West were told by Thalberg to bring in a scenario that stayed as close to Coward as possible while still "opening up" the proceedings for the screen.

The relative frequency of the Shearer-Montgomery onscreen pairings had given rise to gossip in Hollywood, and rumors of a romance between them began to circulate, much to Montgomery's resentment. "Norma wanted me with her in those films because she thought our chemistry was right and because she felt comfortable with me," Montgomery said later. "She claimed I made her laugh, and that she *needed* to laugh." "But," he added, "that did not translate into any mutual romantic feelings off-screen. We had a good friendship and a fine working camaraderie, and that was 'romance' enough for us. If people wanted to read something else into it, that was their problem!"

Oddly, Montgomery's chief memory of *Private Lives* was not a particularly romantic one. He recalled:

> We were engaging in a no-holds-barred fight scene and we were knocking each other around pretty hard. Norma could pack a mean left, and she got so carried away in her enthusiasm, her desire to give 'em a show, that she knocked me into a screen and I landed flat on my derrière and went out cold. I remember her kneeling over me begging me to forgive her. It was a really nice way to "come to" and of course I did forgive her—but Louella Parsons was wrong when she claimed in print that we sealed our reconciliation with a kiss—it was a handshake, as I remember.

To my mind, *Private Lives* does not hold up as well as some of Norma's other pictures of the time. She seems forced and nervous, to be trying too hard. Of course she has her winning moments, and at times her comedy has high style. Montgomery seems to be more at ease; Reginald Denny and Una Merkel as the other pair seem to be just along for the ride. But at the time of the picture's release in December 1931, it won critical huzzahs. "A wild farce idea made snappy by sparkling and at times questionable dialogue," *Photoplay* said, calling the Shearer-Montgomery duo "excellent." Mordaunt Hall in *The New York Times* called Norma's portrayal "sharp" and "alert."

11

The Screen's
First Lady

ARLY IN 1932 Irving Thalberg came to a momentous decision—momentous, that is, in terms of Norma Shearer's future screen persona. He decided that in order to solidify her position as the First Lady of the Screen (as the ads and the publicists continued to tab her), he would have to choose vehicles for her that had a distinct "prestige" feel—and that they would have to be mounted as carefully and lavishly as the story values permitted.

Shearer, too, felt that her years of hard work (she was by then thirty-two, and had been in films for twelve years) entitled her to "superstar" treatment, and many critics and film commentators across the country indicated that she was long overdue for the top drawer. On a visit to New York, Norma had consulted with her old friend, Jimmy Quirk, whose flattering covers on *Photoplay*, notably the April 1932 issue, and constant run of "build-up stories" had pleased both her and her husband mightily. "You're a great star, Norma," he told her, "and a fine actress; I am deeply proud of the way you have developed. Yes, you have your Academy Award [for *The Divorcee*, 1930] but for the *long* haul, on the *topmost* rung, you have to choose your vehicles with great care. And I have two in mind that I pass along to you for what they're worth. One is a 'prestige' item, and the other is surefire romance, but high-level romance. And if you follow one with the other, in short order, they ought to do the trick."

Shearer told me that the two pictures Jimmy Quirk proposed were *Strange Interlude*, the smash Eugene O'Neill drama that had electrified Broadway in 1928, and a carefully mounted talkie remake of *Smilin' Through*, which had been an enormous stage hit of 1919 and a 1922 silent with Norma Talmadge. Shearer remembered asking Jimmy if she was really up to following the brilliant Lynn Fontanne in a play so complex as *Strange Interlude*, and she never forgot his reply: "Just give it your best—no matter what they say, you've got a prestigious item under your belt, and it starts up the cycle you're after." She and Jimmy, she recalled, felt she was able to get across, for both critical and popular approval, the sentimental values implicit in *Smilin' Through*, in which she would have a dual role set in different periods. "And if the one conks out, the other will take up the slack," Jimmy added. Delighted, she went back to Hollywood sold on the two projects, and Thalberg agreed with her. "As Jimmy suggests, we'll do the O'Neill thing first, and *Smilin' Through* second," he said.

Negotiations were opened immediately for the purchase of both projects, which were to be released almost back to back in late 1932. Some exhibitors criticized the closeness of the release dates, as the moviehouse people usually liked to see a star space out pictures by some months. The reason for the close release dates became obvious later; *Strange Interlude* had been too "adult" and "subtle" for the general audience, so *Smilin' Through* was rushed in to clinch the earlier film's "class" success—though even that impact was, the Thalbergs found, to be limited to discriminating, educated audiences.

Jimmy Quirk spent much of the summer of 1932 in Hollywood on his annual tour, and while he visited both sets at MGM, he died that August of pneumonia complicated by a heart attack without seeing the results of either on the screen. "That saddened me greatly," Norma told me. "If only he had lived long enough to see the final product, and learn how things had worked out. . . ."

Strange Interlude, when they got to it, presented a number of special problems, and Norma and Thalberg were depressed to find out that playwright Eugene O'Neill disapproved both the screen treatment *and* the stars, which included Clark Gable. "That Gable and Shearer are in over their heads—way over," O'Neill is reported to have said, though later his advisors got him to make some ambiguous and conciliatory remarks about the filmic outcome that disguised, or at least ameliorated, his true feelings.

Strange Interlude had opened on Broadway in 1928. It was so long that a dinner break was inserted. Stream-of-consciousness techniques, rather novel for 1928, were employed, with the characters disguising their true feelings and reactions in their speeches, while voicing these inner reactions to the audience via what were known as "asides." This played interestingly on the stage, thanks to the inventive art of Miss Fontanne and her colleagues, but Thalberg—*and* Shearer—were worried how this would play on a large screen, where all reactions were of necessity magnified even when underplayed. The story deals with the neurotic, complicated Nina Leeds, who has lost one lover to an early death and who marries a rather ineffectual man on the advice of her admirer, a doctor, who feels motherhood will cure her morbidity. But when her new husband's mother reveals that there is inherited insanity in the family (this was sensational subject matter in 1932, as per *A Bill of Divorcement*), Nina, who is not too stable or clear-minded to begin with, decides to have her child by someone not her husband—and the doctor is elected. The child's birth is a tonic for her husband, who believes himself the father, but when the child grows to manhood he develops an inexplicable aversion for his true father; in the end, Nina loses her husband to death, her son goes off and marries someone she disapproves of, and the doctor withdraws from her, having had enough of the neurotic goings-on. In the denouement, a faithful admirer, Marsden, who has loved her consistently through the years but whom she takes for granted, wins her, even though he, too, is neurotic. One of the famous lines in the play is his—something to the effect that "I am Marsden, to whom all things come—in the end."

Confronted with the monumental task of getting all this, plus asides, plus complex "subtexts," plus the spirit of O'Neill's "sublime perversity" across—and in a "mere" 110 minutes ("mere" for O'Neill, that is)—Shearer and Thalberg proceeded full-speed ahead.

O'Neill, barely disguising his contempt, curtly refused to get involved in the screenplay ("God help *them*—and God help *me*," he told his wife) so the Thalbergs cast about for screenwriters who would not be daunted by the play's complexity. No less than seven writers tried out and then withdrew, and Louis B. Mayer, who had never liked the project, predicted a fiasco. Eventually Bess Meredyth and C. Gardner Sullivan, two tough pros who were not easily intimidated, accepted the challenge. Thalberg himself dissected and pondered their screenplay at such length that MGM execs openly expressed doubts that it would ever reach the camera stage.

Thalberg was determined to keep a close eye on the picture (the "asides" particularly bothered him—he feared they would come out with awkward literalness, moving audiences to laughter), and he made a misguided decision. He put the commercially successful but far from creative Robert Z. Leonard in as director. "Bob is competent and reliable—and we can control him, which is the important thing," he assured Norma. Though she had doubts about Leonard's suitability, she acceded. Lee Garmes was called in and told he had the photography job—"and make her look like a million!" Thalberg implored him. "In fact, make the whole shebang look good—if we fail on the other counts, we'll have some glamour to fall back on—hopefully."

Adrian was told to create costumes that were subdued, in order to catch some of the O'Neill spirit, and did not distract, yet would be effective in establishing the overall mood. "I felt like I was being asked to go in two directions at once," Adrian later said, but he did what he thought was required. Douglas Shearer was called down to the beach house for a whole weekend, in which the mechanics of the "asides" were debated over and over again. Later he recalled that *Strange Interlude* was one of his toughest assignments in all his years at Metro-Goldwyn-Mayer.

Gable was brought in "for box office," as Thalberg told Schenck's New York office, which kept sending him anxious memos after Schenck learned the basic story. "This one time forget the will-it-sell-in-Peoria attitude," Thalberg told anxious executives. "This will add to the studio's prestige, and we always have room for a few of *those*, no?" Even easygoing Robert Z. Leonard had doubts about Gable's ability to get across the complexities of Ned Darrell.

Mayer, however, seemed to brighten at the idea of a plot in which Shearer has an illegitimate child by Gable—"so long as it is done with *taste*," he added. Will Hays, the movie's morals czar, became nervous when he heard of the plot, but Jimmy Quirk in New York and Mayer at Culver City assured him that *taste* would be the keynote and that in the end, Shearer would end up at least relatively unhappy because of her "misdeeds," which seemed to satisfy him.

Gable felt he was in over his head and was nervous throughout the shooting. "All I do is get mad and look worried all through it," he complained to Leonard. "Can't I smile and be affable and romantic once in a while?" He even took his worries to Mayer, who replied: "Hell, you're *knocking up* Norma in this one—you only knocked her in a *chair* your last time out. The fans will eat it up!" Still, Gable returned to the sets nursing serious doubts.

Norma worked harder on *Strange Interlude* than ever before. She went over her lines again and again, sometimes alone and sometimes with coaches. Later she recalled that stage veteran May Robson had offered helpful advice, as did the fine character actor Henry B. Walthall. Ralph Morgan, who had performed in *Strange Interlude* on stage, cued her in on the nuances the gifted Lynn Fontanne had injected into her critically acclaimed rendition of Nina, but in the final analysis, and despite her best and most sincere efforts, Shearer failed to capture the neuroticism that Fontanne had so brilliantly delineated and that was one of the key elements in Nina.

After a lengthy shooting schedule, Thalberg began to supervise cutting and editing; this time, he decided, he would skip out-of-town sneak previews and would rely more than usual on his own judgment. *Strange Interlude* was released as an MGM superspecial aimed at discriminating adult audiences in the big cities in the fall of 1932, with the distribution gradually fanning out on a more cautious basis. Meanwhile, with the role of Nina Leeds scarcely behind her, Norma was rushed into what Mayer and everyone else at MGM considered would be the "sure-fire" box-office item—*Smilin' Through*.

"Maybe that damned *Interlude* will get the critics excited, but *Smilin'* will get the audiences," Mayer said. Eddie Mannix later recalled Mayer striding through a corridor muttering "damned O'Neill high-falutin' la-de-da stuff—we'll go *broke* with it!"

As it turned out, Metro-Goldwyn-Mayer did not "go broke" with *Strange Interlude*. Mayer's original hunch that Clark Gable knocking up Norma Shearer would bring the audiences in was accurate, but when word got around about the "asides"—which Leonard failed to bring off smoothly and which kept the picture static, leaden, and often self-conscious—and the talk-talk-talk and the dearth of Shearer-Gable lovemaking, the picture began to die. Eddie Mannix recalled Thalberg's exasperation when Mayer sent him a publicist-inspired proposed ad along the lines of GABLE LOVES SHEARER ALL THE WAY***AND THERE'S HELL TO PAY! "Let L.B. keep his vulgar ideas to himself!" Thalberg shouted to his aides.

Even critics didn't seem to know what to make of *Strange*

Interlude. Photoplay, mourning the loss of its editor-publisher, went out of its way to be kind, reporting: "Norma Shearer takes her place among the great artists of her day. Clark Gable does his finest technical screen work as he ages over a period of forty years. Ralph Morgan, Alexander Kirkland and Robert Young share honors."

The New York Times's Mordaunt Hall tended to agree with *Photoplay,* writing: "Norma Shearer has given several noteworthy performances in recent motion pictures, particularly her portrayal in the film *Private Lives,* but in this present offering she easily excels anything she has done hitherto." But Richard Watts, Jr., in *The New York Herald-Tribune,* was scathing: "Miss Norma Shearer, apparently filled with reverence at the thought of the classic lines she is reciting, but at the same time, understanding so little about them, makes Nina Leeds, the neurotic heroine, a good, healthy, normal young woman, who ages prettily and isn't bothered much about her tragedies."

But it was one Alexander Bashky in *The Nation* who really nailed it down:

> For once Hollywood has dared to produce a picture that deals with life in terms of adult intelligence. But though the courage thus shown deserves every credit, the outgrowth of this courage, the film itself, is hardly a feather in the producer's cap. It conforms faithfully to its Hollywood type of an uninspired cross-breed of the stage and screen, and it is badly miscast in its two principal parts. Neither the beautiful but cold Norma Shearer, nor the uncouth Clark Gable are the actors for the parts of Nina and Darrell.

I have seen *Strange Interlude* a number of times over the years. While I feel that Shearer gave an earnest and intelligent performance, I don't think she was suited to the role. I feel Gable played Darrell in a dour one-note manner throughout. The asides seem awkward and forced and slow up the action and Leonard was not the man for this assignment, let-

ting the narrative slacken on many occasions. But it *did* give
Shearer what Jimmy Quirk had said she needed: a controversial, much-discussed "prestige superspecial." In that respect,
it was a gain for her.

Smilin' Through, which also appeared in the fall of 1932,
was to be Shearer's greatest popular and critical success.
Sidney Franklin, who directed it, told me twenty-five years
later that everyone connected with it felt instinctively that
it would be a smash. "The set was a particularly happy one,"
he recalled, "and we were swept along with it." Indeed, the
film more than fulfilled Jimmy Quirk's prediction; it won millions of hearts all over the country and abroad and amazed
critics.

As I wrote of it in my 1974 book, *The Great Romantic
Films*:

> One of the great romances on both stage and screen,
> *Smilin' Through* retains its enduring appeal. The secret of
> its charm and power, undiminished through the decades,
> lies in its perfect fusion of the romantic and the super-
> natural, with a story so haunting and emotional as to cast a
> spell over viewers of any era. Even today, when respect for
> the supernatural has reached a relatively low ebb, *Smilin'
> Through* in revival affects even the spiritually alienated
> young. Its sincerity is irresistible, its depth unquestioned, its
> purity of spirit an enchantment in itself.
>
> *Smilin' Through* belongs to an era that was somehow
> more spiritually healthy—a time when Death was accepted
> in the midst of Life. The fear of Death, the constant efforts
> to stave it off, or ignore its inevitability, that characterizes
> more current thinking, was in those days sublimated and
> transmuted into a romanticization of what is after all a natu-
> ral human phenomenon. Death was often regarded as a
> friend, with this life and its appurtenances *not* regarded as
> the Be-All and End-All. Through that time of soul and
> spirit, the 1930s, other highly romantic films played on the
> same principle. They suggest to the society [of the current

era] that the shifting attitudes toward Death have introduced something craven, mean and negative, something
myopic, for what once flourished on the human scene as a
beautiful and fulfilling sublimatory experience.

Smilin' Through first enthralled the nation as a play written
by Jane Cowl (writing under the pseudonym Allen Langdon
Martin) and Jane Murfin, and starred Miss Cowl. It opened at
the Broadhurst Theater, New York, on December 30, 1919,
and co-starred Henry Stephenson (later a well-known Hollywood character actor) and Orme Caldara. After playing 175
performances in New York (a phenomenal run for its time), it
went on the road with equal success. The first film version
came in 1922 as a First National release, starring Norma Talmadge, Harrison Ford (an earlier actor of that name), and
Wyndham Standing. Sidney Franklin also directed the silent
version. In the same year in which the sound version with
Shearer, Leslie Howard, and Fredric March appeared, Vincent
Youmans did an operetta based on it called *Through The
Years,* starring Natalie Hall, Michael Bartlett, Reginald Owen,
and Charles Winninger (in the 1930s the latter two actors
would have conspicuous character careers in Hollywood).

When *Smilin' Through* first debuted in 1919, a shocked and
saddened world had just weathered a terrible world war that
had dragged on for four years with millions of lives lost. Just
the year before, 1918, a terrible flu epidemic had killed many
thousands in the United States. Death was on everyone's
mind, and Jane Cowl as star and coauthor sought to console
and illuminate the spirits of her audience. When the Norma
Shearer version came out in 1932, the country was in the grip
of a terrible depression that threatened to destroy the way of
life Americans had known, and again the story proved a consolation. In 1941 Jeanette MacDonald attempted a version,
costarring her husband, Gene Raymond, and Brian Aherne,
this time directed by Frank Borzage, but the film was static,
stopping dead for interpolated songs by Miss MacDonald, and
fussily overproduced and overscored. The Shearer version still

stands as the most memorable rendition. The song "Smilin' Through," swept the country; Arthur Penn had written it for the 1919 stage debut. It became the haunting theme of the 1932 film, underlining the poignant story most touchingly.

Since *Smilin' Through* is a pivotal film in Shearer's career, and indeed clinched her claim to superstar status from 1932 on, its plot bears recounting at some length.

In the year 1868, in a little Kentish village in England, close to the channel, Moonyean Clare (Shearer) is about to marry her beloved, Sir John Carteret (Leslie Howard). She is accidentally killed by a bullet meant for her groom, fired during the ceremony by her rejected suitor, Jeremy Wayne (Fredric March). Before passing into eternity, Moonyean promises Carteret that she will always be with him in spirit and that one day they will know a blissful reunion in eternity.

As the decades pass, Moonyean comes to her ever-grieving lover as a supernatural vision, consoling him when he is especially lonely and dejected. (The delicately nuanced special-effects photography of Lee Garmes, inspired throughout the film, is particularly commendable in these scenes.)

Some thirty years later, in 1898, Moonyean's niece Kathleen (Shearer in a dual role) comes as a small child to live with Carteret after her parents are killed in an accident. The child grows to womanhood looking identical to the long-lost aunt, and the old man and the sensitive young girl form a deep attachment.

The Great War of 1914–18 comes, and the Kentish villagers can hear the sound of cannon and shellfire from across the channel. Then an American comes to the little village: Kenneth Wayne, son of the murderer, Jeremy, who had fled across the seas in 1868. Neither Kenneth (played by March, also in a dual role) nor Kathleen know of the long-ago tragedy; they meet when Kathleen takes shelter in an old house during a thunderstorm. There are cobwebs and dust everywhere; she notes an overturned chair, a newspaper dated June 14, 1868, and senses that something terrible happened in that room. (In fact, it was from this room that Jeremy, tor-

mented by drink, rushed out to implement the original tragedy.) Kathleen succumbs to the strange spell of the room,
with its portrait of Jeremy Wayne above the fireplace gazing
down fiercely. Kenneth stops off at the old estate en route to
joining the British army.

The two meet there and proceed to fall in love. When Carteret discovers that the man his niece loves is the son of the
man who doomed him to a lifetime of sorrow and frustration,
he forbids her to see him again, and in the same garden where
he and Moonyean had once romanced, he tells her of the
tragic events of 1868.

When Kathleen tells Kenneth of this, the couple realize
that their love is doomed, as he is about to leave for war and
cannot leave her unprotected (her enraged uncle has threatened to break with her if she marries Kenneth).

The ghost of Moonyean appears to tell Carteret that he is
driving her away from him with his bitterness and that they
can never be reunited while he feels as he does. Later Kenneth returns from the war, crippled and tries to alienate Kathleen because he doesn't want to be a burden to her, but
Carteret tells her the truth and sends her to him. When the
spirit of Moonyean appears for the final time, Carteret rises
from the chair a young man, in his wedding garments, and
together they look at the old man who has just died. They go
from the garden into the lane, where the ghostly wedding attendants of 1868 help them into their nuptial carriage, and the
wraiths drive off embracing happily after they have fondly observed Kathleen, coming from the opposite direction, bringing her crippled lover back to the home that Carteret has
thrown open, at last, to them both.

This extremely affecting closing scene overwhelmed 1932
audiences, and I have noted tearful young people emerging
from its recent theatrical revivals. The basics of human
nature, its longings, hopes, aspirations, and dreams, and the
eternal quest for the ideal love, never really change.

Shearer and Thalberg had long admired the work of Fredric
March, who had made a name for himself during his four

years at Paramount and whom MGM borrowed for this role. March had just won an Academy Award for his work in *Dr. Jekyll and Mr. Hyde*; he was to appear with Norma yet again, in *The Barretts of Wimpole Street,* and MGM was to avail itself of his services later in such films as *Anna Karenina* (1935) with Greta Garbo and *Susan and God* (1940) with Joan Crawford.

When I was interviewing March for my 1971 book, *The Films of Fredric March,* he had a great deal to say about Norma Shearer and Thalberg. He confessed that she was his favorite female costar, though he asked that I keep that information a secret, as he didn't wish to offend those he called "the other lovely ladies it was my privilege to work with." Since he died in 1975, a number of his costars have also passed on, and doubtless eighty-two-year-old Garbo is unconcerned, so it does not seem unfair to him to reveal this now. March told me:

> She had a wonderful sincerity and poise, and she was deeply emotional but she knew how to filter that emotion with discipline so that it came off the screen as deeply felt rather than merely sentimental. She had some very strong scenes with me in *Smilin' Through*; I especially recall one in which we were to part as I went to war; she got across her agony in truly eloquent terms. I heard how perfectionist she was supposed to be, but if she gave her best, she expected everyone else around her to give theirs along with her, and as I have always tried to set the highest standards for myself, I could hardly fault her for that.
>
> Yes, she did fuss around with Lee Garmes about "white" lighting and all that, but there was a reason for it as she had a rather peculiar face, beautiful as it could be, with eyes smaller than normal, and it took a combination of the right lighting and the right eye makeup to get her looking at her best. I don't think vanity had a thing to do with it—she just wanted to give—and look—her absolute best, and how can one fault an entertainer for *that*?"

March gave a fascinating summary of the acting styles and on-screen mystiques of MGM's Big Three of the 1930s, Shearer, Garbo, and Crawford.

Garbo was all instinct. She wasn't a trained actress and her love scenes were the best, because she believed them totally and something radiant and wonderful came over her and she was totally true to the mood. She could be awkward at times, and worried a great deal about her looks and her performance—but that kind of instinct and camera magic are so rare that she was in a class by herself. She was a *natural* actress, and followed her own special laws, and they *worked.*

Crawford was probably the least naturally talented of the three. She was at her best in shopgirl-on-the-rise stuff, but she was to be commended for trying to reach the outermost limits of her abilities, and she surprised me and a lot of other people by achieving, by hard work and strong desire, a wonderful, deeply felt technical excellence that got her that deserved Academy Award, in time.

[Shearer] was a tremendously gifted actress, technically the strongest of the three; I always felt she was every bit as naturally talented as Garbo, and with a greater range; there was a sweetness and a sincerity about her that came across with a wallop on-screen, but she was also a strong person with the true artist's discipline and perseverance.

March said he regretted that Shearer had retired relatively early. "But she told me and Florence that she felt she had run her course, and wanted to explore other areas of life. I think her happy second marriage had a lot to do with that."

Leslie Howard, who was to die in 1943 at the age of fifty in a plane accident over Portugal (reportedly while on a war-time mission for the British government) had his best chance yet in American films in *Smilin' Through,* and his sensitive, intense portrait of Sir John Carteret turned him into a major film star. He had appeared with Shearer the year before in a rather thankless part in *A Free Soul,* and was delighted with the range that *Smilin' Through* afforded. As Sidney Franklin told me in 1957:

> That film was probably the happiest, most fulfilling professional experience I ever knew, and people mention *Smilin' Through* more to me than any other. Also, I was glad to be able to make some improvements and embellishments I felt the 1922 film I directed lacked, just as I was to be glad to do *The Barretts* once more for the same reason. My only reservation about the 1932 *Smilin' Through* was its comparative dearth of mood music (Irving Thalberg didn't care for music, one of his surprising oversights, I felt) and when I came to the second *Barretts,* I determined to make up for that, as Irving had kept the music largely out of the 1934 version, to my great regret.

The critics went out of their way to lavish superlatives when *Smilin' Through* premiered. Richard Watts, Jr., of *The New York Herald-Tribune,* who had panned Shearer in *Strange Interlude,* did an about-face, declaring of her *Smilin' Through* performance: "Miss Shearer is so earnest, so straightforward and touching, so entirely in the proper romantic mood, that you are reminded that she is an effective sentimental player if hardly an ideal O'Neill heroine."

Photoplay, in its November 1932 issue, stated: "This is Norma Shearer's picture, and the one adjective that comes to mind upon seeing her is 'Splendid.' That Norma could change so suddenly from the sophisticated heroines which she has been creating lately, to this charming, old-fashioned girl, is a great tribute to her versatility."

Movie Classic noted: "Sentimentality is written large all over it, but it makes no apologies for the fact; it justifies itself, with its beauty, its charm, its wistful moodiness."

The author remembers, at the age of nine, seeing *Smilin' Through* for the first time and being powerfully affected by it. It was my first major movie experience, and it left a permanent imprint on my esthetic awareness. I remember going home and creating a reproduction of Jeremy Wayne's haunted 1868 room out of the cavern of my little rolltop desk and sprinkling baking powder over my little set and its miniature furnishings to reproduce the dust and cobwebby neglect as best my child's mind could conceive of it. Such is the power of the movies, to child or adult, in 1932 or any year. And since my family was in mourning for my uncle Jimmy Quirk that Fall, it added a poignant personal note.

Edwin Schallert in *The Los Angeles Times* had run an interesting story on Shearer in which he quoted her on her film characterizations and her essential approach to a role.

> The starting point in many of my pictures has been idealism. It is that even in several pictures that have been deemed so sophisticated. I can't do the Garbo or Dietrich thing. I admire them both greatly and I wish that I could play such characters as they interpret but I have to go through a transition to become worldly. Hence I had to begin by being very nice and then about the middle of the picture I am likely to go all haywire. That's when things really grow interesting.
>
> But if I just stayed sweet and appealing, I fear the roles I played today would be very dull.

In this period Norma was also giving interviews to the fan-mag mavens in which she stressed her chronic claustrophobia. She told Gladys Hall that she was afraid of small rooms, could never ride in a subway, hated tunnels, and felt she would prefer cremation after death since the confines of the grave would make her ghost restless and keep it moving.

In a grandiloquent statement that smacked more of studio publicity than of her own honest reactions to her "affliction" (if such it was), Shearer added: "It is possible to use this phobia to great advantage. It is chained like to waterfalls and has become an inspiring motivating force working in my blood and brain to drive me on ceaselessly, to force me to grow in time and space, to breathe and work more spaciously. And while I can push back walls and escape treadmills and channels, I am safe and reasonably content."

It is still a moot question as to just how severe this "claustrophobia" actually was. Certainly it smacked more of studio press agentry than of reality, especially as Norma had seemed calm and happy enough emerging from transcontinental trains and had certainly summoned enough intrepidity to live in small rooms in New York early in her career. Billy Grady thought it "an MGM publicist's pipedream."

By 1932, thirty-three-year-old Irving Thalberg was at the height of his power and influence. Though it galled the autocratic and egoistic Louis B. Mayer to admit it, Thalberg was regarded as the creative lifeblood of the studio. Thalberg personally supervised the quality product turned out by the studio, while keeping his eye on everything MGM produced. "Quality" he defined as polished craftsmanship and believable, adult stories, taking special pride in the all-star *Grand Hotel,* which premiered in the spring of 1932 and starred Garbo, Crawford, John Barrymore, Wallace Beery, and other luminaries. He had succeeded in enticing the famous husband-and-wife theatrical team of Alfred Lunt and Lynn Fontanne, who made for him their first and only film, *The Guardsman.* He also lured the brilliant Helen Hayes, one of the leading stars of the Broadway stage, to Metro-Goldwyn-Mayer, where her picture *The Sin of Madelon Claudet,* made her an overnight film star. The stamp of quality was on all the major films Thalberg produced, and he was especially proud of Norma's two 1932 films that had won her both prestige and popular admiration—*Strange Interlude* and *Smilin' Through.* Now, truly, she had become "the First Lady of the Screen."

Hayes and her husband, the rakishly brilliant playwright-screenwriter Charles MacArthur, became close friends of the Thalbergs, and Norma grew very fond of Helen, whose spiritual serenity and womanly dignity matched her own. Thalberg and MacArthur complemented each other well, for the more retiring Irving, plagued as always with concerns about his health, found extroverted, hard-drinking Charlie a spiritual tonic. MacArthur became very devoted to Irving and tried to relax him while not jeopardizing his health.

Some years earlier, Louis B. Mayer had formed what came to be known as The Mayer Group, which enabled him and some of his Loew's cronies to buy options on the company's stock at favorable prices. By 1929 Mayer had become a millionaire. Thalberg, fearful that he would not live long enough to assure the financial future of Norma and their child, and feeling that he had laid the foundation for the quality product for which the Lion Studio was now famous and that he should be rewarded accordingly, had for some time expressed his dissatisfaction with his salary and stock-option terms, and it became a bone of contention among him, Mayer, and Nick Schenck in New York. Mayer accused Thalberg of being spoiled and greedy and claimed the offers he was receiving from other studios, in the wake of the magical MGM product he had generated, was giving him a big head.

In September 1932 Thalberg was greatly shaken by the death of the gentle and sensitive Paul Bern, who had been his associate and close friend for years. A man of impeccable taste, Bern was assigned to the Garbo pictures and others that required special handling. (He supervised the writing and production values.) He had a stage background and was a literate and intelligent man. But Bern, slight and diminutive in build, had some Achilles' heels; he dated beautiful women and got written up as their escort because he was overcompensating for elements in himself he considered "unmanly"—notably impotence and a very small genital development. In July 1932 he had wooed and won Jean Harlow as his wife. The platinum-blonde dynamo had shot to stardom that year in *Red-Headed Woman* (she had worn a wig in that), a naughty Anita Loos–scripted confection in which she had sparkled sexily as a ruthless young woman who uses men to climb to riches. Harlow had liked Bern, who gave her good creative advice, and reportedly his sexual inadequacies didn't bother her because, she told Loos, "I'm sick of sex. I'm sick of being

Two beauties: Norma with her mother in 1901.

A New York modeling photo.

Norma Shearer, film star.

opposite page, top
With John Gilbert again in *He Who Gets Slapped*, 1924.

opposite page, bottom
She fell unrequitedly in love with Malcolm McGregor during *Lady of the Night*, 1925.

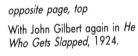

With John Gilbert in *The Snob*, 1924.

Norma in the mid –1920s.

With William Haines in *The Tower of Lies*, 1925.

Conrad Nagel, also in love with Norma offscreen, comes on strong here in *The Waning Sex*, 1926.

With Ramon Novarro and Ernst Lubitsch, the legendary director, on *The Student Prince* set, 1927.

The "boss" and his star: The newlywed Irving Thalbergs, 1927.

Norma with her husband, Irving
Thalberg, 1928.

In her first sound film with Lewis
Stone in *The Trial of Mary Dugan*,
1929. Audiences liked her speaking
voice, unlike that of other big stars.

With Basil Rathbone in *The Last of Mrs. Cheyney*, 1929.

With Robert Montgomery in *The Divorcee*, 1930. They were ideal together and made several films as a team.

With Chester Morris in her Oscar-winning *The Divorcee*, 1930.

To her fans, Norma represented the ultimate in 1930's chic. Her "soigneé" look became the rage.

Norma, her mother Edith, and her sister Athole arrive in New York from Hollywood in 1928 all wearing the same style shoes.

Getting the Oscar from another fervent Norma-admirer, Conrad Nagel, 1931.

Norma with Irving Thalberg, Jr., 1931.

Torn between lovers in a revealing satin gown. With Robert Montgomery and Herbert Marshall in *Riptide*, 1934. Both actors were considered ideal leading men and were extremely popular with audiences.

With Leslie Howard in *Smilin' Through*, 1932.

Louis B. Mayer welcomes the Thalbergs back to MGM, 1933. Norma would soon be a widow due to her husband's fragile health and overwork.

With Marlene Dietrich and Max Reinhardt at a Hollywood event in 1934.

With Frederic March and Charles Laughton in *The Barretts of Wimpole Street*, 1934.

With Frederic March in *The Barretts of Wimpole Street*, 1934.

Showing her famous profile as Elizabeth Barrett: with Maureen O'Sullivan in *The Barretts of Wimpole Street*, 1934.

Irving, Norma, Katherine and Irving Jr.: One of the last family photographs, 1935.

The Widow Thalberg ventures out of mourning for the first time in 1937, escorted by Louis B. Mayer.

With Leslie Howard in *Romeo and Juliet*, 1936. At the age of thirty-five Norma was cast as young Juliet. Howard was forty-one.

Scenes from *Romeo and Juliet*.

Shearer and Power in love in *Marie Antoinette*, 1938. No expense was spared for Norma's elaborate costumes. Even without her husband in charge, she was still the "Queen of MGM." She chose her co-star Tyrone Power, whom she fell in love with offscreen. "When we first met, my heart stood still . . ." Power was considered one of the most beautiful and dashing men in Hollywood.

With Tyrone Power at the Hollywood premiere of *Marie Antoinette*, 1938.

Above, below, and opposite top left:
In her blond wig for *Idiot's Delight*, 1939.

Idiot's Delight: Her co-star, Clark Gable, stole the picture with his song-and-dance rendition of "Puttin' on the Ritz." Norma plays a bogus Russian Countess.

With her gossipy pal Hedda
Hopper, 1939.

Norma had the leading role in Clare Booth
Luce's classic film *The Women*, 1939. But her
co-stars Rosalind Russell, Paulette Goddard,
Joan Crawford, and Joan Fontaine stole the
show, 1939.

Making a foursome of it at Earl Carroll's Cafe in New York, 1939. At left, beautiful Mexican star Dolores Del Rio. Behind, Cedric Gibbons and Sir Adrian Baillie.

Doing the town with new swain, George Raft, 1939.

From *Escape*.

With Alla Nazimova and Robert Taylor in *Escape*, 1940. The three stars gave sterling performances in this war-time thriller.

Robert Taylor, Mervyn LeRoy, Lawrence Weingarten, Norma, and Alla Nazimova on the set of *Escape*.

A more mature-looking
Norma primps for *We Were
Dancing* scene, 1942.

With Melvyn Douglas.

With Robert Taylor
and George Sanders
in *Her Cardboard
Lover*, 1942.

At her wedding to Martin Arrouge, 1942.

In front of her beach house at Santa Monica, 1943. "Let them remember me like this," said Norma. She had retired from film.

With Van Johnson and her discovery Janet Leigh in 1947.

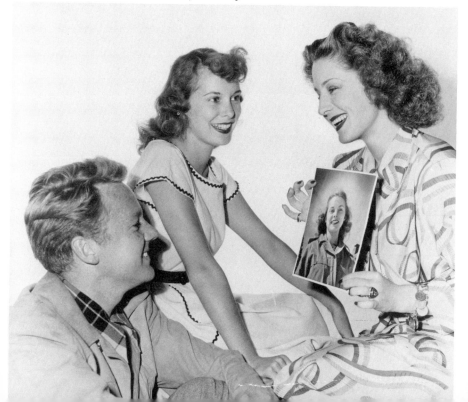

Norma looking very happy with her second husband Martin Arrouge in the late 1940s.

In Sun Valley in 1960, with husband Martin. Norma, still beautiful and happy at age sixty.

Skiing with Martin at St. Moritz in 1950.

pawed and drooled over by predatory men. Paul is kind and gentle and he appreciates my *mind*."

However, by Labor Day 1932, two months after their marriage, Paul Bern shot himself to death. He was alone in the house, as Harlow had spent the night at her mother's. Norma and Thalberg, who had been attendants at their wedding, were the first to be notified. Irving was prostrated by grief, and it was Norma who had the presence of mind to phone the studio's publicity watchdog, Howard Strickling, to warn him of what promised to be a major scandal. Harlow, with a hot new picture with Gable *(Red Dust)* due out in a couple of months, was too valuable a property to risk.

Strickling and Louis B. Mayer rushed to the Bern house. Paul lay nude with a gun at his side, shot through the head. His suicide note to his wife read: "Dearest dear: Unfortunately this is the only way to make good the frightful wrong I have done you and to wipe out my abject humiliation. You understand that last night was only a comedy. Paul." Obviously Bern was referring to his pathetic attempts at sex, which had either disgusted or otherwise alienated his beautiful wife.

Thanks to Mayer's friend, publisher William Randolph Hearst, who told everybody to "just shut up about it," the "scandal" flared briefly, then died out, but Bern's death left Thalberg crushed and depressed. Again he was reminded of his own mortality. "It's a bad omen," he told Norma.

Meanwhile quarrels over money matters kept Thalberg, Mayer, and Nick Schenck in a state of continuous tension. Though his contract ran to 1937, Thalberg signified that he wanted out; he said he was ill and tired, and wanted to rest, and that the burden of supervising the constant movie-house fodder that Schenck demanded was depleting his energies severely. The Mayer Group and Nick Schenck had already tried to accommodate Irving's financial demands; the Mayer Group had an arrangement whereby they received a yearly "bonus" from the net profits of Loew's Inc. In 1929 Thalberg's portion was raised from 20 percent to 30 percent; another partner, J.

Robert Rubin, kept his 27 percent while Mayer surrendered some of his percentage to accommodate Thalberg's raise. In early 1932 a fresh revision guaranteed Thalberg and Mayer 37-1/2 percent each.

Now, in the fall of 1932, Mayer, Thalberg, and Schenck were quarreling again over money. "What the hell are you going to *do* with all that money?" Nick Schenck, summoned to the coast for fresh bickering, yelled at Irving. "To protect the future interests of my wife and son from you blood-suckers," Thalberg yelled. "Oh, it was hell," Mayer told Eddie Mannix later. "The things Irving said to him! And here I treated him like a son all these years, guarded his health, relieved him of stress! And what thanks do I get?"

Finally, Thalberg was permitted to buy up to 100,000 shares of Loew's common stock between 1934 and 1939 at thirty to forty dollars a share, regardless of market price. Mayer was told he could buy up 80,000 shares under the same terms, and this irritated him mightily. Here his "son" and "protégé" was getting the better of this deal. A coolness developed between the two men, a coolness that was never to thaw. Mutually suspicious of each other now, they exchanged surface politenesses only and gave each other a wide berth.

The depression year of 1932 began to affect film business, and this took a further toll of Thalberg's health while he drove ahead all that fall to fulfill Schenck's incessant demand for films and still keep quality, on the pictures he personally supervised, high. Seeking to lighten his moods, Norma threw parties for the top film people, especially favoring the creative types her husband enjoyed. Her tact and kindness were legendary. Years later F. Scott Fitzgerald, who did two hitches at Metro-Goldwyn-Mayer as a screenwriter in the early and late 1930s, recalled her thoughtfulness when he got drunk at a party and told some stories that fell flat. He departed depressed and embarrassed, but the next day Norma sent him a telegram stating she had thought him one of the more agreeable persons at her party. He later immortalized Thalberg, or rather his conception of him, in the person of Monroe Stahr, the producer protagonist of his unfinished, but eventually published, novel *The Last Tycoon,* which appeared in 1941, the year after Fitzgerald's sudden death of a heart attack.

By December 1932 Thalberg had become hypochondriacal over his heart. He insisted to Norma that his years were numbered. They had said he wouldn't live to thirty; now he was thirty-three. Could he make it to thirty-six? Forty? He carried pills of all kinds in his pocket. Norma had mastered a hypodermic-needle technique (he made her practice it for "dry runs") so that she could give him injections if a "heart attack" ever struck. Finally, in late December, one did. Mayer rushed over to the house. Norma refused to let him in the bedroom where Thalberg lay surrounded by specialists. "He cannot be disturbed," she informed Mayer coldly. "Not under any circumstances!" Nick Schenck hurried west from New York. He was given the same treatment.

Feeling that Irving might die at any time, Mayer and Schenck made a deal with Mayer's son-in-law, David O. Selznick, the robust and talented young husband of Irene M. (*"He* won't leave her a young widow," Mayer had said at the time of the Selznick-Mayer nuptials.) Some weeks later, when Mayer told him that Selznick would be supervising the overall film production henceforth, Thalberg shouted "Betrayal!" and accused Mayer and Schenck of trying to undercut him.

In February 1933, after Thalberg had recovered somewhat, he and Norma set out for Europe with their son; also coming along were their close friends Helen Hayes and husband Charles MacArthur and their daughter, Mary. Thalberg and Mayer's letters just before parting were cool. Thalberg accused Mayer of holding up the final shooting of Hayes's *The White Sister* to keep her from accompanying the Thalbergs; she finished shooting and made it anyway.

Norma instigated the European trip. She feared a fresh heart attack if Irving returned to the studio too soon; he had to have rest and a change of scene, she told everyone who asked. In taking an extended vacation she jeopardized her own career, as it was considered unwise for a "superstar" to stay off the screen a year, as she did after *Smilin' Through*. Thalberg never forgot his wife's unselfishness at that time and her constant care and solicitude. Meanwhile, in early 1933, the new president, Franklin D. Roosevelt, declared a bank holiday to combat the effects of the ever-deepening depression, and the West Coast was assaulted by both an influenza epidemic and an earthquake. "Europe," as waggish Charlie MacArthur observed, "certainly seemed the place to be at *that* moment!"

The party went directly to Germany. Norma wanted Irving to see the famous Dr. Franz Groedel, who treated heart patients with the carbonated waters of the Bad Nauheim spa. The Thalbergs had seen Dr. Groedel in 1928 and 1931, during previous European sojourns. But by now Hitler had taken over, and Dr. Groedel had to cope with anti-Semitic attacks, which increased Irving's tension. They stayed in Europe for six months. When the Thalbergs returned to Hollywood in August 1933, Irving, after some initial run-ins with Schenck and Mayer, agreed to take over his own special group, supervising pictures he really believed in. Selznick would relieve him of the onerous production list, and he would retain his financial arrangements of 1932. At first angry and frustrated by these events (though he liked David Selznick personally), Thalberg later came to feel that it was all for the best.

For his first independent production, launched that fall of 1933, Thalberg determined to find a suitable vehicle for his wife. She had been a dutiful, loving wife, had traveled with him and nursed him and, in his own words, "literally kept me alive." Now he wanted to do something for *her*. In 1932 she had been acclaimed one of the screen's superstars, and now her diehard fans were clamoring to see her again. Mayer and others had noted to the Thalbergs, Mayer with considerable emphasis, that it was unwise for her to let so much time elapse, and that there was a distinct danger of her losing her hardwon gains. The exhibitors, too, had registered their impatience over her absence, both at sales meetings and in personal communications to Schenck and Mayer. Obviously there was no time to be lost.

Thalberg had contemplated several projects as possible vehicles for his wife, pondering one, temporarily accepting and then rejecting yet another. For a while he considered hauling out what Mayer called "that tired old chestnut," *The Green Hat,* which Katharine Cornell had played on the stage and which Garbo had starred in under the title *A Woman of Affairs,* one of her last silent films, in 1929. Charles MacArthur was called in to create a new, updated version, retaining some of the plot elements but striking out in new directions to tailor the proceedings to suit the Shearer mystique.

MacArthur made no secret of his distaste for the project, and advised Thalberg that it should be discarded. Thalberg had already come up with a new title, *Riptide,* and he called in Edmund Goulding and asked him to dream up a new story as well as direct.

Norma was not keen on the story that Goulding, after a writing marathon of several weeks, presented, and Thalberg, too, had his doubts. "We'll liven it up," he said. "Pour on the production values, dress Norma up in the snappiest outfits Adrian can devise; we'll get Ray June to photograph her." His colleagues, eager to share his enthusiasm, returned his smiles, but later there was head shaking. Norma, feeling that too much time had already elapsed and concerned for her husband's health, urged that they go ahead with the film. She felt that one of the picture's pluses was its limited, easily fulfilled production schedule; thus it would not overtax Thalberg's energies and would get him back into the production groove without getting him involved in protracted shooting.

Later she regretted agreeing to this film; a more elaborate production on a stronger subject might have assured the success Thalberg was so anxious for on his first time out on his own as an independent producer.

Riptide turned out to be a paltry thing indeed, not quite a fizzle but certainly no blockbuster—and far from the success Thalberg needed so badly to shore up his flagging spirits.

The story was a silly, inconsequential one about an American girl who marries an English lord who tends to neglect her, whereupon she takes up with an American playboy who compromises her and nearly occasions a divorce. But this lord and lady love each other after all, and there is a reconciliation and renewed joy in their child. Edmund Goulding tried his best to inject sparkle into the proceedings, and the studio packed the film with a solid array of character actors, but it didn't help all that much. At the Pasadena preview, as writer Bob Thomas has related, "The august C. Aubrey Smith was required to speak the grandiloquent line: 'Ah, this air of old England; presently I shall hear a nightingale.'" The cynical, depression-jaded 1934 audience greeted the line with razzberries and Bronx cheers, and the ensuing laughter drowned out dialogue for minutes.

Thalberg was frantic and pulled the print back to the studio for more tampering; some scenes were cut outright, others severely edited. Retakes were ordered, and the cast, which included Herbert Marshall as the lord and Robert Montgomery (in his fifth and last appearance with Shearer) as the playboy, were rushed back to the sound stage.

Marshall, who was having problems with his wife, Edna Best, because of his drinking and his excessive womanizing (the big news of 1934, the year of *Riptide*'s release, was to be his red-hot affair with Gloria Swanson), was in a bad mood throughout the shooting. To compound his problems, he was being fitted for a new artificial leg (he had lost his leg in World War I and was having serious pains in his stump), and Norma later recalled her feelings of distaste as she and Goulding, both wishing to be polite and solicitous, were forced to hear about "phantom pain"—one of Marshall's favorite conversational themes. One day, while wearing his new limb, to which he was not accustomed, Marshall crossed over to Norma for an intimate love scene and alarmed everyone by falling down in front of her, while the artificial limb tore through his pants and ricocheted at a weird angle.

As Robert Montgomery recalled: Marshall's drinking and other problems brought Shearer and Thalberg their own problems. "I remember that Irving was rushing down to the set—

it wasn't good for his heart, really wasn't—to calm down everyone. He liked Bart [his friends' nickname for Marshall] and knew he'd wind up giving a fine performance, as he always did, that would enhance the values of the picture, and I remember him commenting that if he had had to hobble around for all those years with an artificial leg, *he* might have wound up an all-out alkie."

Eventually it was Norma and Edmund Goulding who got Marshall to stop drinking for the duration of the picture, and from then on he was fine, but Shearer confessed to Lilyan Tashman, who was also in the film, that every time Marshall took her in his arms she had nightmares of the artificial limb breaking into her own leg.

Tashman, a talented actress, was to die later that year (1934) of cancer. She was a noted blond beauty who was considered one of the best-dressed women in Hollywood and had reportedly given Norma tips to pass on to Adrian about her styles for the picture. But Shearer could see that Tashman's health was failing, and she tried to keep her cheered up. Another supporting actress in *Riptide* was the famous Mrs. Patrick Campbell, the noted stage actress who had been the toast of London at the turn of the century. Mrs. Campbell, who was then pushing seventy, presented Shearer with other problems. Once famous for her wit, beauty, commanding stage presence, and piercingly eloquent voice, Mrs. Campbell was down and out at this point in her life, and had only a few years to live. Long gone were the great days in which she scintillated in *Pygmalion,* written by her close friend George Bernard Shaw, and now she was broke and bitter. Norma and Thalberg had heard of her plight and had given her the role to get her a little money and shore up her morale (she did three more films before fading permanently into a disgruntled retirement).

Mrs. Campbell was unfamiliar with screen technique and tended to overplay and overattitudinize greatly. When Norma tactfully discussed the intimacy of the camera and the necessity of scaling down and so forth, Mrs. Campbell offered ad-

vice of her own, couched in overbearing terms, concerning
Norma's own technique. The last straw was when Shearer
overheard Mrs. Pat commenting to C. Aubrey Smith about
Shearer's lack of stage training and how her eyes were much
too small and needed careful and stringent highlighting, and
so forth. After that the two ladies' scenes together were completed in a rather cold atmosphere, with the venerable C.
Aubrey shaking his head and raising his eyebrows over it all
as he watched them work.

When *Riptide* was released in March 1934, there was a general feeling that Thalberg had fallen short of his usual standards—which left his enemies at the new MGM gleeful, to
say the least. One of his more flagrant mistakes, committed in
a frantic effort to inject excitement (as he conceived it), included a ridiculous on-screen costume party featuring the
stars caparisoned as *insects*—gargantuan ones, too.

When I saw it recently, *Riptide* struck me as forced, contrived, and not a little frantic in its efforts to please, entertain,
and titillate. It bore the earmarks of considerable editing, cutting, and assorted tampering, with a decidedly jerky and self-
conscious result. Shearer was delightful in her role, as were
Marshall and Montgomery; Mrs. Campbell was overassertive,
so much so that she threw the picture off balance at times;
and Lilyan Tashman seemed wan though, as always, competent. Only C. Aubrey Smith, that eminent character veteran
of innumerable films of the time, seemed to be really enjoying
himself.

Photoplay's verdict on the proceedings was: "Norma
Shearer is vivid and compellingly convincing as the wife who
never dreams of being unfaithful until her husband's insistent
suspicions practically force her to be. Miss Shearer has an exceedingly difficult role, and she carries it gallantly and ex-
pertly."

The critic for *New Outlook,* one Cy Caldwell, wrote it as he
saw it: "Into the capable hands of Miss Shearer, Mr. Marshall
and Mr. Montgomery has been placed a luscious, sloppy glob
of whimsical elfishness, and they have done their honest best
with it."

Mordaunt Hall in *The New York Times* wrote that the starring trio gave "performances that are emphatically more provocative than the story."

Though Norma herself felt let down over the results, considering the effort she had put into it, she tried to take the sting out of it for her husband by reminding him that there was always "a next time out." One bit of advice they *did* heed; when one catty critic meowed that she "had had enough of Shearer and Montgomery's cocktail-shaking coynesses," it signaled the end of their screen partnership.

Disappointed with the film's popular and critical reception and more than a little guilt-ridden because he had not, in his view, "delivered" for the "comeback" effort of the wife who had sacrificed so much for him personally, Thalberg determined that her next vehicle would represent the quality for which his name had come to stand. He thereupon purchased the screen rights to the famous play about Elizabeth Barrett and Robert Browning in which noted stage actress Katharine Cornell had achieved one of her more notable successes. Here, Thalberg felt, was the vehicle calculated to continue and reinforce his wife's "First Lady of the Screen" status, circa 1934.

The story bears some recounting as it contains many of the ingredients that appealed to Thalberg's concept of "adult" screen fare. The famous poetess Elizabeth Barrett, who by 1845 has deeply moved many literate English men and women with her lyrical verse, is in private life a lonely woman close to forty who suffers from what we would term today psychosomatic invalidism. Confined for the most part to her couch in an upper bedroom of the grim Victorian townhouse of her father, Edward Moulton-Barrett, forced to content herself with her books and the company of her dog, Flush, she submits resignedly to her widowed father's starchy, rigid, and subconsciously incestuous tyrannies and covertly sympathizes with her frustrated brothers and sisters as they vainly attempt to resist their father's brutal strictures.

Resigned to doing without a meaningful love of the kind her heart cries out for, Elizabeth begins a correspondence with another poet, Robert Browning, who is six years her junior. Robust and life-loving, uninhibited and humanistic, the impetuous Browning forces a meeting and soon Elizabeth is awakened to the fullness of life and womanhood. In time she defies her frighteningly forceful and secretly incestuous father and goes to Italy with Browning. There, to quote one of her loveliest lines from her famed collection, *Sonnets from the Portuguese,* she is "caught up into Love and taught the whole of life in a new rhythm."

The leading role offered any actress of skill and sensibility a wondrous range of emotions and reactions, and Thalberg was convinced that his talented wife was the only woman in Hollywood who could do the role justice. Oddly, Norma, who was no slouch as a persistent seeker of mystique-enhancing parts, did not at first agree with him. She would be consigned to a couch for at least half the film's running time and would have to appear passive, sweetly compliant, and resigned until near the end—actions that ran counter to her own instinctual drive toward dynamic theatrics.

But when Thalberg showed her the literate and intelligent script concocted by such consummate pros as Donald Ogden Stewart, Claudine West, and Ernest Vajda, and when she realized that they had "opened up" the single-set and (in her view) dank play via scenes in Regent's Park, the drawing room of the townhouse, and the church of St. Marylebone, she began to come around to his way of thinking. As the part and the story and its ramifications penetrated her imaginative mind, the possibilities implicit in them fired her up. She looked forward to the start of production with keen interest.

Another development had arisen during preproduction that had doubtless added to her determination to showcase herself successfully in *Barretts.* The autocratic publisher William Randolph Hearst had gotten it into his head that his mistress, Marion Davies, should play Elizabeth Barrett. Davies was a truly talented comedienne, and she could be adorable in pixieish, waifish, lovelorn, ingenuously humorous portrayals, but as a dramatic actress she had distinct limitations that her smitten elderly lover could never face. Hearst was determined to make her a great dramatic star. While she doubted she could extend her narrow but authentic talent range, she was willing to go along with him. Fundamentally, Davies was indifferent to her career. Like Susan Alexander, the singer in *Citizen Kane* who tried to comply with her lover's insistence on forcing her mediocre talents into grand opera (Susan was, rather cruelly and unfairly, modeled on Marion), Davies, out of her admiration and respect for her protector, tried to force herself into roles beyond her range, albeit halfheartedly. Delightful in winsome roles such as *Polly of the Circus* and *Blondie of the Follies* (both 1932), she had gone up to the limit of her range in 1933 in *Peg o' My Heart,* originally a Laurette Taylor stage hit, in which she played a fey and feisty Irish girl who runs up against the starchy mores of the English aristocracy.

Everybody liked Marion. She was a kind and generous woman with a charming little stutter that magically disappeared when she got in front of a camera with memorized dialogue. She could kid and charm the formidable Hearst into a semblance of humorous relaxation, but when it came to her career, he was totally humorless. "The sad thing about it all," as her sometime costar Billy Haines told me, "was that Marion was just delightful in certain parts and could have made the grade if she had never laid eyes on Hearst, but his insistence on artificially inflating her image, often in inappropriate roles, resulted in her becoming, at least so far as her career went, a Hollywood joke." Mayer, who had great difficulty in selling the pictures Marion made under Hearst's aegis— Hearst's Cosmopolitan productions were released through Metro-Goldwyn-Mayer—tolerated the situation for years because of free publicity Hearst offered for MGM films in his many newspapers.

But even Mayer was tiring of these accommodations to Hearst. That same year the publisher had taxed Mayer's patience to the limit by pushing Marion for yet another role for which she was manifestly ill suited, Marie Antoinette. When Hearst learned that MGM had bought the Stefan Zweig biography of the ill-fated French queen because Thalberg had considered it an ideal vehicle for Norma Shearer, he had jumped in tactlessly and demanded it for his girl. Mayer decided that the problems of ramming Davies pictures down the throats of his exhibitors and coping with Hearst's unreasonable demands outweighed the publicity advantages of frequent playups of MGM products in Hearst newspapers. He had had enough; it was time to draw the line, and he told Hearst that both Elizabeth Barrett and Marie Antoinette were Norma Shearer vehicles. Thalberg was relieved and grateful that Mayer sided with him here, but he should not have been so surprised. Mayer had better taste than he was credited for. "I closed my eyes one afternoon while I was getting shaved," he told Eddie Mannix, "and I tried to visualize Marion floundering around in elaborate eighteenth-century costumes and telling off Du-Barry in *Marie Antoinette*; then I tried to imagine her languishing on a couch as *Elizabeth,* and damn it if I didn't cut my chin moving too quickly when I scared the hell out of my barber by shouting 'No, no, a thousand times no!'" He added, laughing, that the frightened barber asked timidly, "No what, Mr. Mayer?" and was puzzled but relieved when Mayer said "No Marion!"

Meanwhile Shearer took matters into her own hands. She went over to see Davies in the enormous "bungalow" that Hearst had constructed for her on the MGM lot and that was known, Mannix once told me, as "The Palace." The girls had a heart-to-heart chat, the substance of which was Marion's unsuitability for the role of Elizabeth. "You're a positive genius in certain types of comedy, Marion," Norma told her tactfully. "In fact, you're a far more natural comedienne than I am!" (Shearer was being honest in saying this; as George Cukor was later to tell me, comedy never came easy to her; only applied technique carried her through.) Norma then went for the jugular, but she applied her standard stiletto rather than a meatcleaver. "But certain types of drama are not up your street, Marion," she said. "We all have our special niches, and we have to stay in them." To her surprise,

Marion gave her no argument. She had, she said, never felt that Marie and Elizabeth were within her range, she was only trying to go along with "Poopsie" (one of her pet names for Hearst), and of course she would try to make him understand.

Thalberg was very angry about what he called "Hearst's damned intrusions on my preserve." Grateful though he was for Mayer's siding with him on the matter, he felt less powerful at MGM than before he left for Europe, as he was now limited to special projects, and Hearst's "damned-fool" insistences and demands grated on him.

Despite all of Marion's tactful cajoleries, Hearst took profound offense when told that his inamorata would have to stay in her own artistic backyard at MGM, and by the next year, 1935, Marion and her bungalow and her entourage were established over at Warners, where, during the last two years of her career, Marion did comedies of epic slightness and vacuity. Scuttlebutt had it that Jack Warner and Marion finally persuaded Hearst that she was never going to be the Bernhardt of the screen, and resignedly he left her to her soufflé-light fare and her flirtations with such as Dick Powell, one of her Warner leading men, who told me years later: "Marion's efforts to undo my fly kept me in a nervous tizzy all the time, wondering if Hearst knew and if he were deputizing 'hit-men' to visit me!"

Hearst might have been out of sight at MGM by then, but he was not out of mind. Norma Shearer was conspicuously missing from the pages of Hearst publications for quite a while, and MGM promotion was heavily reduced while ad rates for its films went dancing upward, to the exasperation of the New York executives.

Shearer later got a revenge of a sort. Mayer and Thalberg got back eventually on a full social footing with Hearst and Marion, and when Marion threw a costume party, Norma showed up in an elaborate gown from *Marie Antoinette* that forced all kinds of adjustments to the decor, so wide and extensive were its folds and flounces. "Norma drove Hearst crazy that night," George Cukor told me, laughing. "He was having trouble with the French at that time over politics, trade, and other matters; Willie could not only dream up artificial wars (such as the 1898 conflict with Spain) via his papers, he could generate the most damnably pointless petty quarrels, and anyway his fuss was with France at that moment. And here's Norma in the costume of a French queen forcing the Hearst minions to take the hinges off doors and move tables around to accommodate her costume! And what did Marion think of it? She thought it was a laugh riot!"

Meanwhile, with Hearst's retreat assured, there was the business of getting *The Barretts of Wimpole Street* on the screen. The tasteful, painstaking Sidney Franklin was assigned to direct, and Fredric March was assigned the Robert Browning role. Charles Laughton was given the baleful part of the tyrannical Edward Moulton-Barrett; at first Thalberg, who admired him greatly, felt the role might be too small for him (Laughton was to join the other two stars as an Academy Award winner, for *The Private Life of Henry VIII* [1933] during the shooting, and they gave him an informal set party). Laughton, however, who always had an eye out for the neurotic possibilities in a role, was eager to do it. To everyone's surprise, he even lost some fifty pounds and adopted side whiskers and a new hairstyle, so as to fit his impression of the tyrant of Wimpole Street.

March recalled to me that Laughton always made him very nervous. He had appeared with "the rotund gargoyle" (as Ray Milland uncharitably termed him) in such DeMille extravaganzas as *The Sign of the Cross (1932),* in which March had been a handsome Roman soldier and Laughton a lascivious emperor. March and Milland had similar reactions to Laughton. Laughton's homosexuality and predilection for the charms of attractive young men were well known in the early thirties, but they were not viewed with the charity and forebearance of later decades, especially since Laughton was a singularly (and sinisterly) unattractive man physically. Milland, who never liked him, had appeared with Laughton in early 1932 in *Payment Deferred* for Paramount. As he later told Mitchell Leisen, he had to play a scene in which Laughton poisons him with drugged wine, then buries him in the backyard. "I'll never forget the expression on Laughton's face as he waited for the poison to work. It was like he couldn't wait to get my pants off before he buried me!" (Note: the scene to which Milland refers in *Payment Deferred* plays, as more than one film student of the 1980s has noted, exactly as Milland indicated.)

March had his own version of his appearances with Laughton, according to George Cukor (possessor, incidentally, of one of the nastiest tongues and most amusingly malicious wits in Hollywood). According to Cukor, Laughton used to try to look up Freddie March's toga in *Sign of the Cross* and when confronted in *Barretts* with March in pants *sans* underwear and cut rather tightly around the crotch, he grumbled, "The man is shameless!" According to Cukor, this was just Charles "being a bitch" because he knew March wore his pants "that way" to entice females. (As one actress later noted in her autobiography, March still was up to these tricks himself in a grossly tight-panted film called *The Buccaneer* four years later.)

When I interviewed Fredric March for my *Films of Fredric March* in 1971, he candidly confessed that he had been nervous with the Browning role because he didn't think he was right for it. "I think Sidney Franklin paid more attention to Norma," he said, "and maybe he let me get out of hand. Let's face it, Robert Browning was a rather flighty, artificial-bonhomie type of guy (perfect for someone like Brian Aherne, who had done it on the stage), bouncing in and out of Elizabeth's room, applying the morale adrenaline, bouncing up and down and sashaying around with Victorian-style flourishes that, to me, bordered on the fey and effeminate." March went on, "I realized that the character was frantically trying to get Elizabeth off that couch, and I tried to get into his psyche, but he brought out the worst ham elements in me, and I feel I failed in the role." March's instincts were humble but true. It is not one of his better performances, and Sidney

Franklin was partly to blame for not toning—and slowing—him down.

As for Laughton, he was in his element—dank Victorian room, heavy drapes, dark ambience, side whiskers, frock coats, and a neurotically supercharged role in which he literally chewed the scenery, sadistically bullying the children he cared nothing about and addressing himself, with a minimum of subtlety, to the seduction of his beloved Elizabeth. Norma later recalled that he went at the climactic scene with such frightening zeal that Franklin had to tone him down in retake after retake. Of course the character's incestuous longing for his daughter was akin to Laughton's not-always-repressed lustings for young males in both his professional and personal life, and Laughton made the most of his opportunities. But the result is a performance every bit as hammy as March's, albeit for radically different reasons. Even when Franklin had the decibels down to what he considered sufficient vibrancies to keep the production code off MGM's back, Laughton merely snickered that "they" couldn't censor the glint in his eye.

Of the three stars, Shearer comes off best; her delineation of Elizabeth is a restrained and touching piece of acting, muted, soft, pliant in the early scenes when an essential receptive passivity is called for, then ever-more forceful and passionate as the love for Browning that revives her spirit, and her hatred and aversion for her monstrous father, bring out her true resources of spirit and purpose.

When the picture was released in September 1934, the critics as a whole liked the result. *The Literary Digest* critic wrote: "Miss Norma Shearer, who has the Cornell part on the screen, is remarkably fine as Elizabeth Barrett, playing with a sensitive skill that makes her performance the best of an interesting cinema career." Andre Sennwald in *The New York Times* called Shearer's Elizabeth "touching" and added: "She is successful in creating the illusion of a highly sensitive and delicate woman who beats her luminous wings in vain against the chains which bind her." Of March, he wrote, "His performance will impress the critical as a highly competent job by a versatile actor rather than an inspired portrayal of the great poet." A number of the critics felt that Laughton as Edward Moulton-Barrett had overacted rather grossly. When I saw the film I thought the first half rather slow and plodding.

Maureen O'Sullivan gave a lively and winning portrayal of Elizabeth's high-spirited sister Henrietta, who determines to pursue her own love objectives with a handsome young officer despite her father's opposition, and has vivid memories of the film and Shearer. In 1983 she told me: "Norma had such a serenity about her, such quiet authority. The role was perfect for her and she shone in it. She inspired the whole cast, and she lent herself to the period and its ambiences as only a true classical actress could. She was uncommonly gifted; to react to her, to play back to her, was a memorable experience I can never forget; I had that feeling with only one other actress, at least to that degree; that was Greta Garbo," with whom Miss O'Sullivan worked in *Anna Karenina* in 1935.

It is, incidentally, interesting to compare the 1934 version of *Barretts* with the 1957 rendition that starred Jennifer Jones and Bill Travers as Elizabeth and Robert and the brilliant John Gielgud as Edward Moulton-Barrett. In my 1974 book, *The Great Romantic Films,* I expressed a decided preference for the 1957 version, which Sidney Franklin also directed for MGM, but this time in England. Later in 1957 I was to interview Franklin, who told me that he had always wanted to have another go at the subject because he felt there had been distinct limitations to the 1934 treatment. He had thought Shearer superb, indeed, he said, reverenced her as artist and woman through the years, but he agreed that March had been rather bouncy and juvenile and that Laughton had been almost grossly self-indulgent.

This second version was enhanced by CinemaScope and Metrocolor and by Bronislaw Kaper's rich, moving theme music, which the earlier version regrettably lacked. Again Thalberg failed to underscore dramatic highlights with appropriate music—he had a strange, indeed creatively myopic, aversion to theme music, an aversion that was to rob some of his best films of the requisite emotional force. Aside from the song "Wilt Thou Have My Hand" by Herbert Stothart, which appeared fleetingly in the 1934 version, the film lacked mood underscorings. One flagrant example: When Shearer struggles to rise for the first time from her couch to get to the window to see her beloved depart after his first visit, there is *no* underscoring; when Jennifer Jones performs the same awkward movements in the 1957 film, she is supported by some of Kaper's most inspired and rousing musical inspirations, and moreover, Jones looks through the window at departing Bill Travers on the street below, whereas the Shearer shot stops with her reaching the window—we do not look out at March.

As I stated in *Great Romantic Films*:

> The 1957 version had also the benefit of Bill Travers's manly, robust, forceful Robert Browning, one of this underrated and overlooked actor's more notable achievements, and though Miss Jones was not up to Miss Shearer's standard, she acquitted herself creditably. But the surprise of the picture was Gielgud, who filled the Edward Moulton-Barrett character with subtle diabolism and rich complexities born as much of the Gielgud genius as of the original Barrett's mystique, which, from all reports, was baleful enough. . . . there was also a more authentic look to the 1957 version, shot as it was in England, in handsome settings and exterior shots that far outranked for verisimilitude and correct atmosphere the Hollywood conceptions of 1934. The cast, all English except for Miss Jones, seemed to fit more truly into every Barrett-Browning aficionado's concept of the time, the place and the people of this immortal story.

Sidney Franklin told me that he wished he could have remade his other notable films of the 1930s, and he mentioned in particular the 1932 *Smilin' Through*. "It is sad," he com-

mented, "that [in the 1950s] we have so much more technological knowledge but we seem to have gone backward in
artistic originality and inspiration. I feel with *Barretts* that I
did improve on the original in a number of respects, but I
note a number of [1950s] films that seem to me slack and care-
less, both in the direction and general conception." Of course
in the 1950s television was making catastrophic inroads into
film attendance, a harbinger of even greater changes to come
in the motion picture field.

When I interviewed Charles Laughton in 1961 on the set of
his final picture, *Advise and Consent* (1962), he seemed
strangely reticent about *Barretts*. I knew, of course, that I was
talking to a desperately ill and unhappy man (he was sixty-two
then), but his face failed to light up when I mentioned this
film as it did for others—the 1935 *Ruggles of Red Gap,* for
instance, a charming comedy that he seemed to have enjoyed
making. *Ruggles,* I felt, connoted happy tomfoolery to him;
Barretts his inner darkness and sexual conflicts.

He said that losing so much weight for the role of Edward
Moulton-Barrett had, in his opinion, depressed and enervated
him, and that he had had to do it yet again for his roles in the
1935 *Les Miserables* (again with March) and *Mutiny on the
Bounty* (also 1935) in which he had given a rousingly vicious
and brutally sinister rendition of Captain Bligh. "Jesus, he
was the only actor who ever frightened the pants off Gable!"
Billy Grady told me years later, using what those of us who
were aware of Laughton's peccadilloes as an unintentionally
(or perhaps intentional, as Billy was a mischievous Irishman)
hilarious turn of phrase. Billy went on to say that Gable had
told him he never wanted to work with Laughton again, which
echoed March's (and certainly Ray Milland's) unease with
him.

In 1961 Laughton did have kind words for Shearer, saying
that she was a delight to work with and that it was regrettable
that she had retired relatively early when she might, like
Garbo, have done even greater things. When asked about
Fredric March, he changed the subject.

Norma always spoke kindly of Laughton. George Cukor told me that she had mentioned being honestly frightened of him in the famed *Barretts* "incest" scene. "I honestly thought he might go out of control altogether," she told Cukor. "Charles is not a happy man, I'm afraid, and unlike many actors, he can't find any emotional release in his roles; they only seem to *add* to his torment."

Having championed the likes of Ramon Novarro and William Haines, and having been the recipient of many sad confidences over the years ("People came to her as to a *mother,*" Novarro told me in 1960), Norma understood the inner agonies of Charles Laughton's complex talent as well as, and perhaps better than, most. Laughton's wife, Elsa Lanchester, who had strong reservations about many people and didn't hesitate to voice them, told me in 1965: "Charles liked Norma; he never felt she was laughing at him, as he said Tallulah Bankhead did. (There is a story that "Tallu" one day on the set of *Devil and the Deep* in 1932 yelped: "Gary [Cooper, their costar] is a *divine* man, but you, *Charlotte,* are a repulsive, fat mess of glop!")

One of Shearer's recorded comments about Laughton, as relayed to me by Fredric March, was: "Poor Charles; his lot in life is not an easy one . . ."

The year 1936 was to bring Norma one of her most ambitious projects at MGM.

Norma had wanted to do *Romeo and Juliet* ever since she and John Gilbert had done the balcony scene in *The Hollywood Revue of 1929.* Now, in early 1935, pregnant for a second time, she first expressed her wish to her husband. He thought it highly amusing. But after Katherine was born, Thalberg began to think about it more seriously, as he wanted Norma's next role to surpass her Elizabeth Barrett Browning.

Louis B. Mayer was dead set against the idea. He reminded Thalberg that he had no Shakespearean experience, and neither had George Cukor, whom Thalberg wanted to direct it. Eddie Mannix, who also opposed the idea, told me many years later:

Louie Mayer was ready to have an apoplectic fit when Irving sprang *that* one on him—in fact I think he did have one—a minor one, but since L.B. was such a good amateur actor himself, I couldn't really tell for sure. Irving tried to tell him that Jack Warner was producing *A Midsummer Night's Dream* over at Warners, but Louie only snapped: "If Jack wants to make a fool of himself messing with Max Reinhardt and that Shakespeare high-falutin' stuff, that's *his* funeral! Why should we run Jack a race to bankruptcy court? Hell, the film would cost a couple of million!" Irving mollified him slightly by stating his estimated cost at $900,000. Furthermore it would be good for prestige. I think he sold L.B. on it—for the moment. Later, when the total cost totaled the very same two million Mayer had prophesied, and the picture went on to lose some $900,000 after distribution costs, Mayer had the last laugh. But it seemed to *me* he did more *weeping* than *laughing*!

Nevertheless, the picture gained the studio some prestige. Shearer, fired up with enthusiasm, worked hard on her diction with the likes of Constance Collier and Mrs. Robinson Duff, both experts in their field, and at the suggestion of John Barrymore, who was to appear as Mercutio, she also took lessons with Margaret Carrington, who had greatly helped Barrymore during his Shakespearean days on the New York stage. As Bosley Crowther later reported it in his book on MGM: "Norma wanted to catch the cadence of Shakespeare's iambic pentameter without speaking in the classical manner. She wanted to make the language vital and real—to speak like a motion picture actress so the dialogue would be comprehensible to general audiences." After working with the Carrington-Collier-Duff trio, Shearer's vocal projection was richly enhanced.

Considerable care was taken to hire the right Romeo. Fredric March was the first choice—it would have been his third picture with Shearer, but he curtly and definitely refused. "I would have looked like a damn fool in tights climbing balconies and making pretty speeches," March told me years later. "My God, I was thirty-eight years old at the time! I would have totally lost my audiences bouncing around like a sixteen-year-old kid!" After Robert Donat and Brian Aherne were tried and found wanting—or rather, Donat was found wanting in the required enthusiasm—an actor even older than March finally stepped into the Romeo part. Forty-three-year-old Leslie Howard had at first rejected the part. He felt a man in the singleminded pursuit of love came off as effeminate and callow; if he were too young no one would take him seriously; if he were older and experienced, he would be a bore. Later, when Howard learned that Jack Warner refused to lend him to MGM, he got his dander up and forced the turn of events. Warner was later pacified when his studio received the services of Clark Gable and Robert Montgomery in exchange for lending Paul Muni to MGM for *The Good Earth*. Hearst wanted Gable and Montgomery to costar with Marion Davies in *Cain and Mabel* and *Ever Since Eve,* respectively, two of her final, and forgettable, films at Warners. She retired in 1937, after Hearst, in deep financial trouble, found he could no longer afford such indulgences.

Years later Basil Rathbone, who played Tybalt, told me of the difficulties John Barrymore presented in his role of Mercutio.

> At fifty-four or so, John was too old for the role; he was very unsure of himself, up to his ears in trouble with young Elaine Barrie, and he was drinking and unreliable on the set. They finally set him up in a sanitarium for alcoholics across the street from the studio, where a male nurse kept a firm eye on him and delivered him daily to [and from] the set. It was so sad to see him in such a state—the greatest Shakespearean stage actor of his time, who had forgotten more about acting than most people around him would ever know. . . .

Barrymore's experiences in the sanitarium were later the source of a scene in the 1937 *A Star Is Born,* in which pro-

ducer Adolphe Menjou visits Fredric March in a similar estab-
lishment while March's character is drying out. March told me
years later that playing the scene made him very sad. "I had
been called the best John Barrymore imitator around at the
time of the film *The Royal Family of Broadway* (1930, in
which March did a telling takeoff on The Great Profile), but
imitating or even recalling him in that sanitarium scene was
no laughing matter—his decline was very tragic."

But once he hit his stride on the set, Barrymore proved he
could still bat out the best Shakespeare around. "He was a
miracle at times like that," fellow actor Reginald Denny recalled. "He somehow pulled himself together and was his old,
great self, for as long as the camera held him." At review
time, a number of the nation's critics were to agree with
Denny.

I have seen *Romeo and Juliet* a number of times over the
years, and even though Shearer was thirty-five when she made
it, she managed to suggest the ardor of a girl in love, her
speech recorded more fluidly and eloquently than ever before,
and she was charmingly natural, relaxed, and serene in the
quieter scenes and convincingly impassioned in the famed po-
tion episode. As the lovers from two great, bitterly feuding
families in medieval Verona, Shearer and Howard are well
matched; though Howard was in his forties, he managed to
catch the poetry and to suggest the uninhibited ardor of a
reckless swain who fought duels and later literally died for
love. In the final scene, when Shearer finds him dead, her
sincerity and emotional projection are noteworthy. Anyone
who doubts that Norma Shearer is an actress of the first mag-
nitude should see her in *Romeo and Juliet*. Shearer was no
O'Neill heroine, true. But within the range she usually chose,
she excelled. Albert B. Manski, one of the most fervent of
Shearer's admirers and a well-known Boston writer and columnist, put it as well as anyone when he wrote: "After all,
Thalberg couldn't get up in front of a camera and act for her,
could he?"

George Cukor had a lot to say about *Romeo and Juliet* when I interviewed him in the 1960s:

> I wish I had given it more of an Italian flavor. I wanted to catch the period, scale it down, make it a little more intimate. When I see it now I see so many things I would have changed. But Norma and Leslie and John Barrymore were wonderful—couldn't be improved on. Rathbone, all of them, were good, too. But in 1936 we were all caught up in production gloss, giving a film a big, stately look. The feeling at MGM was: Let's show them we can put on the dog with the best of 'em. So I guess I got caught up in all that and the picture suffered a bit—maybe more than a bit. There's too much of the old overproduced Hollywood stuff in it, though some of it is handsome—the staged dances, for instance.

Norma herself looked back on the picture most fondly. "It was my last with Irving and he put so much of himself into it; he so wanted it to succeed. And I feel I did expand my range, and I had the benefit of some good coaching that stood me in good stead for the future, and the cast surrounding me would have been an asset to any actress!"

Shearer is credited with saving John Barrymore from getting sacked when Mayer wanted to fire him. William Powell was offered the role but refused because, he said, Barrymore had shown him kindnesses when he supported him in an early picture. On the set Norma treated Barrymore with every kindness, and personally interceded, when he was absent for three days, with Mayer, reminding him that Barrymore had made a lot of money for the studio in earlier years and that firing John would hurt his devoted brother Lionel, who was coping with an ill wife and severe health problems of his own. Mayer acceded to her request, especially when he learned Powell was having none of his replacement ideas.

When the film was released on August 20, 1936, complete

with a lavish premiere, the critics were generally kind and respectful. According to *Literary Digest*:

> [The reviewers] consider *Romeo and Juliet* a triumph of motion picture art, very possibly one of the finest pictures ever made in Hollywood. The most acidulous critics admitted Miss Shearer's Juliet to be a triumph, garlanded Leslie Howard for a curbed, disciplined performance of Romeo. Also, they delighted in the Mercutio of John Barrymore. *Romeo and Juliet* is Hollywood's best joust with Shakespeare to date. Skilled performances, knowing delivery of the lines, an acute sense that cheers would be grudged, jeers easy, combining to set alight the talents of all concerned.

Frank Nugent of *The New York Times* had a few reservations, admittedly, writing:

> Miss Shearer was not at her best in the balcony scene. With more pleasure and with a sense that this memory will endure the longer, do we recall [her] tender and womanly perverse Juliet during her farewell scene with Romeo before his flight to Mantua. Bright, too, with recollection of her surrender to uncertainty, fear and suspicion before swallowing the potion and of that scene in which she finds her lover dead beside her in the tomb. Miss Shearer has played these, whatever her earlier mistakes, with sincerity and effect.

12

Widowhood: The Lion's Consort Protects Her Territory

WITH THE plaudits for *Romeo and Juliet* ringing in his ears, Irving Thalberg began making plans for such pictures as *Camille* with Garbo, *Maytime* with Jeanette MacDonald and Nelson Eddy, and *The Good Earth* with Luise Rainer and Paul Muni. He enjoyed relaxing at home with his six-year-old son and one-year-old daughter, and Norma, too, was feeling happy and relaxed, looking forward to a long vacation while preparations for *Marie Antoinette* proceeded. In August 1936 they were the happiest of families. The three new pictures, Thalberg declared, would bear the stamp of special quality he had always striven for, and at thirty-seven he looked forward to what might yet prove a decent span of productivity.

Then, suddenly in September, disaster struck. Thalberg had gone to Monterey for the Labor Day weekend; the Del Monte Club there was one of his favorite relaxation spots. He had exercised too strenuously and had stayed in the sun too long. Although overheated and exhausted, he had insisted on playing cards. After returning to Santa Monica with what he thought was a slight cold, he woke up the next morning with a

176

raging fever. Norma summoned the doctors and sat tensely while they gave her the grim verdict: pneumonia. As his condition worsened, Norma, panic-stricken, sent for Irving's old friend Dr. Groedel, who had emigrated from Bad Nauheim to New York to escape the Nazis. The doctor arrived a day later at the Thalberg home. This was in a day before sulfa and other drugs that might have saved Irving. As it turned out, Dr. Groedel could do nothing. Reportedly, an agonized Irving roused himself from the stupors that gradually sank into comas to give Norma advice for the future. Attempting a weak jocularity, he told her, "You'll marry some guy who'll get all my money when I'm gone." Then he added, "Just don't marry an actor!" Just before he went into an oxygen tent, he held Norma's hand tightly as he whispered a prayer. His final reported words to her were: "Don't let the children forget me!" On Monday morning, September 14, 1936, Irving Thalberg died.

Mayer and the studio people were plunged into grief. The death got widespread news coverage, with tribute paid the talent and individuality of this thirty-seven-year-old who had won a number of Academy Awards for the studio he had made the most respected and prestigious in Hollywood and the world. The funeral, at the temple of Rabbi Magnin, who almost nine years before had married Irving and Norma, was elaborate and stately, with thousands of spectators grouped outside on the street and along several blocks. Grace Moore sang the Twenty-third Psalm, and every important film personality who was free for the day appeared to honor Irving.

Mayer's grief was genuine and deeply personal. He had loved Irving like a son; there is no reason to doubt his oft-declared sentiments in that regard. There had been disillusionments and estrangements, yes, he said, but now that Irving was gone, he thought of him only with love. This feeling, however, did not prevent him from immediately dismantling what was left of the Thalberg production units and assigning new producers to Irving's last projects. Five months after Thalberg's lavish burial, the credits for *The Good Earth* included the tribute: "To the memory of Irving Grant Thalberg, we dedicate this picture—his last great achievement."

Norma secluded herself for weeks after Irving's death. Her only outside visits were quick ones to Forest Lawn, where she insisted on personally supervising the landscaping of her husband's gravesite. Then the toll of the days of constant nursing and tension caught up with her. She herself came down with a prime case of pneumonia. During its more critical stages, as Eddie Mannix remembered, she could be heard crying out, in her delirium: "Oh, Irving! Irving! Am I to join you in a young death and leave our children orphans?" Henrietta Thalberg, although shattered by grief, helped run Norma's household as best she could, and shared the supervision of the children with Edith Shearer. Norma's recovery was very slow indeed, and it was early 1937 before she really had her strength back. By April, she began to be seen at the more sedate events, escorted by Louis B. Mayer and producer David Lewin, a Thalberg protégè among others. Her expression was reserved, her manner sad. "And it was no 'widow's front,' either," Anita Loos told me. "She had loved Irving deeply in her protective, motherly, sustaining way, and now, suddenly, there was no one to love any more. I think she felt very bewildered and lost and alone—for a while."

Then, as 1937 wore on, the steel returned to the slight, grieving figure. She would be thirty-seven years old on August 10; she had two children who needed her. For *them,* she told friends, she would be strong; for *them,* she would do what had to be done.

Her first instinct, in the months right after Irving's death, had been to retire outright. *Romeo and Juliet* was a good picture to go out on, she reasoned. She had two young children who needed her. And she could walk away one of the richest women in the country. Irving would be leaving her, according to the lawyers, an estate of close to $10 million from savings of his salary plus bonus payments, and the profitable stock options, to say nothing of the residual interests in the bonuses of The Mayer Group.

But there was *Marie Antoinette,* on which Norma and Irving had placed such hopes. The film had been designed and caparisoned, in every department, expressly to her measure; indeed it was built around her, and over $400,000 in preproduction expenses had accrued, a fortune in those days. Although she initially decided to settle her existing contract for $50,000 and terminate her association with the studio, at least as an actress, she had occasion to change her mind.

A quarrel soon broke out among Mayer and Schenck and other MGM executives concerning how much the Thalberg estate would receive from the profits of future Metro-Goldwyn-Mayer pictures. The Mayer Group insisted that the Thalberg estate was entitled to nothing, now that he was dead, adding that earlier arrangements should be abrogated. *"We're* alive," Schenck reportedly said to Mayer, *"he's* dead, and we're the ones with the god-damned headaches on those uncompleted pictures, to say nothing of the uncertain future!" The lawyers for the Thalberg estate presented details of the growing internecine struggle to Norma.

By mid-1937 Norma was back to her old self. "She was determined that those two innocent youngsters would be secure—more than secure—for the rest of their natural lives," Frances Marion told me, "and she wasn't letting anything get in her way—or anyone. She was a lioness fighting for her cubs, and no one understood the law of the jungle more than *that* kind of animal!"

In June Mayer called to invite her to accompany him to Jean Harlow's funeral. Jean had died, suddenly and shockingly, of uremic poisoning, complicated by a cerebral edema, leaving her picture *Saratoga* uncompleted. Mayer was in a prickly, nervous mood. Norma agreed to go with him, and later, riding back to Santa Monica in the car, she "let him have it." "Irving's estate is getting everything that is coming to it," she informed him coldly and crisply. "I am a woman alone with two little children, and you and Nick Schenck are rolling in money. If you don't agree to the original terms, my lawyers will fight you year after year until your legal fees put you back in that junkyard you came from!" Mayer, a man of fierce temper who was not used to backing down before anyone, quailed before the fury of this refined, patrician lady whom he now realized he had underestimated. "God, I thought she was going to pull a gun out of her purse at any moment!" he later told Mannix. "That woman is a lioness, all right!"

Soon Norma was hinting to reporters that she was being "done in" and "put upon." As Hedda Hopper put it, "God, you'd think she was a poor widow with the wolf at the door, about to be put out into the winter cold with her starving children! She felt that way, though she had millions, and in a way I can understand. She had watched all that quarreling between Irving and L.B. and Schenck all those years, and now she was alone, in charge, and determined to have her way, come hell or high water!"

Nick Schenck, apprised of Shearer's frame of mind, came to Hollywood to get "businesslike" with her, as he put it. For his pains he got an icy calldown on the phone, and when he came to the door at Santa Monica, he was barred from the house.

"Norma drove her lawyers like a slavedriver," Frances Marion said later. "Her attitude was: I don't care how you do it, but get me what I want!" Finally, when all of Irving Thalberg's old friends and associates got behind Norma and the atmosphere at the studio grew frigid, Mayer and Schenck gave in. The compromise arrangement gave Norma and her children the full share of all profits paid to The Mayer Group due to the end of the contract at the end of 1938. After then Norma would get 4 percent of all net profits earned by pictures more than half completed from April 1924 to December 1938. To this day the Thalberg estate has cleared millions from residual income, including residuals on old films and various stock deals. Shearer was now a powerful financial figure at Metro-Goldwyn-Mayer.

One condition exacted was that Norma would return to the studio for six pictures under her former arrangement,

$150,000 per picture. The first picture, naturally, would be *Marie Antoinette*.

First, Norma decided to take her children on an extended vacation in Arizona. When she returned, the lion's consort, having proven her mettle as "An Amazon Woman in a Foxy Male World," as her friend Anita Loos put it, was ready for the filmic wars again. "For such a little lady, she had a giant will and determination," Robert Morley, her future costar, was later to say.

13

Marie Antoinette— and the Younger Man

MARIE ANTOINETTE started production in early January of 1938. Earlier, men had been sent to France to purchase authentic antiques; sets were constructed that put the original palace of Versailles to shame—the MGM photographers had even been given permission by the French government to photograph the royal apartments inthe palace. Actual relics of Marie Antoinette (1754–1793) were tracked down, including pieces of her jewelry. Ever since Thalberg had purchased the Stefan Zweig novel in 1933, the script had caused nothing but trouble. But finally, in late 1937, a script presented by Claudine West, Donald Ogden Stewart, and Ernest Vajda made the grade with Mayer, producer Hunt Stromberg, and the director originally assigned, Sidney Franklin. Shearer and Thalberg had long held Franklin's abilities in high esteem, and he had performed well with Norma in the past; he was sensitive, painstaking, careful, and Shearer was confident that he would not only catch the visual elements necessary for a lavish historical drama but that he would showcase and guide her correctly and tastefully, recognizing that, after all, the picture was built around her and tailored to her personality and distinctive mystique.

But Mayer, who had been sullenly pondering the losses on another lavish Shearer film, *Romeo and Juliet,* was nervous about Franklin, who tended to be a very slow shooter given to numerous retakes. This kind of perfectionism might be admirable in its way, but it would add to the cost of a frighteningly expensive project (which eventually cost about $3 million, a horrifically extravagant outlay in 1938). Mayer was determined to keep costs down, no matter what. "How in hell will I explain such losses to the New York office?" he wailed to Stromberg. Norma was called in and told that Franklin was getting the heave-ho; to salve his already outraged feelings, he would be kicked upstairs and made a producer on other projects. "Norma took it very hard," Franklin told me many years later. "She cried about it on the phone. 'God, Sidney, I feel so alone, so exposed to the elements. Irving believed in this project and now he's gone; you did so much advance work on it, and now *you're* gone. What next?' I did not know how to console her. She was still crying when she put down the phone."

Mayer tried to soften the blow. He made a convincing case for the frightening costs. According to Stromberg, he told Shearer that the only way the picture, with a projected running time of nearly three hours and numerous lavish scenes, could begin to turn a profit would be if it were helmed by a director who could rush it through in three months. "Franklin would have taken nine months to a year, Norma—we'd have been ruined." In spite of her reservations Norma understood Mayer's money problems and told him: "Put anyone you want on it."

That "anyone" turned out to be Woody (One-Take) Van Dyke, a clever and facile director but one who was more at home with the likes of Myrna Loy and William Powell in *The Thin Man* and Gable, MacDonald, and Spencer Tracy in *San*

Francisco, both big MGM hits. He was notorious for doing one take, yelling "Print it!" and proceeding directly to the next set. He had completed films in as little as two weeks. "Get it done—cut corners, break speed records, but get it in in a reasonable shooting time, Woody!" Mayer implored him.

Van Dyke did as he was told, and rushed Shearer and her supporting cast of hundreds through the picture in ten weeks—a phenomenal speed considering the many scenes and the eventual 162-minute running time.

Left on her own, with Van Dyke lounging behind the camera and yelling "Print it, boys!" on the first take, Shearer decided to take over not only her own part but everyone else's, too. Van Dyke's attitude was that if he got his print on the first take, he didn't care what they were doing up front; he knew Shearer had not wanted him, and to placate her he acquiesced to all her ideas. Quietly Norma rehearsed herself and the other players, with the result that when the one take was made, all knew their business. "She performed a miracle with that film," Joseph Schildkraut, who played the Duc d'Orleans, told me. "She actually ran the whole show, had her own part down pat, and was wonderfully resourceful in getting us all to play back to her on her own terms and on her own level. The picture would have been nothing without her."

Anita Louise, who played the Princesse De Lamballe, also told me that Shearer's hard-won expertise was apparent everywhere; she had absorbed many lessons from the directors she had worked with and knew as much about lighting and camera angles as cinematographer Bill Daniels, who was often seen conferring with her in her dressing room. "I think that the challenge that picture represented brought out all her hidden strengths," Louise said. "She knew she was on her own and had to get the picture on the move, and Van Dyke's one plus was that he let her and everyone else do what they wanted as long as he got that one take per scene."

The net result of Shearer's efforts for *Marie Antoinette,* was a picture I have always considered a masterpiece. In certain critical quarters it was thoroughly disliked; Bosley Crowther told me he didn't think much of it and said it was a fast, pageant-style film that was long on flamboyance and short on depth, but I did not agree. Neither did Norma, who always defended the film and considered it her best work. As well she might, since she found herself functioning as director, producer, star, cinematographer, and in other assorted roles. Not the least of her problems had involved the costume fittings, featuring over fifty pounds of material, elaborate headdresses, and gorgeous but unwieldy gowns. Before and during the film she kept rereading Zweig's biography so as to get the tragic queen down just right. Reginald Gardiner, who was in the film, later recalled: "Norma's voice had matured tremendously since *Romeo and Juliet.* I think it was because she had grown up a lot during her widowhood and the studio struggles, and those voice lessons from experts during *Juliet*; her diction was impeccable, her whole approach to her acting deeper, stronger." Audiences agreed with him, as did the critics. The Norma Shearer of 1938 had emerged from her crucible a much more authoritative figure, both as actress and as woman.

Van Dyke, being a professional, made his own shrewd if underrated contribution; he kept the crew and cameraman William Daniels on their toes, speeded up the pace, let Shearer and the cast have their heads while watching the overall schedule and progress. But it was Shearer's picture all the way, and her efforts to deepen its quality are everywhere apparent. Actually, between them, Norma and Van Dyke came through with a fast-paced, absorbing historical drama that takes its time when needed, most notably in the love scenes and other introspective sections. I have sat through *Marie Antoinette* twenty-five times over the years and I do not see how it could have been done any other way. Had it been overly painstaking and thorough, it might have lost out in pace and visual interest, though I did not tell this to Sidney Franklin in 1957 when we discussed the film.

Shearer planned to attend the premiere on August 16,

1938, in New York, but then learned that a union was picketing the theater. She decided that it would politically unwise to cross the picket lines, and waited for the Hollywood premiere instead. But even then she was defending the picture itself. Explaining why she had had to skip the New York event, and denying reports of illness, she told a reporter: "I was perfectly well and I looked forward to [the premiere] with a sort of embarrassed egotism-pride in the picture which I think is wonderful, even if the metropolitan press isn't entirely in accord with me, and embarrassment because it takes something like conceit to ogle one's efforts in company with a theater audience."

In September Norma did a version of *Marie Antoinette* on the Maxwell House Coffee Radio Hour, with Robert Young opposite her. "She was sensitive and touching," one review stated, "and her radio voice is deeply compelling."

While the Stewart-Vajda-West scenes admittedly take liberties with history, the dialogue is highly literate, rousing in the more flamboyant scenes, moving in the quieter, more personal and tender sequences. The facts of the tragic queen who perished in the French Revolution are basically there, and presented in entertaining terms a modern audience can understand.

Some scenes are superb: the grotesque honeymoon night of Shearer and the gross, pathetic dauphin, played brilliantly by Robert Morley, who is ashamed of his ungainly ugliness and helpless to please the ambitions of his domineering grandfather, Louis XV, tellingly enacted by John Barrymore. When DuBarry (Gladys George) insultingly sends Marie an empty cradle on her second wedding anniversary to symbolize her barrenness (the Morley character is impotent at first), she changes from passive victim to defiant schemer. "I will become the brightest, highest star in all this court," she icily informs her timid husband, who keeps repeating forlornly, "It will do no good—the king is the king."

Soon she is up to her ears in cynical court intrigue and obsessive pleasure-seeking, leading a coterie of dilettantes and fops led by the scheming Duc D'Orleans (Joseph Schildkraut). She meets a handsome young Swedish count (Tyrone Power) at a gaming house, dallies with him heartlessly, then proceeds to lose a priceless diamond necklace on a wager. At this the Austrian ambassador (Henry Stephenson) reprovingly informs her that she is the first Dauphine of France to be openly spoken of as a wanton.

After she blatantly humiliates DuBarry at a ball, Louis XV wants to send her back to Austria, but he dies before the threat is carried out. Now Queen of France, with a husband who has suddenly recovered his potency and is ready to be a true husband to her and who expresses his total need of her, she forgoes her love for the Swedish count, who had been prepared to champion her in her temporary disgrace. But Morley's Louis XVI shows himself a weak, bumbling, undignified king, however well meaning, and all her efforts to shore him up fail. The words of the cynical old king come true: "After me, the deluge!"

Shearer and Van Dyke then push the picture busily and speedily (but excitingly and dynamically) through the horrors of the revolution, the sack of the palace, the abortive attempt to escape to the border, then the final disaster of imprisonment in the temple and the executions, first of Louis XVI, then of Marie.

The final scenes are poignant and moving, in the finest tradition of quality cinema. Morley is impressive during the sequence showing his final night with his family. Marie's son is taken from her by the revolutionists, and then comes the terrible wait for her own death. When the moment arrives, at long last, as she stands dazed and grimly meditative as the guillotine blade rises inexorably, she is taken back in time and we see her as a girl in Austria declaring delightedly to her mother, Empress Maria Theresa: "Just think, Mama, I shall be a queen! I shall be Queen of France!" (a re-creation of the first scene in the film).

As I reported in *The Great Romantic Films*:

Miss Shearer dominates the film throughout, not only because scriptwriters, director and all concerned have focused on her but because her beauty and talent magnetize the attention. It takes a true star to shine amidst so much glittering splendor and mammoth production opulence; there is pageantry; there are revolutionary onslaughts, palace-stormings, court balls, crowded theatre scenes—in all of them the star is the centerpiece.

I added:

Special commendation should be given Cedric Gibbons's art direction. The magnificent ballrooms, grand staircases, halls, etc. look as authentic as anything can get outside Versailles itself. Herbert Stothart's music is affecting and tender in the intimate scenes where such is required; rousing, martial, alarumed, triumphantly vital when needed—a tour de force of movie musical expression. . . . William Daniels's photography and the dances staged by Albertina Rasch are also a delight.

. . . *Marie Antoinette* is one of those films one ponders long afterward, savoring certain scenes in memory, recalling an inflection here, a gesture there, a line of dialogue that is particularly sharp and apropos. Well written, well acted, lavishly produced with the full resources of 1938 MGM—and that was full indeed—*Marie Antoinette* is one of the more underrated films of that or any era, but thanks to frequent revivals—and unfortunately frequent TV appearances where it is cruelly cut—the film has gathered a cult coterie, and there is little likelihood that it will lose it. There is one truism more true and pertinent than the oft-repeated "True Art Never Dates" and that is that "True Art Sometimes Gets Belatedly Discovered." So with this Shearer gem.

Young Tyrone Power, then twenty-three to Shearer's thirty-seven, was borrowed from Twentieth-Century-Fox, reportedly at Norma's request, to play the young idealist,

the Swedish count Axel Fersen, with whom the queen falls
in love. Since he was committed to another film that was to
start shortly, all of Power's scenes were shot first, out of
sequence. Shearer's love scenes with him carried ultimate
conviction, and in a scene that I consider the finest love
sequence ever filmed, she tries to explain to him why his
goodness and decency, his innocent adoration and manly
affirmation, have so moved her, with the result that for the
first time in her life she has fallen in love. No one could
speak more tellingly than Shearer such dialogue from that
scene as: "When we first met, my heart stood still. I knew
then, really . . . knew that love could be great and terrible
and everlasting. . . . I thought love came more happily . . .
perhaps the great loves come with tears."

She believed every one of those words from the script, for
the fact was that Norma fell in love with Tyrone Power when
they first met on the set. "She was profoundly in love with
him," cameraman William Daniels said years later. "That is
why her scenes with him carried such deep conviction. A glow
seemed to come over her, a radiance such as I had not seen in
her in years. Of course she had been a widow for over a year
and a half then, much of that time immersed in illness and
seclusion. He brought her fully alive, but I don't think Ty
realized to what extent. . . ."

Did Power return her love? Anita Louise, for one, did not
feel that he did: "He was only a kid, fourteen years her
junior, and had only been a star for a year over at Twentieth,
and I think he was trying to get his impressions sorted out."
Louise (later the wife of Twentieth-Century-Fox producer
Buddy Adler) felt Power was honestly in awe of Shearer, and
of course she could be very charming and overwhelmingly
persuasive. It was, moreover, to his interest to stay in her
good graces. A sensitive bisexual, Power was accustomed to
receiving the adoration—and attentions—of both men and
women. He had had a rumored affair with Robin Thomas,
Diana Barrymore's flamboyantly homosexual half-brother,
when he was twenty and unknown. Later he was to be linked

with Errol Flynn and other males, while courting such feminine luminaries as Sonja Henie, Loretta Young, and the
woman he would later make his first wife—Annabella. Director Henry King felt that Power was inescapably forced into
narcissism, with all the power drives that went with such self-
concentration. He was fully aware that costars often imagined
themselves "in love" during intimate scenes—sometimes
those feelings were reciprocated and were consummated off-
set; sometimes they went unrequited. Usually they were dissi-
pated into other interests once the picture was over and real
life intruded yet again.

It is possible that Power, a sensitive, introspective, and
highly intelligent young man, was aware of Shearer's true
feelings. Or perhaps, sensing her loneliness, he felt she had
fallen in love with love, albeit in a highly mature and womanly manner.

"I think that, with the kindest intentions, Ty led her on,"
Billy Grady, the MGM casting director and an old friend of
mine, told me. "He was a singularly guileless and sweet guy; I
don't think he did it to get publicity for himself or the picture;
he wasn't the calculating type when it came to such matters. I
think it was just that he was in love with her being in love
with him—for lack of a better way to put it." Power spent
much time on the set with Norma; he visited her home and
played with her children, then aged eight and three. He accompanied her to the Hollywood premiere of *Marie Antoinette,* and photos taken of them at that event show both
glowing and happy. Did they sleep together? Eddie Mannix
and Hunt Stromberg both doubted it. "Norma was a one-man
woman, and she wanted marriage—she might go all out for
the romantic aspect but at that point in her life consummation
physically was something she took damned seriously. She was
a very controlled woman in that regard, very dignified, very
aware of the realities—a real combination of romantic and
realist." That was how Mannix saw it. Henry King felt that
Power would have slept with her if she had indicated a deep
need of that kind: "Ty was far more casual about bedding

people down than she was—the funny thing was that he could be promiscuous and at the same time basically decent and honorable. That combination was catnip to the women who adored him."

Eventually Shearer sent Power away. His being at a different studio, with different friends and interests, doubtless helped her in her decision. Her common sense, in the long run, triumphed over her womanly needs. "Norma always does the sensible thing—even if it almost kills her," said her brother-in-law, director Howard Hawks. And, as always, she had a strong sense of duty toward her children.

Shearer always remained gracious to Ty Power, and—at a distance—concerned about his career fortunes and personal well-being. When he married Annabella in 1939, she sent them a warm telegram of congratulations. Power always spoke highly of her in later years. "She's a real lady," he told Henry Hathaway, "and one of the most cultivated, refined, sensitive people I ever met."

Jerry Asher, the publicist and fan magazine writer, told me that he was present during a swimming date with Power and Errol Flynn, and he remembers Flynn asking about Shearer: "How was the lady in the sack?" Power's face darkened, he recalled, and he said sharply: "Don't talk about Norma like that!" Flynn, who could be cutting and sarcastic, especially when he was in his cups, snapped, "What do I care for your dirty little secrets, Ty!" and got into his car and drove off.

"Those three years after her husband's death, when she tried to lose herself in movie making and social life, were very lonely for her," Asher remembered. "Joan Crawford, who never liked her, used to make catty, nasty cracks about Norma robbing different cradles. 'I know she liked that young crewman,' Joan would snicker. 'Where did they go when they both disappeared after shooting was over?' But I never believed that about Norma. The quick affair or pickup or whatever you want to call it was never her style." Asher conceded that Norma had affairs but that "she conducted them with class."

She found much happiness with the children, and was delighted to get back to them that April of 1938, after Van Dyke's marathon ten-week shooting schedule on *Marie Antoinette* was over with and the protracted period of cutting and scoring began. She spent much time swimming and taking the children on outings. At three, little Katherine's personality was blossoming; she was a pretty and precocious child, always laughing and mischievous. At eight, young Irving was more serious and introspective. "He was old enough to remember his father, and he took the death hard—very hard," George Cukor told me.

Upon the completion of *Marie Antoinette,* Norma was to find herself smack in the middle of the Search-for-Scarlett competition adroitly staged by David O. Selznick in order to keep interest alive in the 1936 novel he had purchased for filming—Margaret Mitchell's *Gone With the Wind.* It had swept the country the year of its publication, shooting up to the top of the best-seller lists.

From 1936 to 1938 Selznick and his shrewd publicity man, Russell Birdwell, kept the country agog with the "Scarlett" hunt—with all manner of young women getting "tested." The screen tests proliferated, with the likes of the young Lana Turner and the young Susan Hayward doing their bit; Turner was rejected because her talent was found wanting; Hayward because she was considered "a shade too young." Meanwhile established actresses, starlets, and unknowns alike trouped in and out of the testing area.

Katharine Hepburn was one of the top stars who fought hard for the role, and went so far as to declare publicly "I *am* Scarlett," despite the fact that she was a New Englander, replete with the distinctive twang, and angular as against Scarlett's curvy persona—at least as the public visualized it. Selznick knocked Hepburn out of the ring with the statement "I just can't imagine Rhett Butler chasing *her* for ten years." For that matter, neither could anyone else, and Kate retreated sullenly.

Finally, after rejecting the sprightly and feisty Paulette

Goddard because she couldn't prove she was respectably wed to Charlie Chaplin (Selznick feared women's clubs disapproval), his thoughts turned to Norma. She owned a share of Selznick International, because Thalberg had put one hundred thousand dollars into the company when Selznick first formed it—in Shearer's name. She was a major star who was in the process of making a "Super-Comeback" in *Marie Antoinette,* in which she had proved beyond doubt that she could dominate an expensive, lengthy, elaborate production. Selznick also admired her as an actress, and she and Gable had worked together in the past, with notable success.

There was one factor that Selznick left out of his calculations, though: the reaction of Shearer's numerous fans across the country. They thought of her as a lady—queenly, morally impeccable (at least in her more recent films), a model widow, a model mother, refined, womanly, affirmative. Scarlett was a bitch supreme, contrary, willful, ruthless, destructive, given to chasing other women's men, and consummately self-seeking.

For a time Selznick persuaded Norma that the role was right for her. She was eager to top her role as *Marie Antoinette* by delivering another "big" picture that would reinforce her comeback after a two-year absence. Selznick and Shearer conferred; he implied that the "bitchy" aspects of Scarlett could be softened—after all, hadn't the real Marie Antoinette been something of a bitch, before the screenwriters got hold of her? There were many bravura aspects to the role that Shearer could swat home in grand style—and her friend George Cukor, who had done so much for her Juliet, would be at the helm, or so it appeared at the time. And she and Gable had the right mutual chemistry.

So Norma let Howard Strickling of MGM and the Selznick people spread the word via strategically placed items in the gossip columns, that she was leaning toward accepting the role. At that, her fans came alive—they flooded the mails from Maine to California, from Washington State to Florida, begging her to back off. The letters' basic tone was "You're too nice a person to play such a bitch!" With her fans against her accepting the role plus her own strong doubts about her suitability—despite all Selznick's and Cukor's assurances that Scarlett could be "tailored" to her measure and could be "softened" to "win more sympathy"—she decided "graciously" (according to the publicists and spokesmen for all concerned) to withdraw her name from consideration. No one stressed her secret relief, or even so much as hinted at it.

Years later, Norma confirmed her original attitude when she told me: "I felt she was too minxy and mischievous for the persona I had developed in my screen roles." Even so, she indicated that her rejection of Scarlett might have been a major mistake, adding "It *might* have had a *cumulative* effect—with one major production following upon another and all those advantages in the mounting and publicizing." (Her two other mistakes, of course, were refusing the 1940 *Pride and Prejudice* and the 1942 *Mrs. Miniver,* which helped carry Greer Garson to major stardom.)

Selznick, after testing and theorizing on more major stars—even such unlikelies as Joan Crawford and Barbara Stanwyck were interested at one time or another—finally settled on Vivien Leigh late in 1938, after shooting had already begun. In recent years there have been reports that he had Vivien in mind all along, having liked her in the 1938 *A Yank at Oxford* with Robert Taylor and in her English films, such as *Fire Over England* (1937). The famous story that she showed up suddenly during the "burning of Atlanta" sequence and was presented to Selznick with the words "Here is your Scarlett" smack of a publicist's brainstorm. Selznick had simply determined that the search was over—*had* to be over, with production launched, and Leigh, reportedly high on his list all along, was designated to be *it*—leading on to her 1939 Oscar and world acclaim.

Meanwhile, over at MGM, Shearer was giving much thought to what her second picture under the six-picture deal would be. *Marie Antoinette* was obviously a tough act to follow and its long-range box-office returns were not yet in, but she knew that Mayer would not indulge her in another costly extravaganza.

Among the projects suggested was a Pulitzer prize–winning play by her old admirer Robert E. Sherwood, *Idiot's Delight*. It had made quite a splash on Broadway in 1936, starring that peerless theater duo Alfred Lunt and Lynn Fontanne, and had toured successfully for over a year. Later it had been a hit in London with Raymond Massey and Tamara Geva. After it was sold to MGM, Sherwood had been invited to write the screenplay. *Idiot's* antifascist message was even more timely in 1938 than in 1936, and Sherwood was confident that he could make it even more pertinent for an early-1939 release, what with Hitler running wild in one European country after another.

The role of the phony Russian countess, originally a little trouper hailing from Omaha, Nebraska, and other points, had elements of high-gloss glamour and characterization that appealed to Shearer. Mayer had decided that if Norma accepted the role, he would cast Clark Gable opposite her. In September 1938 Gable had three months to go before reporting to *Gone With the Wind*. Mayer wanted to keep him busy and keep him before audiences, and also felt that the pairing of Gable, the future Rhett Butler, and Shearer, who rejected the role of Scarlett, would make for good business.

Mayer promised Shearer a high-gloss production. She asked for George Cukor to direct, but he was being held for *Gone With the Wind*. Mayer suggested Clarence Brown, who had worked with her successfully in the 1931 *A Free Soul*. Gable had been in that, too, and under Brown's guidance he had become a major star. Norma liked Brown personally—he was an amiable teddy bear of a man who worked diligently and proficiently without being an outstanding, auteurlike artist— but she felt that the theme and treatment cried out for Cukor's ministrations. But, with a shrug, she accepted Brown; she could always meddle and direct herself, if need be . . .

Gable had mixed feelings about the project. He saw the logic of Mayer's pairing of him with Shearer, but he felt the role of Harry Van, the song-and-dance man traveling with an all-girl troupe through Europe, a bit tough to get a handle on, and moreover he would have to do a dance number. Norma made him uneasy in more ways than one. He knew that she liked all the special accoutrements of stardom, that he would have to dance attendance on her special lighting insistences and on her assorted perfectionist demands. Between 1931 and 1939 their box-office positions had been reversed; he was the one with the clout now—king of the movies. Would she want to meet him on an equal footing?

"Thalberg is gone—she has to fend for herself now," Eddie Mannix reminded him. "Hell, that makes her even more dangerous—she owns a hunk of MGM stock and she makes her own decisions and she's showing herself a real tigress," Gable replied.

And there was another reason for Gable to feel nervous. Shearer had been a widow for two years, and as the saying went: "Those widows knew their onions." He had heard of her thing for Tyrone Power on her previous picture. Gable frankly considered Power a boy (Power was twenty-four to his thirty-seven in 1938). Norma might be more ready for a man now, since she was a free agent, and could he handle it—off-screen, that was.

His girlfriend, Carole Lombard, shared his fears. She had heard the rumors of Shearer's roving eye for boys *and* men, and when production began she proceeded to make a nuisance of herself on the set, even though she was supposed to be making a picture with James Stewart *(Made for Each Other)* over at Selznick Studios. To Carole, it didn't help that Stewart was also said to be the object of the Widow Thalberg's romantic interest. "It was a confusing foursome, that's for sure," Billy Grady laughingly recalled. "There was Gable acting with a woman who might suddenly express a personal interest in him, while Gable's real gal was acting in a picture with another of Shearer's crushes—Lombard was a feisty, fightin' gal and she didn't like being fenced in—no way—even if it was only in her imagination. And nice old Clarence Brown trying to control it all, too!"

But Lombard, having initially exhausted herself kibitzing on the *Idiot's Delight* set, finally settled down into the Jimmy Stewart picture, directed by no-nonsense John Cromwell, who along with Stewart reportedly assured her that Norma was a nice lady who promptly desisted if her attentions proved unwelcome. Carole wasn't so sure about *that,* but her role was an interesting one and eventually her schedule forced her to leave Gable to the widow's tender mercies. She need not have worked up any sweat.

Clarence Brown later remembered that Shearer and Gable went through their paces dutifully. Yes, their love scenes carried conviction, at least on her part, as he remembered it, but there wasn't any special chumminess off-set. Joseph Schildkraut, again on hand for a Shearer starring vehicle, later recalled a tense Norma hissing to him, after a particularly difficult scene: "I don't like false teeth on men—I'm sure he clacks them to annoy me." (Gable's teeth were false, as was well-known.) When Gable avoided her after a scene finished, she told Pat Paterson (Mrs. Charles Boyer) who had a supporting role: "He's just afraid of Carole." Paterson said to friends later: "I don't think Gable was ever really her type— of course she respected his climb to major stardom but she found him on the crude side—it was a chemical thing." Others felt she was the roving widow out to prove herself with all comers, at least in preliminary skirmishes.

Idiot's Delight, Pulitzer and all, was a heavily political play that Sherwood took seriously, perhaps too seriously. It was a pompous, ungainly, murky affair about a group of people stranded at a Swiss hotel as a world war is about to break out (a portent of things to come); Shearer as the fake countess, complete with snazzy Adrian getups and a long blond wig, is the mistress of munitions tycoon Edward Arnold, who proceeds to desert her; Gable and his girls are also among those stranded; as are Pat Paterson and Peter Willes, a young married couple; Burgess Meredith, a passionate pacifist; Charles Coburn, a research scientist; and Joseph Schildkraut, an officer of indeterminate origins and allegiances. As the war clouds loom menacingly, there is much high-flown, rather stagebound gab about war and peace and the rights of man and the values of freedom. Shearer denounces her munitions-man lover and is left behind to face the bombs, while Gable, who at first recalls with cynical amusement the naive girl in Omaha who had once loved him, finds he returns her feeling and leaves everything and everyone to remain with her at the climax, at which they drink a toast to life and hope while singing "Onward Christian Soldiers." Yes, it is confused, and in the final analysis the mix fails to jell.

Idiot's Delight is primarily an exhibition of MGM Star Power Transcendent. Shearer makes a lot of her wild clothes and hairdo and phony Russian accent and flamboyant continental airs, but the role makes somewhat inexplicable her metamorphosis from Omaha, Nebraska, trouper to such studied and sophisticated elegance. Still it is a star-turn in spades. Well lighted, well dressed, well photographed, and, yet again, to a large extent self-directed, Norma makes a bewitching figure, but the writing and general thematics defeat her attempts at a completely successful portrait. Gable performs well when he sings and dances the hilarious number with six girls called "Puttin' on the Ritz," (Lombard reportedly coached him at home), but he is awkward and seems almost bored during the scenes when he *doesn't* have to look sardonic at Shearer's *grande-dame* flouncings.

Clarence Brown told me years later that he didn't think the picture had come off too well. "The Sherwood high-falutin' polemics got in the way of the romance," he said, "and I for one never felt that a gal like Irene (before *or* after Omaha) and a guy like Harry Van would ever make it in real life."

Sherwood, who had held the Lunts' stage portrayals in high esteem, seemed to have liked its transcription to the screen, calling Shearer "beautiful" in the part and Gable "very funny." But he did admit that something extra was missing: the pathos the Lunts had injected beneath the sparkling comic surfaces. He also felt that much of the bite of the play's message had been cut, with a confusing result.

Lynn Fontanne, with her usual graciousness, had told him:

"It's the play that counts, and it makes no difference who acts it." But Sherwood knew better.

The reviews of *Idiot's Delight* were mixed, as Mayer, who never cared for the final result, predicted to Mannix and others. In some reviews Gable came across better than Shearer, with *Newsweek* declaring: "Clark Gable's hard-boiled hoofer is a fine characterization. Norma Shearer plays a difficult and purposely exaggerated role to the hilt and perhaps a little farther," adding: "With an extra credit for its worthy intention, *Idiot's Delight* is refreshingly intelligent entertainment." *The Nation* was even harsher on her, with its critic snapping "Miss Shearer is even more pretentious than her pretentious part." Edwin Schallert in *The Los Angeles Times* rose to the lady's defense, however: "Miss Shearer displayed a maximum of skill in her impersonation of a peculiarly fantastic heroine." Other critics, not knowing just what to make of the film, tried to have it both ways with adjectives like "meaningful," "intelligent," "classy," "adult," and "worthy."

The picture did make money—due in large part to Gable's 1939 blockbuster box-office clout—but Norma realized that *Idiot's Delight* was not a worthy follow-up to *Marie Antoinette*.

Her next film, however, was to recover all the lost ground—and more.

14

The Women: Cat Fights Deluxe

"T HE CAT Fight of the Century!" That was how they referred to *The Women* in the corridors, dressing rooms, commissary, and executive offices of Metro-Goldwyn-Mayer in the summer of 1939. Soon Hollywood and the whole country were dubbing it just that. Mayer had bought Clare Boothe's scintillating Broadway play about the manners and mores of upper-middle-class wives, mistresses, and assorted hangers-on, their man troubles, bitchy feuds, competitiveness, and assorted high-jinks. Boothe's 1937 theater piece had been a sensation. She said later that it was based on years of dispassionate observation of the ways of her sex, and she had been determined to see her subject "clearly and whole." "I knew it wouldn't make me personally popular," Boothe (later the wife of *Time* publisher Henry Luce) said, "but I was out to tell the truth, the whole truth and nothing but. I was surprised later when I got a lot of fan letters from women telling me they admired my honesty!"

Shearer had seen the play in New York and wanted to do it as a film. The fact that the starring role kept Shearer front and center for most of the action, with the other actresses relegated to what were really expanded character roles, may have sold her conclusively on the project, as she felt she had lost ground with *Idiot's Delight*. Here was a juicy chance to recoup her losses. Mary Haines, the deceived wife and mother, is forced to weather the assorted unkindnesses and gossipy proclivities of her friends while defending herself against a particularly nasty other-woman type who steals her husband and marries him. Eventually, however, she falls victim to Mary's righteous-indignation-inspired retaliation tactics that bring her erring husband back.

The Women also offered Norma strong lines and situations, which she knew she could get her teeth into to good effect. Soon she was off and running with a prime cast that included Joan Crawford (who else?) as her love rival; Rosalind Russell, in a departure from her usual sugary, sedate self as the bitchy gossip who enjoys watching her friends squirm; Paulette Goddard as a chorus girl about town; Joan Fontaine (pre-*Rebecca*) as the wifely wren who is the sweet-and-vulnerable member of the team; and such character stalwarts as Mary Boland as a man-izing, oft-divorced countess, Lucile Watson as Shearer's mother who knows the ways of women, Virginia Weidler as Shearer's daughter, little Mary, and Cora Witherspoon and Hedda Hopper as ladies in attendance, of a sort.

One of the amusing aspects of *The Women* came immediately after the formal credit cards. Each of the principals was portrayed as some type of animal. Shearer was depicted as a species of deer. Crawford, of course, was a tigress. Russell was a black pussycat, Boland a donkey, Fontaine a lamb, Goddard a fox, Phyllis Povah (as an overweight wife with too many children) a cow, Watson an owl, Weidler a doe, and Reno housekeeper Marjorie Main a mule.

Another highlight was the color insert of a fashion show, which ran five minutes and is often cut in television reruns. The principals are trying on clothes at a salon. A slew of beautiful models from the salon appear first in tennis outfits

with accompanying tennis action. They then switch to swimming, and a variety of swimsuits are on display as the girls
sashay around in typical modeling poses. Then follows a "day
at the zoo," with the girls sporting a variety of "afternoon-
outing" apparel. By late afternoon, gardening is the prime
activity, and the models appear in casual afternoon frocks.
The show winds up with a theater sequence, showing hand-
somely dressed models in elaborate evening attire rising from
their "seats" to tour the "theater lobby."

Color was still a sufficient novelty in 1939 to bring this sequence considerable press notice, and though it lasted only
five minutes out of 132, *Variety* commented: "It's a gorgeous
display of fashions from bathing costumes to evening gowns
and wraps . . . it's a dazzling appeal to the women, but even
here it stops dramatic progress and [the] switch back to black
and white photography when the thread of the story is picked
up again requires several minutes for audience adjustment to
[the] change." Despite *Variety*'s opinion, the color sequence
won favorable comments from audiences.

Mayer and producer Hunt Stromberg had originally assigned *The Women* to director Ernst Lubitsch, but when
George Cukor was taken off *Gone With the Wind* because
Gable felt he favored the ladies in the cast and insisted on
"man's man" Victor Fleming, Cukor was put in charge of
"that feminine kennel," as Hedda Hopper dubbed it.

Cukor, a homosexual who was very popular with his female
stars because he understood their psychology and could antici-
pate, control, and soothe their moods, always claimed to me
that he wasn't quite sure why Selznick had taken him off
GWTW, but scuttlebutt later had it that he made Gable nervous by calling him "dear." Furthermore, his presence reminded the film's foremost he-man that he had had a sexual
affair with William Haines in the 1920s to further his career;
of course Cukor knew of this, or so Gable felt.

Lubitsch, who had been expected to lend his cynical continental flair to a film that was essentially mordant, hard-edged,
realistic, and cruelly witty (as against so much of the gooey

"women's picture" material MGM and other studios were turning out at the time), was switched to directing Garbo in the witty and stylish *Ninotchka* ("Garbo Laughs!"). Cukor, who told reporters he felt he was truly in his element with *The Women,* was philosophical about losing *GWTW,* and was prepared to have "the time of his life."

There was so much gossip about how catty, vicious, mean, and cynical *The Women* was turning out to be that MGM's publicity chief, Howard Strickling, asked Norma to authorize a studio publicity release, couched as an interview with her, that set matters straight—or at least brought them into middle ground.

Seeing Strickling's point, Shearer wrote her own statement, then gave it to him to polish for release. Thalberg had always told his wife that she had an excellent "public relations" feel, and the statement bears this out. It went:

> I think women are more romantic than men, but on the other hand, men are more sentimental than women. Women are much better sports nowadays than they used to be. Their feelings are not so easily hurt. They know better how to take it on the chin. They are not as stupidly sensitive as women of another age. Perhaps, along with that, they lack some of the sentimental idealism that Mary has in the picture. When I saw the play in New York, I felt it to be a brilliant observation of women's many-faceted personalities. Each character in the picture represents a definite and recognizable type, even the heavy of the film, the gossip who almost wrecks Mary's life.

When I interviewed Anita Loos on *The Women* (she had cowritten the screenplay with Jane Murfin), she told me something that was then little known—that Norma had actively initiated the choice of Joan Crawford as Crystal Allen, her rival for her husband's affections. (No men appear in the film, even in minor roles, a novel idea for 1939 that was a real draw for the audience.) Crawford, feeling that her last few pictures had been inadequate (they were) and still smarting from the 1938 "box-office poison" label tacked on her by a movie trade paper, had actively campaigned for the role. While George Cukor told her the role was relatively small, Crawford felt it had bite and that she could stand out in it; it would furthermore represent a departure from the stuff she had been doing, which had featured variations on women hurt by handsome heels and shopgirls struggling upward toward minks and diamonds. What Crawford didn't know was that she had a secret ally in Shearer, who always put the good of a picture ahead of any personal considerations. "Norma knew that she and Joan, highlighted as love rivals, complete with the juicy, catty scenes I wrote for them, would bring them into theaters," Loos told me. "I think it helped things along a great deal."

Another ambitious actress, Rosalind Russell, was also trying to get away from type, and she begged for the part of Sylvia Fowler, the malicious gossip. Given her "nice girl," passive image, there was some doubt that she could do it. But Loos was present when Russell put on an informal "preview" for Cukor and Stromberg, aided by lines Anita had fed her— and they were so impressed that the part was hers.

The billing was originally to have read "Norma Shearer and Joan Crawford in *The Women*," but Russell suddenly waxed aggressive and demanded her name over the title with the other two. Stromberg consulted with Shearer. "Why not? She's working hard and giving a good performance that builds up the picture," Norma replied. But Stromberg sensed that Shearer, who was sensitive about billings and always took the top spot, was not overly enthusiastic. Accordingly, though Russell got above the title, her name was somewhat smaller than the others in the credit cards.

Anita Loos disagreed with Bosley Crowther's statement that without Thalberg, Shearer in 1939 was not particularly in favor at court. "She owned a piece of the company, for heaven's sake!" Loos barked. "She got her full share of deference, believe you me! As an individual, she was actually more powerful than before Irving's death! And she knew it. No one tried to upstage her. She could be gracious and kind, but she was never weak or easy; always she upheld her hard-won prerogatives."

Despite getting what she considered a major casting break, Crawford felt herself at a disadvantage, as she always did vis-à-vis the Widow Thalberg. "I worked hard for my success in that picture," she told me more than once. "No one handed me anything on a silver platter." Cukor told me how impressed he had been with Crawford's versatility as Arch-Cat Crystal. After the picture was completed, Norma, who was getting ever more picky about her roles, refused Rachel Crothers's Broadway play, *Susan and God,* about a flighty society matron who neglects husband and child for a religious fad. Cukor persuaded Mayer that Crawford would do well in it; Crawford got the role, and this led to other versatile performances, including the 1941 *A Woman's Face* with Cukor again.

Shearer also actively aided the reports of on-set "feuding" between herself and Crawford; the fan mags and general dailies ate it up, and the girls helped it along, "and they didn't just do it in fun," as Cukor told me. In one famous on-set episode, which Hedda Hopper later told me had never been correctly reported, Crawford and Shearer were doing what was known as a line reading, with one actress who is saying her lines being fed by the other. Crawford, who was to do the "feeding," was rudely inattentive, and sat there clicking away at her knitting. According to Hopper, Norma sharply told her to act professional or go back to her dressing room and Joan called her the biggest bitch in town and walked off the set. Cukor, who secretly enjoyed refereeing temperamental feuds between female stars, rushed off after Crawford to reprimand her but Shearer shouted after him: "George, how dare you leave me standing here!" The scene was eventually finished to everyone's satisfaction, but later Crawford sent Shearer a nasty telegram featuring language so strong that it barely got past the teletypist's standards for decent wording. When I

asked Anita Loos about this, she told me she thought Howard
Strickling had probably drafted the Crawford telegram "just
to keep things percolating for publicity purposes." She added:
"Norma and Joan could never have been personal friends—
they came from different worlds—Norma thought Joan crude
and pushy and Joan considered Norma overbearing and up-
pity—but they both knew the 'feud' was good copy, and so
they helped it along. And why not?"

When Hedda Hopper once questioned Crawford about her
relationship with Norma, the canny Joan volunteered a re-
sponse that, Hedda told me, assured her once and for all that
Joan was a genius at double-edged self-publicizing. "So many
people say Norma and I dislike each other—who are we to
disagree with the majority opinion?"

When *The Women* was remade in 1956 as *The Opposite
Sex,* with kittenish June Allyson in the Shearer role, vixenish
Joan Collins (decades before Alexis) in the Crawford part,
and a generous assortment of male characters (unlike the earlier film), Hedda asked Crawford what she thought about it.
"It's ridiculous," she snapped. "Norma and I might not ever
have been bosom buddies, but we *towered* compared to those
pygmies in the remake!" Which was the nearest thing to a
compliment, public or private, that Miss Joan Crawford ever
paid to Miss Norma Shearer. *The Opposite Sex* was one of the
year's flops.

Twenty years ago, as I was writing *The Films of Joan Crawford,* I told Joan (tactlessly, I fear) that I hoped to do a book
on Norma Shearer one day. Her voice sharpened and her face
grew stony, her eyes cold. "*Someone* should!" she snapped.
"She's all but forgotten." While this was not a true statement
at the time, I let it stand allowing for Joan's quirks. Another
time I asked Shearer if she wanted to contribute anything on
Crawford. "She's said it all herself, hasn't she?" Norma
laughed. "I don't think I have anything to add." This gentle
riposte at Crawford's constant publicity seeking was the nearest Shearer came to malice in speaking of her colleague.

The Women runs for one hundred thirty-two minutes but it

plays fast-paced; it is witty, brilliant, full of good lines. That fine character actress, Lucile Watson, who plays Shearer's mother, is comforting her in a scene in which Norma wonders if her husband has grown tired of her. "He's tired of *himself*," Watson replies. "It's being there with him at the *end* that counts." Crawford, surveying the cats about her after she has been bested in the famous powder-room confrontation, makes a memorable observation about there being no name for those ladies outside of a kennel. The hilarious Mary Boland, countess with an eye for young studs, keeps chanting, "Ah, l'amour, l'amour!" When Shearer tells Crawford that what she is wearing is too vulgar for her refined husband's tastes, Crawford spits back, with venomous wit: "When Stephen doesn't like what I'm wearing, I *take it off*!"

At the end of *The Women*, after Shearer has put on "jungle red" fingernails and gone out to battle for her man with the powder-room cats, she delivers a line that over the years has come to be associated with her. She has won back her husband after exposing Crawford's philandering, and as she rushes to meet him another character asks: "But what about your pride?" "Pride is a luxury that a woman in love can't afford!" Shearer replies.

When *The Women* was released in September 1939, Shearer received some of her best reviews ever. Frank Nugent in *The New York Times* wrote: "Miss Shearer as Mary Haines, whose divorce and matrimonial comeback keep the cat fight going, is virtually the only member of the all feminine cast who behaves as one of Hollywood's leading ladies is supposed to. And even Miss Shearer's Mary sharpens her talons finally and joins the birds of prey. It is, parenthetically, one of the best performances she has given."

Edwin Schallert in *The Los Angeles Times* felt that Shearer had portrayed her character "with deeply-felt finesse." Harry Mines in *The Los Angeles News* felt that her performance was "earnestly expressed," and *Variety*'s verdict was: "Miss Shearer delivers a sparkling performance . . . Miss Crawford is ruthless and tough-shelled as the husband stealer." "Mordant, mature, smart, brilliant, solid" were the adjectives used to describe the picture itself.

Delighted with the reviews and financial returns on *The Women,* Norma decided that it was time to relax and vacation. She went to New York, where she was entertained by Charles Boyer and his wife, (Pat Paterson). It was at their home that she met George Raft.

15

Playing the Field— and George Raft

A T THE time he and Norma crossed paths, George Raft was forty-four years old. He had come into the movies with the first talkies, ten years before, and had reached stardom as the coin-flipping Guido Rinaldo in the 1932 *Scarface,* which had starred Paul Muni as a notoriously realistic Al Capone. A product of New York's Hell's Kitchen, the crime-ridden slum area, Raft had been a professional pugilist, then had danced in ballrooms before debuting in nightclubs and on Broadway. A real-life product of The Roaring Twenties, Raft admitted to close associations with notorious mobsters, some of whom, he said, had proven "real pals in time of need."

Commendable as his loyalty may have been, those early associations were to subject Raft, during the time of his greatest stardom in the 1930s and 1940s, to a host of unpleasant rumors, similar to those that later dogged Frank Sinatra. "Hell, I don't keep tabs on what my old friends do with and to other people," he once told Ruth Waterbury during a *Photoplay* interview. "All I know is that they were good friends to *me.* Friends are friends. It's a cold world out there, honey, and we all need friends." Ruth told me later that they couldn't run the story because Raft had been overly frank about Hollywood moguls and their women friends. She did show me her old notes, and they were sizzlers in which George dished the dirt about such matters as Darryl Zanuck exposing himself and masturbating in front of petrified, goggling starlets "to get those broads' juices running," as Darryl put it, and Harry Cohn's "S & M" games with various actresses and his peepholes into their dressing rooms.

By 1939 Raft was a top Hollywood star specializing in criminals, con men, and other shady types. Earlier in the 1930s he had showcased his dancing-and-romancing skills with such actresses as Carole Lombard in *Bolero* and *Rumba*, but these had given way to the likes of *Each Dawn I Die* and *Invisible Stripes*, 1939 crime opuses in which he held his own with such Warner roughies as Cagney and Bogart.

At the party that night in New York, Shearer and Raft, to the surprise of all around them, hit it off famously. After talking and laughing all night, they left together. Pat Paterson later said: "We knew Norma was lonely and bored and at loose ends; we thought George's brash, natty ways would amuse her. No one ever dreamed she would fall *in love* with the man!"

Soon the Shearer-Raft duo were being seen all over New York. Norma had come primarily to take in the wonders of the New York World's Fair. As it happened, she was seen more frequently in Greenwich Village nightclubs and at the hotter spots with Raft, with the 1939 equivalent of paparazzi having a field day.

Next Norma and George went off to Paris with the Boyers. There they went hand in hand through Montmartre, Versailles, and the Louvre. By late August their romantic interlude in the City of Light was rudely interrupted by the imminence of World War II, and they high-tailed it back to New York via the liner *Manhattan* just in the nick of time. En route, Norma released a rather high-toned statement to the press (considering her giddy romantic fling with Raft) that featured such "First Lady" observations as: "As I come away from these grim preparations for war, I realize how blessed we are in the United States and how much we have to be thankful for."

George and Norma then proceeded on to Hollywood, where they continued their late-night rounds at the leading clubs and restaurants. Louella and Hedda (Hedda had joined the columning contingent in 1938) had a wonderful time with this strange new opposites-attract pairing. Shearer was to say years later that something about Raft had reminded her of Thalberg. But "the gentle, frail, petulant Irving never had *that* kind of pizazz!" Billy Grady told me. "I, for one, never did understand what Raft and Thalberg had in common!" In an interview with another writer, Shearer indicated that George's gamy ways and slightly shady reputation had somehow warmed and excited her patrician nature.

"She and Raft had more in common than people thought," Jerry Asher once told me. "The tough lady who took on the MGM bigwigs after Thalberg died ought to understand where a toughie like Raft was coming from, even if their ball parks weren't the same!" But George had a problem. He was unable to secure a divorce from the wife he had been saddled with since 1923, a former actress named Grayce Mulrooney. Hence he could not offer Norma what she badly wanted from him: marriage. There was also a problem with his recent girlfriend, Virginia Pine, who had resented her "costarring" role in a rather racy (for 1939) *Photoplay* story called "Hollywood's Unmarried Husbands and Wives," and which had made no bones about her six-year affair with Raft. Pine had left him after his European sojourn with Shearer. She later married (in 1942) the famed war correspondent Quentin Reynolds. She and George never met or spoke again.

In Hollywood through the rest of 1939 and through much of 1940, Shearer and Raft continued their red-hot affair. While maintaining separate establishments, they spent almost every night together, and Norma frequently stayed overnight at George's. George became pals with Irving and Katherine, even building a playhouse for the girl, who was then five. Raft cued Shearer in on the goings-on at the races, while she in turn took him to art galleries and museums. At Christmas 1939 he had given her a $5,000 diamond-and-ruby clip, while she had presented him with cuff links initialed in gold. Meanwhile Grayce Raft grew more demanding, irritated possibly by all the Raft-Shearer publicity. In 1940 she sued for, and won, a lump sum of $500,000 from George plus 20 percent of his earnings.

Shearer was forced to consider her duty to her children, who required a kind of order and stability in their lives that her liaison with George could not provide. She ended the affair. George proceeded to tell the press: "I am very much in love with Miss Shearer. She is the swellest person I have ever known, and I wish I could tell you that we are going to be married soon. If I could make the announcement it would be the happiest day of my life!" He then cited, yet again, his inability to win his marital freedom from Grayce Mulrooney. Norma later said of the break: "It was sad but necessary." She and Raft, however, continued to think, and speak, well of each other over the years.

16

The Final Three Films

A FTER relaxing for the better part of a year, during which time she occupied herself with her children, her home, her investments, and romance, Norma finally decided to return to the screen, for the fourth picture under her contract. *Escape,* a film version of the popular novel by Ethel Vance, was similar to *The Mortal Storm,* yet another refugee–escapes–from–Nazi Germany film. Norma's reasons for choosing this film are not entirely clear. She does not have as much footage as in former films, and perhaps she felt that besides being a good and timely theme (anti-Nazi films were the rage in 1940), it would not unduly tax her energies.

Earlier in 1940, Louis B. Mayer had done his best to persuade her to appear in the elaborate costumer, *Pride and Prejudice,* based on the classic Jane Austen novel of five husband-hunting sisters in the Regency period of nineteenth-century England. Mayer felt this would have proven a worthy follow-up to her indisputable triumph in *The Women,* and her role, as the stable, womanly, sensible sister whose "prejudice" against the snobbish "pride" of Mr. Darcy finally melts as they are romantically united, would have showcased her most creditably.

Shearer thought it over. Robert Z. Leonard, a director she
liked and admired, would be at the helm; MGM had counted
itself lucky to obtain the services of the brilliant new star Laurence Olivier, fresh from his *Wuthering Heights* and *Rebecca*
triumphs (Mayer told Mannix that Norma Shearer and Laurence Olivier together on a marquee would be box-office and
prestige magic if he could bring it off); and some wonderful
supporting performers would be on hand, including Mary
Boland (who had also shone in *The Women*), Edmund
Gwenn, and Edna May Oliver.

But Shearer decided against it. This was to prove the first of
two roles she turned down into which Greer Garson stepped,
roles that took Garson, in two years, to major stardom. After
her initial success opposite Robert Donat in his Academy
Award–winning role in *Goodbye Mr. Chips* (made in England
in 1939) Garson (Mayer discovered her in a play in London)
came to America and an indifferent comedy, *Remember?* with
Robert Taylor, which had done little to boost her stock with
American audiences.

The late Anita Louise, who had appeared with Shearer in
Marie Antoinette and who later came to know her well, told
me years ago that she felt that after 1939 Shearer essentially
lost interest in her career, and regarded the six-picture contract (with three films yet to go) as something of a burden.
Also, since the breakup of her romance with Raft, her sense
of loneliness and rootlessness had increased, and the pursuit
of a lasting and permanent new love took precedence over
everything except her two children. In 1940 Irving, Jr., was
ten and Katherine five. "I think she felt there was a big hole,
a vacuum, in the center of her life, and it troubled her
greatly." Nineteen-forty was also the year in which she was to
find herself the exact age as the century, and to a woman who
was essentially a passionate romantic, the loss of a meaningful
love as forty dawned struck a particularly poignant note.

Billy Grady and others at MGM noted Shearer's steady loss
of interest in her career. "Louie Mayer told me he felt Norma
didn't give a damn any more and that was why she turned

down a surefire prestige picture like *Pride and Prejudice,*
which she would have jumped at several years earlier. And
when Greer Garson achieved top stardom via roles Norma
had rejected, she took it very graciously, with an emphasis on
indifference," Billy said.

But from 1940 to 1942 Shearer was actually sending out
mixed signals, according to Hunt Stromberg. "She really felt
she had made real and lasting mistakes in turning down *Gone
With the Wind* and *Pride and Prejudice* and later *Mrs.
Miniver,* but that was later on, after she had been retired for years, and
could look back in retrospect, from the safe and serene van-
tage point of a happy marriage." In 1940, and indeed until her
second marriage in 1942, Norma's strong sense of a void in
her personal life preoccupied her. Louise and others later felt
that had she been enjoying a happy and settled relationship at
that time, she would have had more zest for her career and
would have made wiser, more considered career choices.

As George Cukor recalled it, "You must remember that
she held a lot of MGM stock and was a millionairess many
times over. Financial security had always been important to
Norma and she had that, in permanent terms. But money isn't
everything, as she discovered, and the emptiness of her personal life distracted her and drained her creative energies, and
it was a shame; she had at least another decade and ten great
roles in her if her personal losses had not preoccupied her."

For all these reasons, the year 1940 brought us Norma
Shearer in *Escape,* with Robert Taylor as her costar—the first
of their two on-screen pairings. Taylor, whom I knew well,
always had reservations about Shearer as costar in their pictures. "She was a perfectionist," he said, "and while that can
be fine, and often helps other performers reach the same standard, I always felt she was nit-picking and fussy about lighting
and angles and all the rest of it because she was compensating
for something—some lack in her life. I don't think she cared
much for the picture, wanted to get it over with, but oddly
enough she was, I felt, quite fine in it."

I am not alone in considering *Escape* one of Shearer's more proficient performances. When I covered it in *The Films of Robert Taylor* in 1975, I wrote: "Miss Shearer is charming and restrained, ambivalent in her feelings, what with fondly remembering her native America yet with strong sentiments of loyalty toward her late husband's country, Germany. Her face registers her poignant dilemma when she realizes she is in love with Taylor and that she is betraying her adopted country."

Escape, directed by the able Mervyn LeRoy, has to do with an American, Taylor, who is trying to rescue his mother, Nazimova, playing a once-famous actress, from the hands of the Nazis, who have jailed her for trying to get her property out of Germany, a cardinal offense under their laws. He enlists the help of Shearer, a widowed, American-born German countess, who is under the protection of Conrad Veidt, a German general. Via complicated strategms, Taylor succeeds in smuggling his mother out of the country, leaving Shearer, with whom he has fallen in love, with her duty to the ill Veidt who begs her not to leave him.

Mervyn LeRoy directed with expert pacing and characterizational sharpness, seen especially in the performances of Veidt, Albert Basserman, Philip Dorn, the always-dependable Felix Bressart, and above all Nazimova, who had been the legendary silent star of such outrè films as *Camille* and *Salome* and had later won additional laurels on the stage. A native of Russia, where she had worked with Stanislavsky, Nazimova had been absent from the screen for fifteen years when she did *Escape.* She was by then sixty years old and her fortunes were in decline, but the old creative spark was still there, and she gave a highly creditable performance.

Robert Taylor remembered that Shearer went out of her way to be kind to Alla Nazimova, as she had done years earlier with Mrs. Pat Campbell in *Riptide*. "The old gal [Nazimova] could be very testy and temperamental; I don't think she had faced, even past sixty, the fact that she was no longer the star and the centerpiece of whatever environment she found herself in," Taylor told me. "I found her a drag at times; in fact she got on my nerves no end, but Norma was just wonderful with her." Others on the set commented that Shearer had treated Nazimova more as a costar than as a supporting player. "That was Norma," Felix Bressart later recalled. "She instinctively understood people either already down and out or on the *way* down, and she was the soul of tact. She could be very tough and imperious when she felt people deserved the one-up treatment, but she was the soul of kindness when she sensed tragedy or failure in someone's life."

In his autobiography, *Take One,* Mervyn LeRoy mentions that Paul Lukas, who originally had been hired as the German general, "didn't play it the way I wanted. He was the only person I ever had to take out of a picture and it wasn't because he was untalented, but he simply was misinterpreting the part. I was lucky; when I had to make the change, Veidt was available." (Veidt had been LeRoy's first choice for the role.) LeRoy also recalls that when he offered the celebrated German actor Albert Bassermann (who had fled the Nazis in real life) a small but telling role and apologized for its brevity, he replied, "It isn't how long the part is, but how good it is."

Veidt and Basserman both enjoyed working in the picture, and Veidt, according to Billy Grady, took a special shine to Shearer, calling her a lovely and womanly person with an astonishingly subtle acting technique. Grady recalled the two talking animatedly together over tea during the late afternoons. "It is a joy to play with such a richly gifted actor," Norma told Grady. (Oddly enough, in his autobiography LeRoy mentions practically everyone *but* Shearer, nor could he be coaxed into any comments via letter or other means. They worked together only in that one picture.) Whatever their personal interplay (or lack of it), LeRoy got a very fine performance out of Shearer; it ranks among the ten best of her career. *Modern Screen* wrote: "One of the most poignantly dramatic films of the year is *Escape,* [a] gripping and spine-tingling melodrama. Both Norma Shearer and Robert Taylor are excellent, and the subject matter is very provoca-

tive." *The New York Daily News* felt that Shearer had given
"a fine dramatic fillip to the fadeout."

Time magazine took a swipe at Taylor's admittedly modest
acting skills, remarking "Only Robert Taylor, unfairly injected into big league competition, falls behind the pace. But
director LeRoy's combination is too strong to be defeated by
this single handicap."

In retrospect Shearer seemed to like this picture, stating:
"The part wasn't awfully long but its content was strong and it
gave me some good opportunities that I hope I exploited."
She never seemed any more enthusiastic about Bob Taylor,
either as a man or costar, than he was about her. Their chem-
istries meshed only fairly well, and they never seemed com-
panionable or at ease with each other off-camera, as several
associates attested. Lawrence Weingarten later said that he
heard Norma say that she didn't think Bob Taylor was a naturally talented actor, that he had to work at it all the way, and
the strain showed. Taylor's remarks to me about Shearer indicate that he felt uneasy up against talents he knew to be
greater than his own. He somehow *complemented* Garbo in
Camille because the role of Armand was that of an essentially
unformed and callow youth. With the aid of a good director
like LeRoy, Taylor could rise above himself, and in later
years he became more proficient in his technique than he himself ever realized. But Billy Grady, who liked Taylor but considered him a thespian lightweight, summed it up best: "He'll
never cop an Oscar—ever," he said.

With *Escape* completed in the late summer of 1940, Shearer
again found herself at loose ends. She relaxed with friends,
went to parties and premieres, but essentially seemed un-
directed again. Yet another year went by before she took on a
picture—the fifth of the six for which she was contracted.
Mayer sent her script after script, "some of them first-class, of
really high quality," Eddie Mannix later remembered. "But
she didn't want to do anything she considered heavy. She was
after light, fluffy comedies, and that's what the last two
were." Later she had the grace to admit to Bosley Crowther:

"On those last two, no one but myself was trying to do me in."

One of the reasons Shearer had refused *Mrs. Miniver* was her feeling that it would harm her image to be seen as what she called "a middle-aged wife and mother of two grown children." In 1942 she would turn forty-two, at that time considered an advanced age for an actress, and appearing youthful and vivacious, on screen as well as off, had become one of her main preoccupations. She was determined, she told her sister Athole, to get a new lease on life—*and* love—and had developed what we would now term a mind-set—*her* mind was firmly set on fresh horizons, maximum physical attractiveness, the maintaining of peak energies. Since she had to do two more pictures to get free of her contract, and since she had set her happiness-goals elsewhere than in movies, she determined to find something light, fluffy, even frivolous.

"I just don't know what's come over Norma," Hunt Stromberg recalled saying to L. B. Mayer at the time. "She's become so flighty, so flibbertigibetty, so nervous—scared, somehow." "Of course she's scared," Mayer replied, his voice registering a kind of gruff compassion. "She's scared of growing old. . . ."

Gail Patrick, who had come to know Shearer well about this time and who was to appear in her upcoming picture, told me that she felt Norma was well into a midlife crisis and was determined *not* to let life pass her by.

> She wanted to do those soufflé-light comedy things because they kept up her spirits, made her feel youthful and expectant about future life possibilities. The things they offered her, like *Mrs. Miniver* and even *Madame Curie* [which Garbo had turned down and which Greer Garson later snapped up] seemed too somber, too heavy. It was a sad world out there, that second year of the American engagement in the war, and Norma, I'm sure, felt she had had enough sadness and conformity and staidness and responsibility in her personal life to last her a lifetime. Sure, the

kids were of cardinal importance in her scheme, but she had
nannies and governesses for them—she felt her prime responsibility was to *herself*; after all, she had spent years of
living for others, while stifling her own impulses, to say
nothing of her real needs.

In view of the life philosophies she was steadily evolving at
the time, it is not surprising that she ferreted out, without any
encouragement from anyone at Metro-Goldwyn-Mayer, a tri-
fling playlet from Noel Coward's dramatic property, *Tonight
at 8:30*. She is said to have even chosen the title for it—something that to her mind sounded amusing, euphonious, and
lighthearted: *We Were Dancing*.

A year had gone by since her last appearance, and Mayer
was eager to get her going in something, especially since the
New York office and the exhibitors were clamoring for a
"Norma Shearer vehicle." Nick Schenck is said to have remarked at the time that while "Norma is not such great
shakes at the box office unless she has a strong male star up
there with her, she does have a certain class and panache and
a lot of the women around the country like her and will turn
out to see her." He told Mayer: "She offers prestige, so give
her anything she wants, no matter how you may dislike it. It's
a safe bet that if she likes it she'll give her best efforts to it."

Shearer reportedly ran the show on *We Were Dancing*. She
was given the kindly and compliant Robert Z. Leonard, who
did what he was told and went along with her every directorial
suggestion. She bossed both the screenwriter and the photographer, changing lines she didn't like and driving lenser Robert Planck up the wall with her lighting suggestions and
perfectionist ideas on angles, shadows, and camera place-
ment. Even Cedric Gibbons, the art director, who usually did
as he pleased, was told she expected something "fresh and
unique" from him. Kalloch, who provided the gowns, found
Shearer's endless nit-picking during fittings a prime-size head-
ache, and Norma stayed late at the studio getting everything
as form-fitting as she thought warranted. Norma even told

brother Douglas that his sound was not coming through in the rushes that she studied obsessively: "You're letting my voice *drop* in the wrong places; keep it *soaring*," she told him. Planck recalled that if she didn't like how she looked in the rushes, she would insist that scenes be done over and over. When Mayer protested that costs were going up, she would remind him that the picture was only a society comedy that had a limited budget to start with, so what were a few extra takes? She adopted a radical new hairstyle of the kind she had never appeared in before—a fluffy, curly concoction that softly framed her face. To call attention to it, she even wrote in words for Melvyn Douglas along the lines of "Vicki, there are little lights in your hair." "Then," Gail Patrick recalled, "she saw that Planck followed suit with the correct lensing to bear out what Douglas said."

"I was somewhat taller than Norma was," actress Heather Thatcher remembered—"and so was Gail Patrick, for that matter. This bothered Norma no end, and she devised ingenious means to increase her height—little steps, small boxes—I remember she almost broke an ankle hopping on and off them."

More often, she would arrange the shot (with all hands complying like hired servants) to her satisfaction, putting a tall actor like Lee Bowman between herself and Thatcher. Bowman told me:

> I felt she was very nervous during that picture—and she worried about everything, her clothes, her makeup, and especially the lighting. She wanted her face "white as snow," to use one of her phrases, and the guy found himself in the shadows. In one scene she was wearing a white dress and I was up against her in white tie and tails and there was a protracted debate (instigated by her) as to whether my tie and shirt blanked out her dress and the little bowed hat she was wearing. I felt throughout the film that something was bothering her, though I had heard tales of her perfectionism in other films.

She had also been instrumental in the choice of Melvyn Douglas as her leading man; in fact, she literally wrested him from a reluctant Mayer, who told her: "Melvyn has been doing too many comedies—he just came off one with Garbo [the ill-fated *Two-Faced Woman,* her last film]." Mayer suggested Herbert Marshall, with whom Shearer had appeared eight years before in *Riptide.* Shearer was in no mood to be reminded of *Riptide* or of Marshall. "He's too *old* now, he must be *fifty,*" she snapped, "and his limp is even *more* pronounced!"

Douglas had romanced on-screen such female stars as Garbo (three times), Crawford, Roz Russell, Marlene Dietrich, and Merle Oberon. In fact, it was Oberon, a good friend of Shearer's, who had recommended Douglas to her for the picture. "He's forty but acts and looks thirty-two," she told her, "and his lovemaking is smooth and makes the lady look good."

Many years later Douglas told me: "Norma was delightful to work with but she did want everything her own way, and we had to wait around for what seemed forever while she got the lighting and angles she felt were necessary for herself. I have felt since that I was photographed more lousily in that picture than in anything I did in that period. I was kept in shadows and half shadows and never realized I was developing a double chin until I saw myself in *that*!"

According to Douglas, Norma was annoyed with the production code that would not allow her to get into bed with him for a "morning-after" honeymoon scene—even with the one-foot-on-the-floor rule that the blue-nose overseers considered a must. "We wound up in a kind of twin-mattresses-thrown-together set-up with a common headboard in the back—and Norma thought it was ridiculous and unrealistic. I got the feeling," Douglas added, "that she wanted to make the film as sexy and sparkling as possible."

We Were Dancing had the most gossamer plot conceivable. Shearer and Douglas are two impoverished aristocrats who specialize in professional house-guesting among the rich. Engaged to "veddy-social" stuffed shirt Lee Bowman, she meets Douglas on a weekend party, dances one dance with him, and proceeds to elope. Many silly misunderstandings follow as they find themselves financially embarrassed, then split up, and start divorce proceedings; he resumes with old flame Gail Patrick and Norma gets reengaged to Bowman, but they get back together again after dancing once more, at yet another house party, to the romantic waltz that had first led them into each other's arms.

Reginald Owen, the crustily authoritative old character actor, fell afoul of Shearer when he inadvertently stepped on one of her lines during a heated exchange. Heather Thatcher remembered that Norma stormed off the set and told the hapless Leonard to lay down the law to Owen. "No one upstages me in my own picture!" she snapped, slamming her dressing-room door behind her. Billy Grady, who was on the set at the time, said Owen harrumphed around grumpily for the rest of the day and later told him: "That woman can get so *difficult*—maybe she should have played Scarlett after all!"

We Were Dancing was no world-shaker when it came out in early 1942. Americans were at war, and high-society stuff about parasitical house guests was no longer amusing. The picture did only fair business, and came and went rather quickly on the nation's screens. Actually, Shearer's fussing and nit-picking paid off well for her, at least, because she looks beautiful and is sparkling and witty throughout, despite a weak script. Douglas is ingratiating as always. The critics split down the middle on the picture and Shearer. She was "grand," *Motion Picture* said. She "acts with dazzling aplomb and wears clothes that will knock your eyes out," Bosley Crowther observed in *The New York Times,* while *Photoplay* said, "Too utterly utter and all that sort of rot, my deah . . ." *Time* applied the coup de grace with "Tailor-made for Miss Shearer. . . . *Dancing* is a costly, embarrassing picture whose mood and manners are both dated and false."

Blithely unfazed by the critical and popular reception of *We Were Dancing,* Shearer rushed into yet another comedy, *Her*

Cardboard Lover, based on a 1920s trifle by Jacques Deval.
The Broadway play had been made into a silent movie, then
refurbished in 1932 as a comedy for Buster Keaton. Film critic
Bosley Crowther wrote of *The Passionate Plumber,* "It should
have stood on that production and that title!"

Crowther had been my friend and mentor when I wrote
stories for *The New York Times* years ago on a free-lance
basis, and I discussed Shearer with him when his 1957 book
on MGM, *The Lion's Share,* came out. "I always liked and
admired Norma," he said, "and I still don't quite comprehend
how she could have been so self-destructive with those last
two pictures—they were really trifles, quite unworthy of her,
and they were real comedowns from the work she had done
just before. And she couldn't blame Mayer or anyone else for
it—she did it to herself, and she did have the grace to admit it
to me and others in later years—which was very much to her
credit."

Her Cardboard Lover is a silly story about a silly woman
who is hopelessly in love with a charming cad, George Sanders. To make him jealous, she hires Robert Taylor and pre-
tends to be in love with him. Of course she and the
"cardboard lover" eventually fall in love, and the mounte-
bankish object of her previous affections is given the gate.
That is the sum total of the plot, though there are many silly
and superfluous side issues such as boudoir masquerades and
even a knock-down, drag-out fight between cad and freshly
elected lover.

Deval, the author of the original, was drafted to do the
screenplay. MGM powers-that-were proceeded to insult him
by adding three more writers—John Collier, Anthony Veiller,
and William H. Wright—who promptly generated a babble of
conflicting ideas that, Deval later reminisced, drove him up
the proverbial wall. Billy Grady recalled going by the writers'
section and hearing the foursome propounding their individual ideas about dialogue at the top of their voices. "I thought
for sure we'd need the studio cops before someone ended up
dead," he recalled. It was distinctly a case of too many cooks

ruining the broth, for *Her Cardboard Lover* proved as ill-
starred a swan song for Shearer as Garbo's *Two-Faced
Woman* some months earlier had been for *her*.

Years later Crowther told me that Norma, with whom he
eventually became friendly, had either been consummately
gracious and forebearing or completely forgetful (hopefully
the latter) of his blistering July 17, 1942, *Times* review in
which he said, among other things:

> . . . the screen play by four weary writers is just a lot of
> witless talk, and the performances, under George Cukor's
> direction, are often close to ridiculous. Miss Shearer either
> overacts deliberately, but without any comic finesse, or she
> has been looking at the pictures of fancy models in the high-
> tone fashion magazines. Mr. Taylor, who had finally gotten
> somewhere as an actor, is back where he began—back as a
> piece of well-dressed furniture—compelled to make the
> most inane remarks. And George Sanders, the only other
> character of any consequence, is just a stock cad.

Photoplay felt, on the other hand, that "if this is Miss
Shearer's movie swan song, as has been intimated, she leaves
us with a very fine performance to remember her by. True, at
times Miss Shearer spreads on the histrionics a bit thick, but
the role is difficult and why shouldn't a love-frustrated woman
be a bit hysterical at times?" Other critical observations
ranged from "dated" to "generally dull."

Mayer had thrown up his hands when Norma, after going
through a pile of scripts of a more contemporary vintage,
phoned him and informed him "that she was high on *that* old
chestnut!" He tried to persuade her yet again to go for something more timely and more attuned to the predilections and
interests of 1942 audiences ("This is 1942, Norma! 1942! Not
1926!" he reportedly yelled; whereupon she slammed down
the phone and didn't speak to him for a month.)

Later, having calmed down, Mayer told Mannix, Grady,
and producer J. Walter Ruben: "It will be her last picture for

us, and if she is hell-bent on rushing for the exit with *this* thing, so be it!" Ruben was assigned to the picture with the injunction: "Keep the god-damned budget down!"

Shearer, through intermediaries (she couldn't trust her temper at the moment), asked for George Cukor as director. He was at liberty and altogether willing, for, as he told me years later, he liked Norma and had a high regard for her talent. "Comedy was not really her thing," he told me, "but she was charming in that—she really needed very little guidance."

Cukor particularly remembered a telephone scene in which Norma was supposed to react to what her lover was saying on the other end of the line. He told me: "It was a virtuoso piece of acting. I had directed Laurette Taylor in the stage version many years before, and she was every bit as good as Laurette was. Of course she was a different kind of actress, but she got the identical effects, colored by her own personality, of course."

Cukor and Shearer got on extremely well during the shooting. "I wasn't a doormat for her, as I know Bob Leonard and others tended to be. I let her come up with her own inspirations, but I would head her off at the pass, so to speak, if I thought she was overdoing things a bit. One of Norma's problems was that she tended to go the distance and a little beyond if she wasn't reined in. But believe you me, it is infinitely easier to tone down too much than be forced to try to dredge up—if possible—too little, and I won't name the actresses who were trials to me in *that* area!"

Robert Taylor frowned when I mentioned *Her Cardboard Lover* to him.

I didn't think I was all that hot in it. The war was on by then, and I had more serious things on my mind. Of course George [Cukor] was a great help, and he was kind enough to tell me that he liked my work. Norma? She was as perfectionist as ever. I was surprised when she asked for me as leading man; I felt she didn't care for her *Escape* experience with me. She could be very gracious when she was in the mood, but I often felt I exasperated her in some of the trickier comedy moments; comedy of that high-style kind was never really my thing. I feel I was a stick in it from start to finish.

In my *Films of Robert Taylor* (1975) I wrote: "I saw *Her Cardboard Lover* yet again only a few months ago, and it confirmed my original 1942 impression as a sparkling little comedy, cleverly acted—a creditable effort within its limited range. There are tedious stretches and the situations and dialogue are contrived, but the telephone scene Cukor thought an admirable Shearer tour de force holds up well."

Norma herself dismissed the picture as "not one of my better efforts," adding, "but I worked quite hard on it, getting the comedy nuances just the way I felt they should be, and George Cukor was a darling, so helpful and clever with ideas. He was a gentleman; always talked things over with me first; never tried to push anything on me."

George Sanders later complained that the dialogue stuck in his craw. One piece of dialogue that he thought particularly horrendous went something like: "We have a choice, Consuelo—a nasty quarrel, at which you are not very good—or reconciliation, at which you are adorable." Shearer made him nervous, he reported. It was their only picture together, and he felt that their styles did not blend well, his being sardonic and clipped and emotionally reticent and restrained, and hers, as he put it "so bravura, so emotional." Oddly, Norma spoke well of Sanders in later years, saying he was a fine actor who complemented her very well and that she wished they had worked more together. She even named Sanders, Joseph Schildkraut, and Conrad Veidt as being supporting actors whom she remembered working with to maximum advantage.

The amusing character comedian Frank McHugh, who had made his name at Warners in the 1930s in fast-talking rough-tough pictures with Cagney and Pat O'Brien, remembers laughing when he was assigned to a Norma Shearer picture. "I didn't feel I had the class for *that* act," he told me years later. "And I remember the ridiculous name of the character I was assigned—*Chappie Champagne*; it sounded like something Reginald Gardiner or Charles Butterworth should have been sporting. I don't remember all that much about the picture, but I did get the feeling that Shearer was running the whole show and telling everyone what to do."

McHugh recalled that "while Shearer may have been the prima donna on the set everyone said she was, she did go out of her way to be helpful and kind to that fine character actress Elizabeth Patterson, who was ill and had personal problems at the time. Elizabeth told me that herself."

Shearer had one annoying problem on *Her Cardboard Lover*. The vagaries of conveyor-belt studio scheduling resulted in her having not one but *two* photographers on the film—Harry Stradling and Robert Planck, two gentlemen with somewhat different styles. Because of this, she looks somewhat different in some shots compared to others. The budget-conscious Mayer refused to accede to her request to reshoot with Planck, and some sharply worded phone conversations resulted. But as she was "rushing for the exit and couldn't wait to be done with it and her contract," as Mayer put it, she didn't insist. When shooting for *Her Cardboard Lover* was finally over in April 1942, Shearer packed her things and departed with considerable relief.

Metro-Goldwyn-Mayer might now be a thing of the past for her so far as acting went, Shearer told Hedda Hopper and others in early 1942, but she had every intention of keeping her hand in the financial end, as she did own a large block of stock and had various dividends and returns coming in to her regularly from the 1937 agreement.

She went to her beach house to relax after, at her insistence, approving the final rushes of *Her Cardboard Lover*. Twelve-year-old Irving and seven-year-old Katherine got her complete attention, and they did much swimming and driving and general catching up with family life.

Norma was just getting into a relaxed frame of mind ("It's so wonderful not to have to think of movies for a while, not to care, just to let my mind go blank and my thoughts go free," she told Louella Parsons) when she received a surprise S.O.S. call from Bette Davis at Warners. Shearer had known Davis socially for some years, though their relationship was far from intimate. In the 1939 Oscar ceremonies, when Davis's *Jezebel* had beaten out her *Marie Antoinette,* Norma had graciously congratulated the fiery star whose rise at Warners had since been dramatic. In 1942 Davis was acclaimed the biggest female star in the business, so Shearer couldn't help being flattered and not a little surprised when Davis offered her the costarring role in *Old Acquaintance.* It was based on a 1940 Broadway play that starred Jane Cowl and Peggy Wood and concerned two writers, one a blatant commercialist who specialized in woman's-fodder pap and the other a serious artist whose novels won critical raves but never sold. The movie would trace the women's friendship through the years, with the serious novelist nobly sacrificing her chance to go off with the bubblehead commercialist's husband and later losing a younger lover to her old friend's daughter.

When she saw the script, Norma recalled that no one had specified which part she would play. She thought the script literate and intelligent, and was pleased when she learned that her old friend Edmund Goulding, who had guided her through *Riptide* in 1934, was to direct. (Goulding later took ill and was replaced by Vincent Sherman.)

Still, she had her reservations about doing any more films for a while. She was contemplating war work and some radio shows, but her primary intention was to rest, relax, and enjoy her children.

In the course of a phone conversation with Goulding, Norma asked idly if he felt she was right for the part of Kit Marlowe, the noble, self-sacrificing author who carries loyalty and friendship to the point of masochism with such lines as "There's a certain ecstasy about wanting something you know you can't get"—meaning friend Millie Drake's husband, of course. "But, Norma," Goulding told her, "Bette wants you to play the bitch who writes the trash—Millie, of course!"

In subsequent conversations Shearer announced firmly that playing a flighty bitch was not her thing and did not accord with her established persona. "I didn't want to play Scarlett O'Hara for that reason," she told a commiserating George Cukor, "so why should I play this mean-spirited, brittle hussy?"

Reportedly Jack Warner, who had gotten into his head (prompted by Davis?) that "Bette Davis and Norma Shearer in *Old Acquaintance*" would look great on marquees in Dubuque and Davenport, Iowa, and titillate fans cross-country, tried to persuade Norma to take the role. "It would also put Louie Mayer's nose out of joint to have *me* starring Norma after she left *him*," Jack told friends, chortling.

But in the end Shearer was having none of it. She didn't like the idea of her character aging into her forties; she also didn't like having a grown daughter as in the later scenes, and above all she wasn't going to play Millie Drake, whom she characterized to Cukor as "the biggest bitch in that or any other town!" Since Davis preferred to be noble Kit Marlowe, which Norma thought up her *own* street, Miriam Hopkins eventually waltzed off with the role. "The perfect off-screen bitch to play the perfect on-screen bitch," Warner said, laughing.

17

Total Love, Marriage, and Travel

A FTER DOING a radio show for Arch Oboler's Every Man's *Yesterday, Today and Tomorrow* series, entitled "The Women Stayed at Home" (dealing with "a woman who meets war on a lonely beach"), Shearer turned down other radio offers in 1942. "The Women Stayed at Home" had a supernatural theme regarding servicemen whose spirits returned after their deaths to haunt the living, and fans complimented Norma on the loveliness of her voice, which at forty-two had attained a loamy richness. But she had finally decided to put acting, whatever the medium, behind her for a while. Stage offers had come in, also, but these did not appeal to her.

She decided that some fun and relaxation were in order, and in the spring of 1942 she took Irving and Katherine to Sun Valley, Idaho, for some skiing. It was there that she met Martin Arrouge, a ski instructor. The unmoneyed offspring son of a prominent family in San Francisco, Arrouge was of Basque-French descent. He also promoted Squaw Valley, a popular vacation resort, enjoyed racing sports cars, and flew a great deal, as he was a licensed pilot.

At the time they met on the ski run, Norma was forty-two and Arrouge was twenty-eight. An immediate mutual attraction sprang up between them. Arrouge physically resembled Thalberg vaguely; but he was far more virile and vital, and in robust good health. He enjoyed the outdoors, exercised a great deal, and had, according to Anita Loos, "a beautiful body; he knew how to handle it, too; he moved with grace and assurance, and I think that, for once, Norma felt an honest sexual attraction as well as romantic interest. She had loved Irving deeply, but he had been gone six years, and a woman's physical needs grow more intense as she matures, and she did need love and closeness and—well, Marty was made to order for what she was looking for."

Though a shy, unassertive man, Arrouge had his own brand of self-assurance that, combined with his evident virility and youth, made a deep impression on Norma. Frances Marion later said: "He was smart, too. He didn't chase her; he let her come to him. That intrigued her considerably."

Arrouge also had a way with children, and soon Irving and Katherine were following him up the ski slopes, where he turned them, in short order, into excellent little skiiers. Shearer came to watch the lessons, and though she had done some skiing, she found she had much to learn. Soon Marty was helping her with the finer points of the sport. Quick lunches near the ski slopes soon led to candlelit dinners at a nearby club after the children were in bed. Marty told Norma about his early life and about his ambitions for Squaw Valley, where his father had once grazed sheep. "The plans he had for the area—they were galvanizing, dynamic!" Norma later recalled.

Though for perhaps the first time in her forty-two years Norma felt, full force, that magical synthesis of sexual desire and romantic excitement (here was no older man to be dependent on, no frail invalid to be nursed, no wolf to be rebuffed), she reminded herself that she was a world-famous star, a widow, and the mother of two impressionable young children—and also a very wealthy woman. She tried to be objective when she sized up Marty. He had no money but he was ambitious and hardworking. He seemed to have no bad habits. His attitude toward women was chivalrous in a reserved sort of way, but she saw in his flashing dark eyes his sexual and romantic potential, and she also believed that she had cast the same spell over him that he had over her.

"It was a dynamite mutual attraction, and it brought Norma the first true and complete man-woman sexual and romantic fulfillment she had ever known," Hopper told me years later.

First there was the matter of religion. Since Marty was a Catholic, Norma would convert to Catholicism. "The same God rules us all and loves us equally" was her reply to her brother Douglas when he questioned her decision to convert yet again.

According to fan-magazine writer Ruth Waterbury:

> In 1927 she had gone from Anglican to Jewish for Irving's sake because she felt that it would make them truly one; now, for the same reason, she went from Jewish to Catholic to bring her and Marty closer. To Norma all religions were right and good and served the Creator equally, even if they approached the Mystery from a different angle. She didn't believe in mixed marriages, but in the case of the children she determined to leave their choice of religion up to them. They were being brought up in the Orthodox Jewish faith, but most Jews believed that a true Jew sprang from a Jewish mother and that she was not.

"Norma didn't waste time splitting hairs about religion," Hunt Stromberg said. "Her attitude essentially was that if the greatest theological minds of the ages hadn't figured it all out completely, who was she to penetrate the mystery? Treat others as you wish to be treated; forgive as you wish to be forgiven, was essentially her philosophy. She refused to let anything interfere with her inner serenity."

Norma began to take instructions in the Roman Catholic faith, and on August 23, 1942, she became Mrs. Martin Arrouge at the Church of the Good Shepherd in Beverly Hills, with Father John O'Donnell, known as The Padre of the Stars, on hand to unite them. Little Katherine was a flower girl, and among the attendants was Greer Garson, the lucky inheritor of the plum roles that Norma had earlier refused. Louella Parsons wrote, this time around: "If ever a woman deserved full and total happiness it is Norma. For six years she has been lonely and she has had to bring up those two kids all by herself. She lived for others in so many ways and now she should live for herself. She has paid her dues many times over."

The memory of Irving Thalberg was not forgotten, however. Shearer used her original wedding ring, which Arrouge had remodeled with bands of gold welded on either side. Norma asked that an inscription be placed on it: *Everything leads me to thee.* Those had been the words inscribed on the ring she had given Tyrone Power during their famed love scene in *Marie Antoinette*—they were the last words to appear on the screen when the camera focused on the ring in the fadeout, where Power stood in mute grief as the mob howled in satisfaction after the guillotine blade fell.

Lady Sylvia Ashley, widow of Douglas Fairbanks, Sr., and skiing enthusiast Otto Lang were in attendance, with Lang as best man. The couple went back to the Santa Monica home she had shared with Thalberg (they would later move to a large house in Beverly Hills). The honeymoon was brief, because Shearer was due out on a bond-selling tour. Classified 3-A in the draft because he claimed he was the chief support of his mother, Arrouge began attending navigation school with the Ferry Command in mind, but by the end of 1942 he was in an aviation instructors' course in Phoenix, and on May 27, 1943, he became one of thirty-two naval aviators graduated from the U.S. Naval Air Station in New Orleans. "Now an ensign, he blushed slightly," according to a news report, "but managed a broad smile when his wife pinned the Wings of Gold to his jacket." "I'm so proud of him," Norma told reporters, but she expressed disappointment that they would have to transfer from New Orleans to Oakland, California, where he was to be stationed. Shortly after that, Arrouge became a test pilot and was promoted to lieutenant. He ordered, in addition to the original wedding band, two heart-shaped rings that they both began wearing, each with Norma's favorite inscription, *Everything leads me to thee.*

"With *three* rings carrying that inscription," Ruth Waterbury later said, "it was small wonder why Norma valued those words so much. For Martin Arrouge represented that *total* womanly fulfillment she had been denied all her life and now, in 1943, it seemed that everything in her life had led her to Marty."

During 1942 and 1943 there was the usual unkind gossip that Marty had married Norma for her money. "It's so unfair to him!" Norma complained to Louella Parsons. "I've lived long enough to know a fortune hunter when I see him and Marty is just not that kind of man." She then let it be known that he had signed a premarital agreement in which he waived all rights to her community property, with her first husband's estate retained in trust for her and her children.

In 1940 Norma's sister Athole had divorced Howard Hawks after an unhappy marriage, that had produced two children, David and Barbara. Athole was for some time an invalid, and around 1941 Norma found a place for her near her own home, where they could be in frequent contact.

Among the family problems Norma had to face during the 1940s was the case of her father. Andrew Shearer had divorced her mother, remarried a woman named Elizabeth, and by 1943 was living in California. At this time Norma and her brother Douglas appeared in court to get Andrew removed from the psychopathic ward of the Los Angeles General Hospital and placed in a private sanitarium. Andrew's wife Elizabeth contested the action, feeling that he should remain with her. In any event, Andrew Shearer, consumed by a wasting mental illness, died the following year, 1944, still the subject of a family battle over his custody.

In the early 1950s Norma found it necessary to place her mother, Edith, in a sanitarium, and there she died, at age eighty-five, in 1958.

After the war, and despite happiness in her marriage, Norma thought about resuming her career. (Marty had become a promoter for Squaw Valley, among other pursuits, after leaving the Navy.) In August 1946 it was announced that Norma had signed a contract with Enterprise Productions, where David Lewin, a former Thalberg aide, was a producer. The contract called for her exclusive services for three years; she would also have script approval. Soon Lewin was announcing that an original romantic story was being written for her by Harry Joe Brown. All these ambitious plans fell through, however, when Enterprise Productions failed financially soon after. Norma did not register any undue disappointment, and even said to Hedda Hopper that perhaps it was better that they remember her at the height of her beauty and photogenic appeal, as they were to remember Garbo, who retired a year before her, and never returned to the screen. Assured by George Cukor that she was as lovely as ever, Shearer replied: "Oh, but I'd be giving the cameraman lighting problems by *now,* for sure," and added, "an actress must never lose her ego. Without it she has no talent and is like a clock without a mainspring."

Reportedly in 1947 Louis B. Mayer, feeling that she missed her work, offered her an arrangement similar to the one he proposed to Jeanette McDonald, who returned to MGM for two pictures after a five-year hiatus. But Shearer decided against it. "Let's wait and see how Jeanette does," she said. (By 1949, when the two MacDonald pictures demonstrated that Jeanette's popularity was spent and she retired permanently, Norma told Mayer, "I'm glad I didn't have to wind up like that. It is better to go, when I did, while still on top of things.")

But since she still retained her financial interest in MGM,

Norma kept her hand in, in other ways. In 1947 she had discovered lovely Janet Leigh at the Sugar Bowl Ski Lodge in
northern California; she had happened to see Janet's picture
in an album there, and she recommended her to MGM talent
people. A test was arranged, and to Janet, who had no acting
background whatsoever, it was like a dream come true when
she found herself being groomed at MGM's talent school and
eventually assigned to the lead opposite Van Johnson in
Romance of Rosy Ridge, a Civil War–period drama set in Mis-
souri. This led to an MGM contract for Janet and the start of
a solid film career.

In 1957, on a visit to New York, Leigh told me how grateful
she would always be to Norma for her initial break. She called
her "a lovely, gracious lady whom I will always be proud to
call my friend."

As the years went on, it became apparent that acting no
longer interested Norma. When in 1952 theatrical producer
John Merrick offered her the Gertrude Lawrence role in a
revival of *Lady in the Dark,* she turned him down with the
words: "I am fifty-two years old, happily married, with two
children I adore. I am content, deeply content. I also have my
friends, we travel a lot, and I have more money than I will
ever need. That phase of my life is firmly behind me now.
Everything in its season, and now I am living a new kind of
life."

In April 1954 Norma and Irving's daughter, Katherine,
then eighteen, married Jack Reddish, who was then twenty-
seven. A skiing enthusiast and a former student at the
University of Utah, Reddish had been a member of the 1948
Olympic ski team. By 1960 they were divorced, with Katherine telling the judge, "He was mean, disagreeable, argumen-
tative, and bad-tempered to me. He expected me to support
him." Katherine Reddish waived alimony and kept the title to
her $60,000 home in Beverly Hills.

The following year, Katherine married the actor Richard
Anderson, who had formerly been the husband of Carol Lee
Ladd, Alan Ladd's stepdaughter. The Ladd-Anderson mar-

riage had lasted a year. At the 1956 divorce hearing, Carol
Lee said of Anderson: "He said I wasn't doing anything for
his career and he should have married someone who could
help him more than I was doing." Anderson, who later won a
measure of fame as the intelligence agency bureaucrat on
ABC-TV's *The Six Million Dollar Man* and *The Bionic
Woman,* was described in a 1975 *TV Guide* as having earlier
been "a *Room at the Top* kind of guy"—that is, an oppor-
tunistic young man who stopped at nothing to get ahead. According to *TV Guide,* Anderson later changed to "a good
man—modest, calm, sometimes shy, a simple man who believes in God. . . ." Anderson later explained his character
change (which occurred *after* his divorce from Katherine
Thalberg in 1972) as the result of his feeling that his "moor-
ings were slipping away." Katherine had three children by
Anderson, Ashley, Brook, and Deva.

Irving Thalberg, Jr., served in the Korean War, then in
1956 married Suzanne McCormick of Napa, California. Irving
went on to take his Ph.D. from Stanford University in 1960.
From 1960 to 1963 he taught philosophy at Oberlin College,
then, in 1965, he switched to the University of Chicago,
where he remained until his death on August 21, 1987. He
had also been a visiting professor at a number of universities,
including Fudan University in Shanghai. His articles and es-
says appeared in many philosophy journals. At the time of his
death in Syracuse, New York, he also maintained residences
in Chicago and Aspen, Colorado, where his sister, Katherine,
who has resumed her maiden name of Thalberg, now operates
a bookstore. He was survived by his second wife, Deborah
Pellow, and three daughters, Shoshana, Deborah, and Elana.

Through the years Irving's and Norma's children deter-
minedly and deliberately avoided the public eye, Katherine
for many years as wife and mother, Irving as educator. Photographs of them in adult life are extremely difficult to obtain,
and their aversion to public notice at times assumed phobic
proportions. Jerry Asher later said he felt their attitude was
inspired by their horror of a goldfish-bowl Hollywood exis-

tence. "They saw what it did to their contemporaries, being brought up in the spotlight and forced to compete with parental images. There was too much stress and emotional overkill involved, and they wanted no part of it." Jerry added: "And they were *smart* to feel as they did."

Shearer and Arrouge spent much time in Europe. After a sojourn of many months there in 1956, they returned to Hollywood, and Norma learned that Universal was looking for a young man to play Irving Thalberg in the James Cagney film about Lon Chaney, *Man of a Thousand Faces,* released in 1957. At a party Norma encountered a young New York clothing manufacturer named Robert Evans; he reminded her greatly of Irving, and she recommended him to Universal executives, who tested him. The test proving satisfactory, he got the role.

After some years as an actor, with only so-so results, Evans, uncannily enough, was to follow in the path of Thalberg and become a highly successful film producer. In 1959 he told me, "Miss Shearer is a wonderful lady, and I am proud to count her and her husband as my dear friends. She opened up new opportunities for me that would otherwise never have been possible."

In 1957, fifty-seven-year-old Shearer had to cease her skiing activities after sustaining a severe leg fracture that healed too slowly. When her friends commiserated with her on her "retirement" from her favorite sport, she was philosophical. "Everything has to end some time," she said, laughing, "even life itself." Asked by a reporter if she ever missed her film career, she firmly answered, "No! I believe a movie star should keep them crying—or laughing—for more!" She added, "Anyway, there are a lot of things I want to do, now that I have leisure. I want to learn to speak French fluently, to play the piano like Horowitz or Van Cliburn, and to write a book about life."

It was about this time that Shearer began to think about writing her autobiography, as she felt she had much to tell. She continued her efforts off and on, and years later told Leatrice Gilbert Fountain that she had some 450 pages written, which she hoped to one day publish. Ruth Waterbury, who in the 1960s got a look at some of what she had written, told me that Norma had glossed over too many things and tended to tell only the positive aspects of her own and others' careers. "They all tend to do that; they're too close to things and they can't be objective the way an outside writer can," Waterbury said. In any event, no autobiography of Norma Shearer was ever published to date.

After years of relative silence, in 1959 Norma got into a public quarrel with millionaire sportsman Alexander Cushing when he failed to mention her husband as one of the prime instigators of the Squaw Valley resort project. Arrouge, she added, had been one of the original partners of Wayne Poulsen when Poulsen pioneered there, and Arrouge had remained a stockholder.

18

Twilight and Night

B Y THE 1960s, Shearer had all but disappeared from
public notice. While by no means a recluse, she confined herself mostly to the society of close friends from
the old days, as well as her children and grandchildren. Her
marriage to Marty Arrouge continued to be happy. She was
always accessible to people she liked, however, or who wished
to see her for good and sufficient reasons, and she was always
gracious to me when we met in Hollywood. She enjoyed reminiscing about the old days. "I had my day," she said to me in
1964, "and each thing in its season. We go through various
phases in life, and I'm enjoying the current phase and have no
complaints." She was, at the time, sixty-four years old but
looked much younger, was impeccably groomed and dressed
and superbly coiffed. "One can know, realistically, that one is
not young anymore," she said, "and still want to look one's
best." But she added laughingly, "I don't fuss over myself like
I used to in my screen days. What a trial I must have been to
everyone then! Now I can dress to please just myself, my husband, and those I care for."

By 1970 she had won the grudging respect of her old rival,

Joan Crawford, who told me: "Norma was, I always felt, a highly sexed woman; it showed in her performances. And she was the oddest combination of romantic and realist when it came to men. She was not the kind who spread herself around. She was meant to be a one-man woman. Her two happy marriages prove that. We had our run-ins, but I always had a grudging respect for the way she channeled her romantic and sexual urges." Then, in what was, for Crawford, a surprising burst of humility, she added ruefully, "She did better in *that* department than *I* did, I must admit. . . ."

In 1971 Norma mourned the death of her brother Douglas, founder of MGM's sound department. During his forty-one years at MGM he had won twelve Academy Awards. He had retired in 1968, and was survived by his second wife, Avice, and two sons, Stephen and Mark.

Ed Franks, a writer for *Movie Digest,* met with seventy-two-year-old Shearer in Beverly Hills in 1972. He wrote: "She looks neither younger nor older than her years. Her hair (is it a wig?) is modishly short and gray-blonde. In a stylish pants-suit, she seemed happy and in excellent health, striding vigorously from shop to shop, holding hands with husband Martin Arrouge."

But by 1974 rumors were spreading that Shearer was seriously ill. One of her friends, George Cukor, denied it, saying that Norma suffered from a mild form of atherosclerosis but still looked amazingly youthful and had retained her verve and zest for life. "Marty's devotion to Norma is very touching," George later told me. That same year, when MGM's publicity department was questioned about her, a spokesman said: "She has become a semi-recluse. She hasn't been in touch with us for years." He added: "We couldn't even reach her to invite her to a big party to launch *That's Entertainment* (an anthology of highlights from classic MGM musicals, including the number from *Idiot's Delight* in which Clark Gable sang and danced "Puttin' on the Ritz" with his girls). According to the MGM spokesman, Norma's large, glittering parties used to be the talk of the town, but at age seventy-four she confined herself to small, intimate dinner parties with only relatives and close friends. At that time she and Arrouge maintained two homes, one in Beverly Hills and the other in Squaw Valley.

But after 1976 Norma's health began to slip rapidly. The atherosclerosis grew worse and her eyes began to fail. Soon she was getting a special treatment for her condition available only at the Motion Picture Country House and Lodge (the MPCH), the famous retirement hospital for film people at Woodland Hills, California. Since the frequent trips between her Beverly Hills home and the hospital became too much for her, it was decided that she would take up residence there in September 1980. She was then past eighty.

Some eyebrows were raised when Norma went to live at the MPCH, as it was reputed to cater mostly to ex-film figures who were in financial difficulties. Actually the well-off (and in 1980 Norma was many times a millionaire) were as attracted to the place as were the indigent, because the quality of care was far superior to that in sanitariums and nursing homes, however plush they might be. According to film historian Anthony Slide, who often visits there, "There is nowhere to compare with the MPCH in terms of surroundings, quality of service and treatment, food and facilities. If you are too infirm to take care of yourself, and you are eligible for the MPCH, then you would be foolish not to try and get a room there."

Among those former screen personalities who have recently enjoyed the facilities were the late comedian Allyn Joslyn and actresses Mary Astor and Mae Clarke. Joslyn, who died there at age eighty in 1981, told friends that the MPCH people had provided him with one of the happiest, most peaceful times of his long life and that he "blessed them for it." Astor and Clarke often sang praises for MPCH and lived there contentedly, alternating between rooms and bungalows, depending on the fluctuating state of their health.

According to MCPH spokesmen, those with limited funds hand over what they have to the hospital; it is put into a drawing account, and should it become exhausted, the hospital continues to pay for everything until death or discharge. The wealthy who go there make their own special arrangements. Rules forbid access to their private files on patients, but according to friends, in 1980 Norma was in full possession of her mental faculties and elected to go there of her own volition. She had a dread of conventional sanitariums and nursing homes, and she felt it would be comforting to be among her own kind in an institution to which she had made heavy contributions over the years, as had other great stars, producers, and directors.

For the first years, 1980–1981, Norma seemed content enough there, according to fellow patient DeWitt Bodeen, a noted film historian and screenplay writer and longtime friend of mine. DeWitt recalled Norma engaging in animated discussions with another resident, former top MGM executive Benny Thau, about the long-range future of MGM. At that time still a big MGM stockholder, she kept herself fully informed on the company's doings. At that point, as DeWitt recalled, her long hair, by then completely white, flowed down her back. In December of 1981 she was well enough to receive a plaque in recognition of her induction into the Motion Picture Hall of Fame for her contribution to the motion picture art. Douglas Wright, the Hall of Fame spokesman, later let it be known, however, that the presentation had to be private because of her physical frailty.

By early 1982, DeWitt wrote me that Norma was failing rapidly. On her eighty-second birthday, August 10, 1982, she didn't recognize her children, grandchildren, nieces, nephews, or even her ever-loving and loyal husband, whose visits were constant. Norma's eyesight failed almost completely, and her weight fell drastically. DeWitt lived in the room next to hers, and reported that her mind also failed. James Robert Parish, a film historian who visited DeWitt regularly, remembered seeing Norma being led across the lawn outside her room by an attendant, moving very slowly and wearing dark glasses.

Anthony Slide remembered visiting actress Kathryn Perry

in 1982 out at the MPCH. "While we were talking a white-haired woman in a bathrobe wandered into the room. A nurse came after her, telling her that she had entered the wrong room, and gently led her away. The woman was Norma Shearer and, to me, was totally unrecognizable."

DeWitt Bodeen felt that she resembled, in her final months, the imprisoned Marie Antoinette, blinded by her dark, cold cell, her mind failing as she awaited her execution. In the 1938 film, her hair had gone white; her face was color-less, lined, gray; her figure emaciated; her eyesight had been affected, and she was a pitiable figure indeed. DeWitt also remembered that in 1938 Shearer had been congratulated for eschewing makeup of any kind for those scenes and for allow-ing herself to appear as ravaged as Marie Antoinette must have. In all respects, Shearer had dumped glamour to em-brace reality. Now, in 1982, the realities of age and illness were only too apparent, but she was beyond knowing or car-ing.

Writer Albert B. Manski, Norma's longtime loving and loyal fan, also heard from friends who had seen Norma at the MPCH. Tears came to his eyes when he read their letters de-scribing her condition just before her death. "How terrible that a woman who stood for love and beauty, a star so bril-liant and so charismatic, should end up in such a manner," he told me. "It is terrible what life and time do to even the strongest and best of us. . . ."

Norma did not live to see her eighty-third birthday. On Sunday, June 12, 1983, in the late afternoon, too weak to fight bronchial pneumonia, Norma died. That same pneu-monia had killed Thalberg, and almost killed her in 1936. Ser-vices were held for her at Forest Lawn Memorial Park on Thursday, June 16, where she was buried with Thalberg. Ar-rangements for the funeral and burial were announced as "strictly private" at the request of her family.

When I heard the news of Norma's death, I thought again of myself when as a nine-year-old-boy I had first come under her spell after seeing *Smilin' Through* in 1932. Hers had been a long and full life. She had been nurturing mother, loving, sustaining wife, passionate adorer and pursuer of the male; she had been ruthless, power-driven, determined to meet men on equal terms in a male-dominated world. She had known great fame, great wealth, ultimate respect in the seats of power. She had been vain, proud, intense, combative, and had seen life at the top and at the center of the main action. And at forty-two, at the halfway point, she had known the blessing of a totally fulfilled mutual love, in the safe and peaceful confines of what turned out to be a forty-year marriage.

I wanted to believe that Norma had gradually faded into a blessed and sweet oblivion, all passions spent, all strivings mercifully quieted, and that at the end and beyond, liberated totally by ultimate peace, she was "smilin' through" at all of us who remembered and loved her. I thought of something she had once said to me—something that, on the surface, had seemed to deny the passionate turbulences and fierce life engagements of her eighty-two years. What she had said was: "I always sought serenity and beauty."

And knowing the totality of her intense and complex life as I now do, that is how I, for one, want to remember Norma Shearer now—as serene and beautiful.

A Norma Shearer Filmography

1. *THE FLAPPER.* 1920. Directed by Alan Crosland. Original story and screenplay by Frances Marion. *Cast:* Olive Thomas, Warren Cook, Louise Lindroth, Theo Westman, Jr., W. P. Carleton, Katherine Johnston, Arthur Houseman. *Selznick.* (Shearer was an extra.)
2. *THE RESTLESS SEX.* 1920. Directed by Robert Z. Leonard and Leo D'Usseau. Scenario by Frances Marion from a story by Robert W. Chambers. *Cast:* Marion Davies, Carlyle Blackwell, Ralph Kellard, Charles Lane, Robert Vivian, Etna Ross, Stephen Carr, Vivienne Osborne, Corinne Barker. *Cosmopolitan.* (Shearer was an extra.)
3. *WAY DOWN EAST.* 1920. Directed by D.W. Griffith. Scenario by Anthony Paul Kelly. Based on the play, *Way Down East,* by Lottie Blair Parker. *Cast:* Lillian Gish, Richard Barthelmess, Lowell Sherman, Creighton Hale, Josephine Bernard, Burr McIntosh. *United Artists.* (Shearer was an extra.)
4. *THE STEALERS.* 1920. Directed by William Christy Cabanne. Original story and scenario by William Christy Cabanne. *Cast:* William H. Tooker, Robert Kenyon, Myrtle Morse, Norma Shearer, Ruth Dwyer, Walter Miller, Eugene Borden, Matthew Betz. *Robertson-Cole.*
5. *THE SIGN ON THE DOOR.* 1921. Directed by Herbert Brenon. Screen adaptation by Mary Murillo and Herbert Brenon. Based on the play by Channing Pollock. *Cast:* Norma Talmadge, Charles Richman, Lew Cody, David Proctor, Augustus Balfour, Robert Agnew, Mac Barnes. *First National.* (Shearer's part cut entirely from final print.)

6. *TORCHY'S MILLIONS*. 1921. A two-reeler with Johnny Hines and Norma Shearer. Detailed information unavailable. *Educational*.

7. *THE LEATHER PUSHERS*. 1922. Directed by Harry Pollard. Based on *Collier's* magazine stories by H.C. Witwer. A series of six two-reel features. *Cast:* Reginald Denny, Hayden Stevenson. Denny was later replaced by Billy Sullivan. (Shearer appeared only in two early segments in 1922. The series ran until 1924.) *Universal-Jewel*.

8. *THE MAN WHO PAID*. 1922. Directed and produced by Oscar Apfel. Story and scenario by Marion Brooks. *Cast:* Wilfred Lytell, Norma Shearer, Florence Rogan, Fred C. Jones, Bernard Siegel, David Hennessy, Charles Beyer. *Producers Security/Apfel Apfel Productions*.

9. *THE BOOTLEGGERS*. 1922. Directed by Roy Sheldon. Original story and scenario by Thomas F. Fallon. *Cast:* Walter Miller, Jules Cowles, Norma Shearer, Hazel Flint, Paul Panzer, Jane Allyn. *Film Booking Offices*.

10. *CHANNING OF THE NORTHWEST*. 1922. Directed by Ralph Ince. Scenario by Edward J. Montage. Based on a story by John Willard. *Cast:* Eugene O'Brien, Gladden James, Norma Shearer, James Seeley, Pat Hartigan, Nita Naldi, Harry Lee. *Select*.

11. *A CLOUDED NAME*. 1923. Directed by Austin O. Huhn. Scenario by Austin O. Huhn. Based on a story by Tom Bret. *Cast:* Norma Shearer, Gladden James, Yvonne Logan, Richard Neill, Charles Miller, Fred Eckhart. *Playgoer's Pictures*.

12. *MAN AND WIFE*. 1923. Directed by John L. McCutcheon. Scenario and original story by Leota Morgan. *Cast:* Maurice Costello, Gladys Leslie, Norma Shearer, Edna May Spooner, Robert Elliott, Ernest Hilliard. *Arrow Film Corporation*.

13. *THE DEVIL'S PARTNER*. 1923. Directed by Caryl Fleming from his original story. *Cast:* Norma Shearer, Charles Delaney, Henry Sedley, Edward Roseman. *Iroquois*.

14. *PLEASURE MAD.* 1923. Directed by Reginald Barker. Scenario by A. P. Younger. Based on *The Valley of Content* by Blanche Upright. *Cast:* Huntley Gordon, Norma Shearer, William Collier, Jr., Mary Alden, Winifred Bryson, Ward Crane, Joan Standing, Frederick Trusdell. *Metro.*

15. *THE WANTERS.* 1923. Directed by John M. Stahl. Scenario by J. G. Hawks and Paul Bern. Based on a story by Leila Burton Wells. *Cast:* Marie Prevost, Robert Ellis, Norma Shearer, Gertrude Astor, Huntley Gordon, Lincoln Stedman, Lillian Langdon, Louise Fazenda, Hank Mann, Lydia Yeamans Titus, Vernon Steele. *First National.*

16. *LUCRETIA LOMBARD.* 1923. Directed by Jack Conway. Scenario by Bertram Milhauser and Sada Owen. *Cast:* Irene Rich, Monte Blue, Norma Shearer, Marc McDermott, Alec B. Francis, John Roche, Lucy Beaumont, Otto Hoffman. *Warner Brothers.*

17. *THE TRAIL OF THE LAW.* 1924. Directed and produced by Oscar Apfel. Scenario by Marian Brooks. *Cast:* Wilfred Lytell, Norma Shearer, John Morse, Richard Neill, Charles Beyer, Herbert Holcombe, George Stevens, Baby Florence Rogan. *Producer's Security Corporation.*

18. *THE WOLF MAN.* 1924. Directed by Edward Mortimer. Scenario by Frederick Hatton. From a story by Reed Heustis. *Cast:* John Gilbert, Norma Shearer, Alma Frances, George Barraud, Eugene Pallette, Edgar Norton, Thomas R. Mills, Max Montisole, Charles Wellesley, Richard Blayden, Mary Warren. *Fox.*

19. *BLUE WATERS.* 1924. Directed by David M. Hartford. Scenario by Faith Green. Based on the book by Frederick William Wallace. *Cast:* Pierre Gendron, Jane Thomas, Norma Shearer, John Dillon, Alice May, Harlan Knight, Louis D'Arclay. *New Brunswick.*

20. *BROADWAY AFTER DARK.* 1924. Directed by Monta Bell. Adaptation by Douglas Doty. Based on the play by

Owen Davis. *Cast:* Adolphe Menjou, Norma Shearer, Anna Q. Nilsson, Carmel Myers, Edward Burns, Vera Lewis, Willard Louis, Mervyn LeRoy, Otto Hoffman, Ethel Miller. *Warner Brothers.*

21. *BROKEN BARRIERS.* 1924. Directed by Reginald Barker. Based on the novel by Meredith Nicholson. Scenario by Sada Cown. *Cast:* James Kirkwod, Norma Shearer, Adolphe Menjou, Mae Busch, George Fawcett, Robert Agnew, Vera Reynolds, *Metro-Goldwyn.*

22. *MARRIED FLIRTS.* 1924. Directed by Robert Vignola. Scenario by Julia Crawford Ivers. Based on the novel by Louis Joseph Vance. *Cast:* Pauline Frederick, Conrad Nagel, Mae Busch, Huntley Gordon. Among the guest stars: John Gilbert, Norma Shearer, Mae Murray, May McAvoy, Aileen Pringle. *Metro-Goldwyn.*

23. *EMPTY HANDS.* 1924. Directed by Victor Fleming. Scenario by Carey Wilson. From an original story by Arthur Stringer. *Cast:* Jack Holt, Norma Shearer, Charles Clarey, Hazel Keener, Gertrude Olmstead, Ward Crane, Hank Mann. *Paramount.*

24. *THE SNOB.* 1924. Directed by Monta Bell. Adapted by Monta Bell from a story by Helen R. Martin. *Cast:* John Gilbert, Norma Shearer, Conrad Nagel, Phyllis Haver, Hedda Hopper, Margaret Seddon, Aileen Manning, Roy Laidlaw. *Metro-Goldwyn.*

25. *HE WHO GETS SLAPPED.* 1924. Directed by Victor Seastrom. Scenario by Carey Wilson. Based on the play by Leonid Andreyev. *Cast:* Lon Chaney, Norma Shearer, John Gilbert, Tully Marshall, Marc McDermott, Ford Sterling, Brandon Hurst. *Metro-Goldwyn.*

26. *EXCUSE ME.* 1925. Directed by Alf Goulding. Original story and scenario by Rupert Hughes. *Cast:* Norma Shearer, Conrad Nagel, Renée Adorée, Walter Hiers, John Boles, Bert Roach, William V. Mong, Fred Kelsey. *Metro-Goldwyn.*

27. *LADY OF THE NIGHT.* 1925. Directed by Monta Bell.

Scenario by Alice D. G. Miller. Based on a story by Adela Rogers St. Johns. *Cast:* Norma Shearer, Malcolm McGregor, George K. Arthur, Fred Esmelton, Dale Fuller, Lew Harvey, Betty Morrissey. *Metro-Goldwyn.*

28. *WAKING UP THE TOWN.* Directed by Vernon Keyes and Jack Pickford. Based on a story by James Cruze and Frank Condon. *Cast:* Jack Pickford, Norma Shearer, Claire McDowell, Alec B. Francis, Herbert Pryor, Anna May. *United Artists/Mary Pickford Company.*

29. *A SLAVE OF FASHION.* 1925. Directed by Hobart Henley. Scenario by Bess Meredyth. Based on a story by Samuel Shipman. *Cast:* Norma Shearer, Lew Cody, William Haines, Mary Carr, James Corrigan, Estelle Clark, Sidney Bracy. *Metro-Goldwyn.*

30. *PRETTY LADIES.* 1925. Directed by Monta Bell. Adapted by Alice D.G. Miller. From a story by Adela Rogers St. Johns. *Cast:* ZaSu Pitts, Tom Moore, Ann Pennington, Lilyan Tashman, Bernard Randall, Helene D'Algy, Conrad Nagel, Norma Shearer, George K. Arthur, Lucille LeSueur (later Joan Crawford), Paul Ellis, Roy D'Arcy, Gwen Lee, Dorothy Seastrom, Lew Harvey, Chad Huber. *Metro-Goldwyn.*

31. *THE TOWER OF LIES.* 1925. Directed by Victor Seastrom. Scenario by Agnes Christine Johnston. Based on a novel by Selma Lagerlof. *Cast:* Lon Chaney, Norma Shearer, Ian Keith, William Haines, Claire McDowell, David Torrence. *Metro-Goldwyn.*

32. *HIS SECRETARY.* 1925. Directed by Hobart Henley. Scenario by Louis D. Lighton from a story by Carey Wilson. *Cast:* Norma Shearer, Lew Cody, Willard Louis, Karl Dane, Gwen Lee, Mabel Van Buren, Estelle Clark, Ernest Clark, Ernest Gillen. *Metro-Goldwyn.*

33. *THE DEVIL'S CIRCUS.* 1926. Directed by Benjamin Christiansen. Scenario and story by Benjamin Christiansen. *Cast:* Norma Shearer, Charles Emmett Mack,

Carmel Myers, Claire McDowell, Joyce Coad, Buddy (a dog). *Metro-Goldwyn.*

34. *THE WANING SEX.* 1926. Directed by Robert Z. Leonard. Adaptation and continuity by F. Hugh Herbert. Based on a story by Raymond and Fanny Hatton. *Cast:* Norma Shearer, Conrad Nagel, George K. Arthur, Mary McAllister, Charles McHugh, Tiny Ward, Martha Mattox. *Metro-Goldwyn.*

35. *UPSTAGE.* 1926. Directed by Monta Bell. Original story and scenario by Lorna Moon. *Cast:* Norma Shearer, Oscar Shaw, Tenen Holtz, Gwen Lee, Dorothy Philips, J. Frank Glendon, Ward Crane, Charles Meadin. *Metro-Goldwyn.*

36. *THE DEMI-BRIDE.* 1927. Directed by Robert Z. Leonard. Story and continuity by F. Hugh Herbert. *Cast:* Norma Shearer, Lew Cody, Lionel Belmore, Tenen Holtz, Carmel Myers, Dorothy Sebastian, Nora Cecil. *Metro-Goldwyn-Mayer.*

37. *AFTER MIDNIGHT.* 1927. Directed by Monta Bell. Scenario by Lorna Moon. From an original story by Monta Bell. *Cast:* Norma Shearer, Lawrence Gray, Gwen Lee, Eddie Sturgis, Philip Sleeman. *Metro-Goldwyn-Mayer.*

38. *THE STUDENT PRINCE.* 1927. Directed by Ernst Lubitsch. Based on Wilhelm Meyer Forster's *Old Heidelberg* and the musical play by Dorothy Donnelly and Sigmund Romberg. Scenario by Hans Kraly. *Cast:* Norma Shearer, Ramon Novarro, Jean Hersholt, Gustave Von Seyffertitz, Philippe De Lacy, Edgar Norton, Bobby Mack, Edward Connelly, Otis Harlan, John S. Peters, George K. Arthur, Edythe Chapman, Lionel Belmore, Lincoln Steadman. *Metro-Goldwyn-Mayer.*

39. *THE LATEST FROM PARIS.* 1928. Directed by Sam Wood. Original story and scenario by A. P. Younger. *Cast:* Norma Shearer, George Sidney, Ralph Forbes, Tenen Holtz, William Bakewell, Margaret Landis, Bert Roach. *Metro-Goldwyn-Mayer.*

40. *THE ACTRESS*. 1928. Directed by Sidney Franklin. Scenario by Albert Lewin. Based on a play by Arthur Wing Pinero. *Cast:* Norma Shearer, Ralph Forbes, Owen Moore, Gwen Lee, O. P. Heggie, Roy D'Arcy, Lee Moran, William Humphrey, Effie Ellsler, Andree Tourneur, Cyril Chadwick, Margaret Seddon. *Metro-Goldwyn-Mayer*.

41. *A LADY OF CHANCE*. 1928. Directed by Hobart Henley. Adapted by Edmund Scott. Based on a story by John Lee Mahin. Dialogue by Mahin. *Cast:* Norma Shearer, John Mack Brown, Lowell Sherman, Gwen Lee, Eugenie Besserer, Buddy Messinger. *Metro-Goldwyn-Mayer*.

42. *THE TRIAL OF MARY DUGAN*. 1929. Directed by Bayard Veiller. Scenario by Becky Gardner. Based on the play by Veiller. *Cast:* Norma Shearer, Lewis Stone, H. B. Warner, Raymond Hackett, Lilyan Tashman, Olive Tell, Adrienne D'Ambricourt, DeWitt Jennings, Wilfred North, Landers Stevens, Mary Doran, Westcott B. Clarke, Charles Moore, Myra Hampton. *Metro-Goldwyn-Mayer*.

43. *THE LAST OF MRS. CHEYNEY*. 1929. Directed by Sidney Franklin. Scenario by Hans Kraly and Claudine West. Based on the play by Frederick Lonsdale. *Cast:* Norma Shearer, Basil Rathbone, George Barraud, Herbert Bunston, Hedda Hopper, Moon Carroll, Madeline Seymour, Cyril Chadwick, Maude Turner, George K. Arthur. *Metro-Goldwyn-Mayer*.

44. *THE HOLLYWOOD REVUE*. 1929. Directed by Charles Reisner. Dialogue by Al Boasberg and Robert E. Hopkins. *Cast:* Norma Shearer, John Gilbert, Joan Crawford, Bessie Love, Lionel Barrymore, Cliff Edwards, Stan Laurel, Oliver Hardy, Anita Page, Nils Asther, Marion Davies, William Haines, Buster Keaton, Marie Dressler, Charles King, Polly Moran, Gus Edwards, Karl Dane, George K.

Arthur, Gwen Lee, Jack Benny, Conrad Nagel. *Metro-Goldwyn-Mayer.*

45. *THEIR OWN DESIRE.* 1929. Directed by E. Mason Hopper. Scenario by James Grant Forbes. From a story by Sarita Fuller. *Cast:* Norma Shearer, Robert Montgomery, Lewis Stone, Belle Bennett, Helen Millard, Cecil Cunningham, Henry Herbert, Mary Doran, June Nash. *Metro-Goldwyn-Mayer.*

46. *THE DIVORCEE.* 1930. Directed by Robert Z. Leonard. Scenario by Nick Grinde, Zelda Sears, John Meehan. Dialogue by John Meehan. Based on the novel by Ursula Parrott. *Cast:* Norma Shearer, Chester Morris, Conrad Nagel, Robert Montgomery, Florence Eldridge, Helen Millard, Robert Elliott, Mary Doran, Tyler Brooke, Zelda Sears, George Irving, Helen Johnson. *Metro-Goldwyn-Mayer.*

47. *LET US BE GAY.* 1930. Directed by Robert Z. Leonard. Scenario and dialogue by Frances Marion. Based on the play by Rachel Crothers. *Cast:* Norma Shearer, Rod La Rocque, Marie Dressler, Gilbert Emery, Hedda Hopper, Raymond Hackett, Sally Eilers, Tyrell Davis, Wilfred Noy, William O'Brien, Sybil Grove. *Metro-Goldwyn-Mayer.*

48. *STRANGERS MAY KISS.* 1931. Directed by George Fitzmaurice. Scenario and dialogue by John Meehan. Based on the novel by Ursula Parrott. *Cast:* Norma Shearer, Robert Montgomery, Neil Hamilton, Marjorie Rambeau, Irene Rich, Hale Hamilton, Conchita Montenegro, Jed Prouty, Albert Conti, Henry Armetta, George Davis. *Metro-Goldwyn-Mayer.*

49. *A FREE SOUL.* 1931. Directed by Clarence Brown. Scenario and dialogue by John Meehan. Based on the novel by Adela Rogers St. Johns. *Cast:* Norma Shearer, Clark Gable, Leslie Howard, Lionel Barrymore, James Gleason, Lucy Beaumont, Edward Brophy. *Metro-Goldwyn-Mayer.*

50. *PRIVATE LIVES.* 1931. Directed by Sidney Franklin.

Scenario by Hans Kraly, Richard Schayer, and Claudine West. Based on the play by Noel Coward. *Cast:* Norma Shearer, Robert Montgomery, Reginald Denny, Una Merkel, Jean Hersholt, George Davis. *Metro-Goldwyn-Mayer.*

51. *STRANGE INTERLUDE.* 1932. Directed by Robert Z. Leonard. Scenario and dialogue by Bess Meredyth and C. Gardner Sullivan. Based on the play by Eugene O'Neill. *Cast:* Norma Shearer, Clark Gable, Alexander Kirkland, Ralph Morgan, Robert Young, May Robson, Maureen O'Sullivan, Henry B. Walthall, Mary Alden, Tad Alexander. *Metro-Goldwyn-Mayer.*

52. *SMILIN' THROUGH.* 1932. Directed by Sidney Franklin. Scenario by Ernest Vajda and Claudine West. Based on the play by Jane Cowl and Jane Murfin. Dialogue by Donald Ogden Stewart, James Bernard Fagan. *Cast:* Norma Shearer, Leslie Howard, Fredric March, O. P. Heggie, Ralph Forbes, Beryl Mercer, Margaret Seddon, Cora Sue Collins, Forrester Harvey. *Metro-Goldwyn-Mayer.*

53. *RIPTIDE.* 1934. Directed by Edmund Goulding. Story and scenario by Edmund Goulding. *Cast:* Norma Shearer, Robert Montgomery, Herbert Marshall, Mrs. Patrick Campbell, Ralph Forbes, Lilyan Tashman, Arthur Jarrett, Helen Jerome Eddy, George K. Arthur, Halliwell Hobbes. *Metro-Goldwyn-Mayer.*

54. *THE BARRETTS OF WIMPOLE STREET.* 1934. Directed by Sidney Franklin. Screenplay by Claudine West, Donald Ogden Stewart, Ernest Vajda. From the play by Rudolf Besier. *Cast:* Norma Shearer, Fredric March, Charles Laughton, Maureen O'Sullivan, Katherine Alexander, Una O'Connor, Ian Wolfe, Marion Clayton, Ralph Forbes, Vernon Downing, Neville Clark, Matthew Smith, Robert Charlton, Ferdinand Munier, Margaret Seddon, George Kirby, Winter Hall, Lowden Adams, Robert Bolder, Flush (a dog). *Metro-Goldwyn-Mayer.*

55. *ROMEO AND JULIET.* 1936. Directed by George Cukor. Screen adaptation by Talbot Jennings. Based on the play by William Shakespeare. *Cast:* Norma Shearer, Leslie Howard, John Barrymore, Edna May Oliver, Basil Rathbone, C. Aubrey Smith, Andy Devine, Ralph Forbes, Reginald Denny, Maurice Murphy, Conway Tearle, Henry Kolker, Robert Warwick, Virginia Hammond, Violet Kemble Cooper. *Metro-Goldwyn-Mayer.*

56. *MARIE ANTOINETTE.* 1938. Directed by W. S. Van Dyke. Screenplay by Claudine West, Ernest Vajda, Donald Ogden Stewart. Based on the biography by Stefan Zweig. *Cast:* Norma Shearer, Tyrone Power, John Barrymore, Gladys George, Robert Morley, Anita Louise, Joseph Schildkraut, Henry Stephenson, Reginald Gardiner, Albert Dekker, Barnett Parker, Cora Witherspoon, Joseph Calleia, Ivan Simpson, Alma Kruger, Marilyn Knowlden, Scotty Beckett, Henry Daniell. *Metro-Goldwyn-Mayer.*

57. *IDIOT'S DELIGHT.* 1939. Directed by Clarence Brown. Screenplay by Robert E. Sherwood. Based on Sherwood's play. *Cast:* Norma Shearer, Clark Gable, Edward Arnold, Charles Coburn, Joseph Schildkraut, Burgess Meredith, Pat Paterson, Skeets Gallagher, Peter Willes, Fritz Feld, Paula Stone. *Metro-Goldwyn-Mayer.*

58. *THE WOMEN.* 1939. Directed by George Cukor. Screenplay by Anita Loos and Jane Murfin. Based on the play by Clare Boothe. *Cast:* Norma Shearer, Joan Crawford, Rosalind Russell, Mary Boland, Paulette Goddard, Joan Fontaine, Phyllis Povah, Lucile Watson, Virginia Weidler, Florence Nash, Esther Dale, Virginia Grey. *Metro-Goldwyn-Mayer.*

59. *ESCAPE.* 1940. Directed by Mervyn LeRoy. Screenplay by Arch Oboler and Marguerite Roberts. Based on the novel by Ethel Vance. *Cast:* Norma Shearer, Robert Taylor, Conrad Veidt, Alla Nazimova, Felix Bressart, Albert Bassermann, Philip Dorn, Bonita Granville, Edgar Bar-

rier, Elsa Bassermann, Blanche Yurka. *Metro-Goldwyn-Mayer.*

60. *WE WERE DANCING.* 1942. Directed by Robert Z. Leonard. Screenplay by George Forschel. Based on playlets by Noel Coward. *Cast:* Norma Shearer, Melvyn Douglas, Gail Patrick, Lee Bowman, Reginald Owen, Heather Thatcher, Alan Mowbray, Connie Gilchrist, Nella Walker, Florence Shirley, Russell Hicks, Norma Varden. *Metro-Goldwyn-Mayer.*

61. *HER CARDBOARD LOVER.* 1942. Directed by George Cukor. Screenplay by Jacques Deval and John Collier. Based on a play by Jacques Deval. *Cast:* Norma Shearer, Robert Taylor, George Sanders, Frank McHugh, Elizabeth Patterson, Chill Wills. *Metro-Goldwyn-Mayer.*

A list of Norma Shearer's short films follows.

Norma Shearer's Short Films

1. *VOICES ACROSS THE SEA.* 1928. Directed by Jack Conway. Running time: twelve minutes. Norma Shearer, Joan Crawford, John Gilbert, Ernest Torrence and George K. Arthur played themselves. Was shot to plug MGM film, *Alias Jimmy Valentine,* starring William Haines (November 1928) and to commemorate opening of new Loew's Empire Theatre in London. Torrence broadcast the London premiere from the stage of the Empire, via telephone hookup and chatted briefly with Shearer and other stars about the event. Shearer's voice was called "pleasing." *Metro-Goldwyn-Mayer.*

2. *THE STOLEN JOOLS.* 1931. (British title, *THE SLIPPERY PEARLS.*) Produced by the Masquers Club of Hollywood. Director never listed. Running time: twenty minutes. Released in U.S. April 1931; in Britain September 1932. With Norma Shearer as a robbery victim (her jewels, of course) and among the "suspects" such top stars as Joan Crawford, Edward G. Robinson, Laurel and Hardy, Doug Fairbanks, Jr., Barbara Stanwyck and Maurice Chevalier, plus many lesser lights. Wallace Beery was a police sergeant and Eddie Kane "investigated" the robbery. *Hollywood Masquers Club, Producers.*

3. *JACKIE COOPER'S CHRISTMAS PARTY.* 1931. Director not listed. Norma Shearer, Jackie Cooper, Clark Gable, Wallace Beery, Marie Dressler, Polly Moran, Marion Davies, Lionel Barrymore, Leila Hyams, with a special appearance by studio head Louis B. Mayer. Running time: nine minutes. Shearer asks Mayer to arrange a

Christmas party for Jackie's football team. Since there isn't enough room at Mayer's home, Norma gets a sound stage. The stars serve a festive meal. Released December 1931. *Metro-Goldwyn-Mayer.*

4. *MISTER WILL SHAKESPEARE.* 1936. Directed by Jacques Tourneur. Script by Richard Goldstone. Narration by Carey Wilson. Anthony Kemble Cooper plays Shakespeare in this two-reeler meant to publicize (and double as a trailer for) *Romeo and Juliet.* Norma Shearer and Leslie Howard are seen briefly (in *silent* sequences) in their roles. Presented highlights from life of Shakespeare. *Metro-Goldwyn-Mayer.*

Source Notes

Note: Many sources are already credited by name in the text itself.

Page 5 "Some years ago, film historians and commentators . . ." "The Glamorous Norma Shearer," in *Screen Stars Album*, 1964. Defense of her by Lawrence J. Quirk in that article. Slighting references in *Films in Review*, 1960, *The New York Times*, 1942, etc.

Page 6 "Of course Thalberg helped her . . ." From articles by Quirk, books by Bob Thomas (*Thalberg*) and Bosley Crowther (*The Lion's Share*), numerous references in major newspapers and fan magazines.

Page 6 "Norma Shearer was also a much finer actress than . . ." Defense of her by Quirk in *Screen Stars Album*, 1964, etc. Also Quirk defense of her in *Great Romantic Films*, 1974.

Page 9 "Shearer was born . . ." Many authorities, including Quirk, Crowther, Thomas, in their respective books, Jack Jacobs and Myron Braum (*The Films of Norma Shearer*), *The New York Times*, Shearer's own life story in *True Story*, October 1936, and such articles as "Norma," *Screen Book*, 1934; *Films in Review*, 1960.

Page 10 "As a child, mine was a glorious life . . ." Shearer in *True Story*, 1936.

Page 11 "Norma was particularly fond . . ." Shearer in *True Story*, 1936.

Page 12 "Norma gave an interesting clue . . ." Shearer to author, 1965.

Page 13 "She remembered also having a gentling influence . . ." *Photoplay*, 1932.

Page 14 "But again death interposed itself . . ." Shearer to author, 1965.

Page 14 "Her mother sat the children down . . ." Shearer in *Modern Screen*, 1933.

Page 15 "She then talked her mother . . ." *Photoplay*, 1931; *True Story*, 1936.

Page 18 "At home that night . . ." Shearer to author; also *Photoplay*, 1933.

Page 21 "Everything in New York bewildered . . ." Shearer to author; also *Modern Screen,* 1931; *Photoplay,* 1934.

Page 22 "As Norma later remembered . . ." *True Story,* 1936.

Page 24 "Father, in Montreal . . ." Shearer to author, 1966; also Shearer to Ruth Waterbury in *Photoplay,* 1936.

Page 25 "He was a dynamic Irishman . . ." *Quirk of Photoplay,* by Lawrence J. Quirk, in *Films in Review,* 1955; "Jimmy Quirk, Hollywood's Father Confessor" by L. J. Quirk, *TV Radio-Movie Guide,* 1966; foreword by L. Quirk to anthology of *Photoplay,* 1971; memories of Margaret Ettinger, Anita Loos, etc.

Page 26 ". . . felt an instant attraction to Norma." Margaret Connery Quirk in text to author.

Page 30 "With the cast in her eye . . ." Ruth Waterbury to author.

Page 30 "Arnold Genthe's distinctive portraits . . ." Shearer to Ruth Biery in *Photoplay,* 1931; *Modern Screen,* 1936.

Page 31 "Finally a talent agent . . ." Jacobs-Braum.

Page 35 "Ralph Ince and Eugene O'Brien were 'coming on' . . ." Helen Ferguson to author; Anita Loos to author.

Page 35 "I was afraid of drinkers . . ." Shearer to Ruth Waterbury, 1934.

Page 36 ". . . Hays let it be known . . ." Will Hays to author, 1949.

Page 36 "My mother . . . recalled Jimmy's growing interest . . ." Margaret Connery Quirk to author.

Page 37 "Norma was deeply fond of Jimmy . . ." Anita Loos, Margaret Connery Quirk, Allan Dwan to author; Terry Ramsaye to author.

Page 37 "To my mother, it was obvious . . ." Margaret Connery Quirk to author.

Page 38 ". . . after numerous flings . . ." Joan Crawford to author; Phyllis Haver to author; director Eddie Sutherland to author.

Page 38 "Norma went to Hollywood in the winter . . ." Bosley Crowther to author; Crowther's *The Lion's Share* and *Hollywood Rajah, Photoplay,* 1923.

Page 39 "The other man who was to loom large . . ." Bob Thomas on Thalberg; Crowther on Mayer; Crowther to author.

Page 41 "Having read reams of newspapers and magazines . . ." *Photoplay,* 1927; *True Story* 1936.

Page 42–43 First meeting with Thalberg. Shearer to author. Also in Jacobs-Braun, Thomas, Crowther, Sam Marx books. Anita Loos to author.

Page 45 "I'm Hollywood's wandering orphan girl . . ." James R. Quirk papers.

Page 46   "She and Athole and her mother . . ." Helen Ferguson to author; Phyllis Haver to author; Shearer to Ruth Waterbury, who told author.

Page 48   "Jack and Norma had been sweethearts . . ." King Vidor to Leatrice Gilbert Fountain; Leatrice Fountain to author.

Page 50   "Leo the Lion was on his way . . ." Crowther, Thomas, Quirk in *Screen Album; Films in Review,* 1960; *Photoplay,* 1927; James R. Quirk files.

Page 53   "Norma later remembered Chaney . . ." Shearer to author.

Page 54   "There were so many infatuations . . ." Helen Ferguson to author.

Page 55   "Don't get overjoyed too soon . . ." Joan Crawford to author.

Page 56   ". . . I was the rinso-white knight . . ." Conrad Nagel to author.

Page 56   ". . . involved with Jimmy Quirk and . . . with Jack . . ." King Vidor, Phyllis Haver, Eddie Sutherland to author.

Page 56   "The part provided a real opportunity . . ." Leatrice Fountain to author.

Page 57   "Douglas knew . . ." Douglas Shearer to author; Thomas, Crowther.

Page 59   "In love with love . . ." Helen Ferguson to author.

Page 62   ". . . lacked John Boles's gentle tact . . ." Helen Ferguson to author; Frances Marion to author.

Page 65-66   "He was a heavy drinker . . ." Frances Marion, Anita Loos to author.

Page 67   "I can't get rid of him . . ." Frances Marion to author.

Page 72   "Thalberg doubtless felt he was giving . . ." Thomas, Crowther.

Page 74   "Cody continued his persistent . . ." Frances Marion to author.

Page 77   ". . . again she found herself fending off . . ." King Vidor to author.

Page 86   "She asked Mayer for a revised contract . . ." Crowther, Thomas, Jacobs-Braum.

Page 87   "Thalberg's mother, Henrietta . . ." Thomas, Crowther. Loos to author.

Page 89   ". . . keep up a front . . ." Jerry Asher to author.

Page 89   "When I began to go with Irving . . ." Crowther, Jacobs-Braum, Thomas.

Page 90   "Never has Norma looked lovelier . . ." Louella Parsons in *New York Journal-American,* Sept. 30, 1927, etc.

Page 91   "Henrietta had no objections." Thomas, Crowther, Frances Marion to author.

Page 94   ". . . love affairs [of Novarro] with various males . . ." King

Vidor to author; Anita Loos, Frances Marion, Blanche Sweet, Eddie Sutherland to author.

Page 95 ". . . Lubitsch was taking obvious pleasure . . ." George Cukor, Jerry Asher, King Vidor to author.

Page 98 "That drive . . ." Sam Wood to author.

Page 100 "Owen Moore proceeded . . ." Adela Rogers St. Johns, *Photoplay,* 1928.

Page 104 "Thalberg was also worried." Thomas, Crowther.

Page 114 "Motherhood suited her." Robert Z. Leonard to author.

Page 117 ". . . a warm affection . . ." Frances Marion to author.

Page 118 ". . . time they went their own way . . ." Helen Ferguson and Anita Loos to author.

Page 119 "I want nothing show-offish . . ." Helen Ferguson to author.

Page 124 ". . . I sensed a new restlessness . . ." Robert Montgomery to author.

Page 127 "Thalberg knuckled under . . ." Adela Rogers St. Johns to author.

Page 131 "Norma assured everyone . . ." George Cukor to author.

Page 137 "O'Neill, barely disguising his contempt . . ." Terry Ramsaye and Ruth Waterbury to author; Katherine Albert to author.

Page 138 "Will Hays . . . became nervous . . ." Will Hays to author, 1949.

Page 150 "The Mayer Group . . ." Crowther, *The Lion's Share.*

Page 151 ". . . just shut up about it . . ." Terry Ramsaye and Adela Rogers St. Johns to author.

Page 152 "Finally, Thalberg was permitted . . ." Crowther, *The Lion's Share.*

Page 153 "By December 1932 Thalberg . . ." Thomas.

Page 155 "MacArthur made no secret," Thomas.

Page 157 "Mrs. Campbell was unfamiliar . . ." Katherine Albert to author.

Page 160 "The leading role offered . . ." Quirk, *Great Romantic Films,* 1974.

Page 161 "Everybody liked Marion . . ." Anita Loos, Joan Crawford to author.

Page 163 "Hearst's damned intrusions . . ." Jerry Asher, Eddie Mannix to author.

Page 176 "Then . . . disaster struck . . ." Quirk, Crowther, Thomas, Jacobs-Braum.

Page 178 "Then . . . the steel returned . . ." Crowther, Mannix.

Page 179 "I am a woman alone . . ." Frances Marion and Eddie Mannix, Anita Loos, Billy Grady to author.

Page 183   ". . . nervous about Franklin . . ." Crowther, Quirk, Jacobs-
            Braum.
Page 189   "Did Power return her love?" Anita Louise, Adela Rogers St.
            Johns, Anita Loos, Billy Grady to author.
Page 190   "How was the lady in the sack?" Jerry Asher to author.
Page 193   "There was one factor . . ." Bob Thomas in *Selznick*; Loos to
            author.
Page 200   "The Cat Fight of the Century!" Anita Loos, Eddie Mannix,
            Howard Strickling.
Page 206   Joan–Norma relationship. Joan Crawford and Hedda Hopper
            to author.
Page 209   "At the time he and Norma . . ." Ruth Waterbury in
            Photoplay; Waterbury and Anita Loos to author.
Page 220   "Shearer . . . ran the show . . ." Melvyn Douglas, Robert Z.
            Leonard, Billy Grady to author.
Page 226   "I wasn't a doormat . . ." George Cukor to author.
Page 227   ". . . not one of my better efforts . . ." Shearer to author.
Page 228   ". . . while Shearer may have been the prima donna . . ."
            Frank McHugh to author; Robert Taylor to author; Quirk's *The
            Films of Robert Taylor* (1975).
Page 229   "In the course of a phone conversation . . ." Jerry Asher,
            George Cukor to author.
Page 232   "Arrouge also had a way with children." Jerry Asher, George
            Cukor to author.
Page 232   ". . . for . . . the first time . . ." Frances Marion, Anita Loos
            to author.
Page 233   "Norma didn't waste time . . ." Hunt Stromberg to author.
            Also *Photoplay*, 1942.
Page 235   "With *three* rings . . ." Ruth Waterbury, *Modern Screen*, 1942.
Page 236   "All these ambitious plans fell through . . ." Reports in
            periodicals; Jerry Asher and Frances Marion to author.
Page 243   "There is nowhere to compare . . ." Anthony Slide to author.
Page 244   ". . . Norma seemed content enough . . ." DeWitt Bodeen to
            author.

A Selective Norma Shearer Bibliography

Crowther, Bosley. *Hollywood Rajah, The Life and Times of Louis B. Mayer.* New York: Henry Holt, 1960.

——— *The Lion's Share.* New York: E.P. Dutton, 1957.

Eames, John Douglas. *The MGM Story.* New York: Crown Publishers, Inc., 1979.

Goodman, Ezra. *The Fifty-Year Decline and Fall of Hollywood.* New York: Simon and Schuster, 1961.

Jacobs, Jack, and Braum, Myron. *The Films of Norma Shearer.* Secaucus, N.J.: Citadel Press, 1977.

Jacobs, Lewis. *The Rise of the American Film.* New York: Harcourt, Brace, 1939.

Marion, Frances. *Off With Their Heads! A Serio-Comic Tale of Hollywood.* New York: MacMillan, 1972.

Pickford, Mary. *Sunshine and Shadow.* New York: Doubleday & Co., 1955.

Quirk, Lawrence J. *Anthology of Photoplay* (foreword). New York: Dover Publications, 1971.

——— *The Glamorous Norma Shearer.* New York: Screen Stars Album, 1964.

——— *The Films of Robert Taylor.* Secaucus, N.J.: Citadel Press, 1975.

——— *The Films of Joan Crawford.* Secaucus, N.J.: Citadel Press, 1968.

——— *The Films of Fredric March.* Secaucus, N.J.: Citadel Press, 1971.

——— *The Great Romantic Films.* Secaucus, N.J.: Citadel Press, 1974.

Ramsaye, Terry. *A Million and One Nights.* New York: Simon and Schuster, 1964.

Thomas, Bob. *Thalberg: Life and Legend.* New York: Doubleday and Co., 1969.

——— *Selznick.* New York: Doubleday and Co., 1970.

Tornabene, Lyn. *Long Live The King, A Biography of Clark Gable.* New York: G.P. Putnam, 1976.

SELECTED PERIODICALS

Quirk's Reviews, Photoplay, Modern Screen, Films in Review, Picture Play, Time, Life, McCall's, Cosmopolitan, Variety, Saturday Evening Post, Vanity Fair, Screen Album, Screen Book, True Story, Exhibitor's World, Motion Picture Herald.

Index